PONTY 1911?

DARYL LEEWORTHY was born in 1986 and, despite numerous efforts to escape, has lived in Pontypridd for most of his life. His previous books include biographies of Gwyn Thomas and Elaine Morgan, and several landmarks of historical scholarship, most notably *Labour Country: Political Radicalism and Social Democracy in South Wales, 1831-1985* and *A Little Gay History of Wales*.

PONTY IS IT?

Travels in A Valleys Town

DARYL LEEWORTHY

PARTHIAN

Parthian, Cardigan SA43 IED
www.parthianbooks.com
First published in 2024
© Daryl Leeworthy 2024
ISBN 978-1-914595-94-3

Editor: Richard Davies

Published with the financial support
of the Books Council of Wales

Designer: cover, text and typesetting
by Lyn Davies *lyndaviesdesignfolio.com*
Text set in Sabon Std, titles in Gill Sans Nova Inline

Printed and bound by 4edge Limited, UK

British Library Cataloguing in Publication Data
A cataloguing record for this book is available
from the British Library
Printed on FSC accredited paper

I left Pontypridd but it never left me

ALUN RICHARDS

For Grampa, who pointed the way

Contents

Part 1

CENTRE GROUND

I.

I HAVE TRAVELLED INTO Pontypridd thousands of times. And so, like most commuters on the A470 north out of Cardiff, I rarely pay attention to my surroundings. Usually, I am stood in the aisle of a cramped bus trying not to fall over whenever the vehicle jerks forward, or, if I have been lucky enough, I am sat in the seat immediately behind the driver and hidden from everyone else. Where better to read a novel or to scribble some notes for my next article or book. This is how I write: by hand either with the stub of a pencil or the ink of a fountain pen and always in narrow-ruled notebooks.

On this occasion there are not many passengers, and those onboard seem to know each other. Their accents sing a Merthyr song with a Rhondda chorus. Out of nowhere a disembodied Carmarthenshire voice tells me *don't forget to tap off when you get off*, but there is no advice about what I should have done when I got on. Next comes a half-garbled indication of the next stop: Pontypridd Bus Station.

I fell out of the habit of travelling during the pandemic, when we were compelled (or should that be condemned) to live our lives within our own habitat – what they call in Welsh *cynefin* or

1

German *heimat*. A French *milieu*. I had been living near the centre of town for about twelve months when the first lockdown was announced in early March 2020 and approached the place much as I had always done: with the sidling malicious obliquity of someone from Ynysybwl, a former mining village that lies in the hills a few miles away.

Restricted to a daily walk, I began to pay closer attention to Ponty itself. To the scars left by Storm Dennis, our perverse preamble to the coronavirus, to the relics of industries long gone, and to the small plaques informing passers-by, especially those like me still angry at what had happened in 2016, what had led to The Mistake, that this or that had been supported by collective continental endeavour.

As spring turned to summer and the rain-sodden ground dried out, I extended my range. I took to the hills, to the empty country lanes, to long-forgotten footpaths, and there perambulated like a Victorian explorer. A friend cycled up from Cardiff once or twice and we made socially distanced tours of landmarks that, hitherto, I had taken for granted and about which they knew nothing.

'It's bloody marvellous this,' he says, in a Leodian accent flattened off by years spent studying in Cambridge. He flicks the fastenings of his helmet which dangle from the handlebars of his bicycle. 'I feel reet at home.'

'I don't,' I hear myself say under my breath.

For years I've been trying to leave, feeling that I don't belong here, but each time I get away I come back. The reason why escapes me. I was determined as a teenager not to be one of those who lived here for ever and ever, who settled. The very sound of that word made my stomach turn. But here I am, still in Ponty.

The twelve miles from Cardiff takes about half an hour. We pass Castell Coch, the hunting lodge intended for the Marquess of Bute, but now a tourist attraction managed by Cadw. We pass what remains of the railway viaduct that once carried coal from one side of the valley to the other and now details the jubilees of Elizabeth II. We pass the engine sheds belonging to Transport for Wales, then the industrial estate, then Tesco, then the university, and finally the bus pulls up the ramp onto the roundabout. To the left is the ship, a public artwork paid for by Europe. It is bright red. A memorial to industry: anchors, chains, and steam coal. To the right, on the site of the old Brown Lenox Chainworks, is Sainsbury's supermarket cast in a burnt-orange colour scheme, a half-empty retail park lies behind the ship-shaped store.

I press the bell and alight at the park gates. The Carmarthenshire voice is back again: I hear *Clwydi Ynysangharad* from the pavement. On any given day, the park is busy with dog walkers, runners, parents, children, amateur sportspeople, and so on. Today is no different. There are plenty of familiar faces about, but no one stops for a chat, and it is no surprise as there's drizzle in the air. I get thrown a look that says, 'where's your coat, butt'. It rains so often that certain types of downpours, including drizzle, can be safely ignored. Sure, you get a bit damp, but it is nothing that hanging around for ten minutes in a shop or the public library won't fix. And so that's where I go to dry out: the library.

As I walk through the automatic doors and pass by the main desk, one of the librarians says, 'eh up.' Before I get chance to reply, 'how do' or 'hiya,' they have turned to apologise to another user who has missed this week's supply of dog bags. The disappointed are recompensed with some sacks for recycling food, plastics, and cardboard, and a leaflet reminding them what can go in each. Before long, an excited yelp echoes through the building. The librarians turn towards the toilet. Noises emanate from the reference department upstairs, where someone has found their great-grandmother on a census return. One of the librarians is unconvinced and raises their eyebrow like Mr Spock.

Over the years, I have worked in many of the world's greatest libraries – it is one of the advantages of being a historian. We have an idea, I think, that such places should have neoclassical columns and frontages, that they should have wooden desks that have been warmed by the bums of Oscar Wilde or James Baldwin, or perhaps Alan Bennett and Kenneth Williams, and then by you and me on a wet Thursday afternoon. Alas, modern architects missed the memo. This new one looks as though it was inspired by a woodlouse or a minor sports stadium in the American Midwest. It was fated to be opened during the year of the plague. Officially, it is called Llys Cadwyn and in addition to the library there's a gym and various hot-desked advice services, including what remains of many of the town's banks. Welcome to *Books, Bods, and Banks* how may I help you? After a rummage through the shelves, I leave with a previously missed le Carré and the next volume of Henning Mankell's Wallander series.

This part of town has changed a lot, even in my lifetime. The more I say that, the more I realise I am getting old: it's the fast approach of middle age that's the cause. It'll be backache and waterworks trouble next and then anxiety about my PSA score. My eyesight is already on the way out and my hearing was always selective. Back in the 1990s, the corner of Taff Street and Bridge Street, now occupied by the library, was the site of a rather sorry-looking branch of the value supermarket, Kwik Save. Lots of the products, as I recall, this being the era of price wars with the recently arrived German upstarts Lidl and Aldi, were wrapped in a white plastic embossed with the company's brand, No Frills. The building itself was an ugly, cream-painted, mostly concrete monstrosity with large aluminium-framed windows. Next door was the Taff Vale Shopping Centre. Neither venue would win architectural awards.

Notorious for its dank, permanent stench of urine, for junkies and their drugs, and for various shops that were out of time as much as they were out of place, The Precinct as the Taff Vale Shopping Centre tended to be called, was a failed idea from the

1960s, which lingered well past its sell-by date. No one mourns its demolition and almost everyone has forgotten what was there before The Precinct. Answer: cafés, shops, and a row of houses. The colourful office blocks of today are much better looking than either of those earlier iterations and, best of all, they afford residents and visitors a healthier relationship with the river. There are fewer discarded shopping trolleys in the water and the smell of piss has gone, *deo gratias*, although marijuana and cheap lager has not.

One other thing remains. The omnipresence of government administrators. The tax office, which jutted into the sky from the centre of The Precinct, has gone, but Transport for Wales has its offices here instead, as does the local council and the Traffic Commissioner. The lanyard class mixes with pensioners in the queues at a nearby coffee shop - or at the Gatto Lounge after five o'clock - and that's where I join them.

'Tea please,' I say to the barista before tapping my debit card and taking a seat as instructed.

Everyone else is drinking some variant of frothy coffee: a latte, cappuccino, or a flat white. Hissing steam mixes with chatter, the smell of toast about to burn, slices of cakes, and the gurgle of warming milk, and I begin to lose sense of where I am.

2.

I wake up in a daydream. It is 1989, at least I think so.

'Where are we going?' I say, as my parents are packing the car and hoping that my baby sister, Katrina, her age still measured in weeks rather than months, will not wake up and cry.

I pull on my Grampa's burgundy cardigan and ask him the same question.

'South Wales,' he replies, before turning back to help Mum and Dad.

'Oh.'

'It's where your Grampa comes from,' says Granny, as I lean in for a cuddle. She points at my sweater. 'And Fireman Sam.'

'Oh! Can I meet him?'

The adults laugh, as if to say it will be okay.

We reverse out of the driveway, along Garsdale Road, then Locking Road, and onto the motorway. The M5 carries us north towards Bristol, the M4 and the old Severn Bridge takes us across the sea, and finally the A470 brings us into The Valleys for the first time. My parents argue in the front of the car about mundane things until Dad presses a lever to indicate he is turning off. When we are stationary again, I say:

'Dad.'

There is no reply, so I lean forward in my seat and say it again.

'Dad, how do you say that?' I'm pointing at a road sign. 'Where are we?'

More silence.

I fall back in my chair and let out a disappointed sigh.

Mum looks over with a face that says, not now, and so she answers my question herself:

'Pont-ee-Prid.' (A hard *d*, the Preeth of the Welsh *dd* came later.)

I try to repeat, saying the word under my breath, each syllable distinct as though hyphenated and with a pause that I do not yet know to call a fermata.

'But Pont-ee for short,' she reassures me.

That I can get my lips around. My new word for home: 'Ponty.'

We have arrived now. On our new street, more a slope really, there are thirteen terraced houses plus a bungalow at the top, which I count using my fingers. Two hands and four more. Each of the houses is the same: two windows on the first floor: a larger one to the left, a smaller one to the right; on the ground floor, a window to the left, and a door to the right. Around each of the windows are crenelations painted in a unique colour, some bright, most muted. Ours is white but some of the paint is flaking and so I know the bricks are yellow underneath. As an adult, I recognise this style of housing as Rhondda vernacular. But as a toddler I just noticed the colours.

The house – our house – is strange to me. On entering, I see a set of stairs leading upwards. To my left there are two doors, both the same: one to the front room, which is destined to be my bedroom, the other to the living room. Through the second, I find the stairs that lead down to the kitchen and to the bathroom, which I insist on being the first to use. Dad says okay, but that I must not flush. I hear him tell Mum something about turning the water on, but I do not understand. I spend ages sat on the white plastic seat swinging my legs back and forth watching a house-spider move around on the cold tiles. Eventually, I hear a rush of water through the pipes and there is a knock at the door.

'Hurry up,' Mum says.

When I emerge, I find her unpacking some sandwiches.

In the morning, Dad heads off to work and Mum takes my sister and I out into the garden to play. There is no fence, yet, or a wall, to separate our strip of grass from those either side of us. Nor do we have the swing that will be a present from Mum's parents, nor the rabbit that will keep escaping, nor the BMX bike that will be handed down by my cousins. I am fascinated by the view. It is not the beach at Weston-super-Mare anymore, I will not see my old playground again until Christmas, but it is beautiful: a mountainside slowly coming back to life after a century as a coal tip. The remains of a colliery are visible.

Mum goes to sit by the kitchen stairs with her back to the wall as I run around. She can feel the residual heat of a coal fire on the other side. It is like the embrace of a long-lost friend. Our neighbours work for the National Coal Board and still take their weekly allowance. I walk to the bottom of the garden, down some steps, and there I find a shed. I imagine it to be like Grampa's. I have my own set of yellow- and green-handled tools – a spade, a fork, and a Dutch hoe – which I use to poke at his compost heap, but when I open the door, I discover something else instead. I shout:

'Mum, Mum, come and see what I've found.'

Failing to notice that she is busy feeding my sister and unimpressed at being ignored, I stomp back towards the kitchen. I arrive just as the lid of the SMA formula milk is replaced.

'There's a toilet at the bottom of the garden, Mum.'

'Oh. Well, stay out of there. Stay on the grass where I can see you.'

Still in a huff, I explore upstairs instead. From the living room window, which looks out across the valley, I can see that our shed is one of three on the street. The others have all been knocked down. I soon learn that only one of our neighbours uses theirs as a toilet except on the coldest days when they use a chamber pot. This is Sadie, who lives a few doors down the hill. She is older than almost anyone I have ever met before. To me she looks older even than my grandparents' neighbour, Mrs Phillips, and I believe, because Grampa has told me so, that Mrs Phillips is almost a hundred years old.

3.

Sadie and her *ty bach* form one of my earliest childhood memories. In my mind's eye, I can still see her walking down to the bottom of the garden at night with toilet paper wrapped around one hand and a flickering battery-powered torch in the other. My parents must have wondered, and not for the last time, if they had made a mistake moving to the village. Whatever its faults as a town, no one in Weston, my birthplace and theirs, lived in so Victorian a way. But ten years and as many months from the start of the new millennium, this was the living standard of some of the Welsh. It was hardest on Mum, of course, because she was on her own most of the time and knew no one for miles around. Dad at least had his colleagues for a bit of company. This was before we had a telephone or a television of our own. We were cut off, as though sent into exile.

Eventually, Mum and Dad grew accustomed to valleys life. The locals sounded just like my Grampa who had grown up not that far away in Llanharan and Nantyffyllon. When he died in March 1991, his voice was all around us still, and that mattered to Dad who struggled with the loss for a long time. For Mum, the rooting echo was of her two grandmothers, Pomeroy and Thomas: the one from Treherbert, the other from Ebbw Vale. Our neighbours, Sherie and Gwyn, Jeanette and Dilla, Dawn and Nigel, Phil and Sam, the Rowlands, and Sadie, were as warm and friendly as any stereotype would have them be. In fact, my sister, despite what it says on her passport, refuses to acknowledge anywhere else as home. She has no memories of our life in England and, unlike me, has never felt the urge to return. If I ask her about it, as I have done again writing this book, she says, 'but this is where I come from, it is where I belong.'

Had I been a little younger, I might not have questioned my relationship with the village or the surrounding area. I might have grown comfortable with the accent, the culture, the habits, the sustained beliefs, the post-industrial poverty that was to be our way of life. I might even have found solace in the way these things were, and still are. But I did not. I wriggled against them. In certain circumstances I railed against them. I felt like an alien, which is why I knew I had to leave – to get the anxieties of dislocation and unbelonging out of my system. If I had stayed and gone to Cardiff University with my schoolfriends and then settled as they have done, these words would never have been written. In fact, I am certain that I would not be alive to write anything at all.

At seventeen or eighteen, I felt like Laurie Lee when he walked out on his people and his valley on that midsummer morning in

1934. Like him, I was convinced something better lay elsewhere. Somewhere out there. Somewhere in the distance. With my own violin and books in hand, I left Ynysybwl and took myself off to England. To Oxford, to be precise. I imagined a homecoming, for I was never Welsh as a child. After receiving so much physical and verbal abuse from my peers – 'fuck off back to England' was thrown at me often enough along with punches and bottles of urine – how could I be that. I thought that after holding on to as much of my old identity as I could, my Englishness unencumbered by anxiety would now flourish. But it did not. I learned what it was to be an alien again, if not an exile this time.

Arriving at university a curious, even hopeful, fresher, I talked with others about where they had come from – the more affluent English counties, of course, or well-to-do parts of Scotland – and naturally we compared our experiences. Few believed me when I told them my story. Fewer still accepted that Sadie was real. Even now, thirty-five years later, I sometimes question whether I have, in fact, made it all up in my mind or if I have over-embellished certain details. Surely everyone in Britain in the last decade of the twentieth century had an indoor toilet and hot running water, didn't they? Well, apart from those who lived off the grid or chose to reside on a minor Scottish island with post arriving once a week. But no, this really happened. It was a measure of the place to which we had moved as a family in 1989 and its memory serves a measure of how far we have all travelled since then.

Few believed that I would be gone from the valleys for good. They knew instinctively that I would return. Perhaps they were right. It is why I became a historian, I think, rather than any other kind of scholar – a geographer, say, or a linguist. But why a historian of the place I hated so much as a child and about which I remain ambivalent? It was partly an accident. I could have chosen a topic other than the social history of rugby football for my undergraduate dissertation – doing so would have been the career-minded thing to do – and so become a historian of the United States or the Soviet Union as I once intended, but I turned back instead. Others assure me that it was a calling. I don't believe that. If anything, I was looking for an answer to the question of where I belong. In England, in South Wales, or perhaps in another place. I remain on that journey.

4.

Isolated from the rest of the world during lockdown, I re-read Laurie Lee. First his memoir of childhood, *Cider with Rosie*, then about his departure from Slad, his adventures in Spain, his journalism, his portraits of the seasons, his essays on being a writer. I followed him as he recovered his sense of place. Then I turned to Dennis Potter's *Changing Forest* and the people of that 'strange and beautiful place' of his childhood who were 'as warm as anywhere else, but seemed warmer to me'. When I was done, I moved on to the big books of world literature – *War and Peace*, *Don Quixote*, *The Count of Monte Cristo*, *Madame Bovary*, *Sons and Lovers*, and so on – an immersion in the classics like the one I had undertaken as an overly precocious teenager twenty years before. Finally, I turned to vintage travelogues: the Durrells in the Mediterranean, Eric Newby across the Hindu Kush, Graham Greene in Mexico, John Steinbeck in America, Alan Sillitoe in Russia. The books arrived in packages through the post from Blackwells, as if I was back in Oxford and had the run of the famous Norrington Room once more.

One volume stood out among the rest: Daniel Defoe's *A Journal of the Plague Year*. I know I was not alone in picking this up in 2020. It was discussed often enough on the radio to convince me of that. But re-reading the book I became gripped with the desire to look again at the place I called home and which I could not leave, and so I began to take notes. I wrote down what I saw on my walks, wrote down my feelings and other thoughts as they occurred to me. Some emerged as fiction. This behaviour was out of the ordinary since I have never kept a diary, and never will again. But in that moment, it seemed the right thing to do.

To my surprise, I noticed just how much in common there was between a plague outbreak in the seventeenth century – Defoe's book was first published in March 1722 – and my own experience of the coronavirus pandemic hundreds of years later. There were those who 'talk[ed] of locking themselves up and letting nobody come near them.' There were walks through streets marked by a 'profound silence'. And there were plenty of people who could not work as normal. Too young to recall the plague of 1665 for himself, being a child of five at the time, Defoe instead blended historical research and fictional invention, casting his account as a true record of what had happened, not as a novel or something else. Readers have debated what sort of book he wrote ever since.

When I first encountered Defoe properly as a teenager, I knew him as the author of *Robinson Crusoe* and *Moll Flanders*, and so I took this, the third book of his I found at the library, to be fiction. Later, when I read his historical and travel writing, I reconsidered the label and so moved my copy of the *Journal* to the nonfiction section of my bookshelf. Now I think of him as someone coming to terms with an event that had a lasting social and cultural resonance. I think of him as a writer using whatever creative technique he could to achieve his aim.

Officially, around seventy thousand people died in London in 1665, with unofficial estimates of more than a hundred thousand deaths, the equivalent of one in every five of the city's population. As history and as lived experience, this was as stark as any numerical summary of Covid-19's impact upon us. After all, how do we come to terms with the fact that Covid-19 caused the biggest fall in life expectancy in Britain since the Second World War? How do we acknowledge our losses: of time, of family members, of life chances? How do we tell the truth of what happened except through fiction and personal reinvention?

Going through empty streets was how I experienced those eerie, sun-filled but anxious days of March and April 2020. My thoughts were fixed on those I could not visit, on those I knew to be vulnerable, and on my close friend David who was fighting for his life in a Norwegian hospital. He caught the coronavirus early in the pandemic and was very nearly one of its first victims. Messages from his partner, Miriam, flew around the world to relatives and to friends, through her pain we were brought face to face with the stark reality of an illness that dark-web conspiracy even then dismissed as 'just a bad cold'. It was never that.

David has since written about his experiences in a deeply moving, poetic memoir called *Pacemaker*. In its pages he charts his recovery using a calendar marked up with the year as planned in January and as it became when he fell ill. He records the simple joy he takes wandering around, paying attention to the landscape, being a walker. As he puts it:

At heart I am a pedestrian... walking slows things down. Walking is something that provides many things to me. Time alone. Time to think. Exercise.

This is not a book about the pandemic, of course, any more than it is a straightforward essay in memory or history, biography or urban geography, but it has been shaped by that period and by the nine months I spent almost completely alone. Walking was how I coped with my isolation. My constant companion during the pandemic was Ponty itself. We argued with each other, we revealed ourselves anew, and in the end, we learned to live together - like a couple, long married, who have threatened divorce but who realise, in moments of travail, that they were once in love and perhaps still are.

5.

There is only one Ponty, if we are honest.

We have the bridge. The famous crossing of 1756, I mean. Or is it 1755, no one is quite sure anymore. What I do know for certain is that the bridge was built by William Edwards, an amateur stonemason and nonconformist minister, and that it was his fourth attempt in a decade. He was commissioned in 1746 to build a bridge across the Taff. If successful, he would be paid £500 (about £90,000 today) by the local gentry. A fair sum. His first attempt, made of wood, was swept away by a heavy storm in 1748. His second collapsed in on itself. As did his third (by now the bridge was made of stone). This one after a period of just six weeks. For a fourth, Edwards went back to the drawing board: he needed to know how to make his bridge lighter and so better able to withstand heavy rain. The answer was to drill three holes on either side of the keystone, six in total and with varying diameters. This version has stood ever since. But it was a costly endeavour. In total, Edwards spent more than £1,500 on this one project (more than £250,000 today), three times the original budget, leaving himself heavily indebted and with plenty of regrets. Nevertheless, the achievement speaks for itself.

Contemporaries called the crossing New Bridge. These days it is the Old Bridge. For more than two hundred and fifty years it has drawn tourists to this, the true capital of Wales. In fact, I reckon that the Old Bridge has been painted, sketched, and photographed almost as often as Michelangelo's *David*. And just like their Florentine cousins, Pontypriddians have learned how to flog an icon. The town museum holds examples of illustrated souvenir jugs, plates, teacups, and teapots. There is even a maniacal porcelain pig that would not look out of place in Napoleon's army of occupation at Manor Farm. Most of these things were made at the Nantgarw China Works, which was established by Derby-born potter, William Bilingsley, in 1813.

It's the fault of the Romantics, really, this trade in tourist tat. Those who reacted to the gathering pace of the industrial revolution in Britain – and to the social and political upheavals then apparent in France – by looking again at the landscape, did so in the belief that previous generations had taken it all for granted. You can't do that if a copy is sat there on your mantelpiece. One of their number, the rather obscure artist E. B. Edwards, painted the Old Bridge in about 1760. His work typifies the spirit of that soon-to-be revolutionary age: our eye is drawn (as it is meant to be) to mountains, to woodland, to the river, and, of course, to the Old Bridge, but the effect could hardly be described as remarkable. Bland would be a better word. This other Edwards was evidently a second-rate artist. Still, his painting has found its way into the collections of the National Library of Wales – the Aberystwyth graveyard of the amateur – and there it is certainly admired by those who know no better.

More able painters arrived soon enough. Richard Wilson, the pioneer of landscape painting and co-founder of the Royal Academy, produced his much-imitated view, *The Great Bridge over the Taaffe in South Wales*, at some point in the mid-1760s, all but erasing any popularity accrued to E. B. Edwards' artwork. Wilson's 'Great Bridge' was then translated into a mass-reproducible form by the French-born but London-resident engraver, Pierre Charles Canot. His edition was exhibited at the Society of Artists in London in 1766 and then in July 1775 it was included in a volume of Wilson images entitled *Six Views in North and South Wales*, issued by the publisher John Boydell. Together they put Pontypridd on the map.

Copies and reproductions abounded, so that by the time J. M. W. Turner created his own fine portrait of Edwards' crossing in 1798, there were scores of images in circulation, with no apparent let-up in the rate of production. One of the better ones was by John Lewis. His *Pontypridd*, which likely dates from 1767, bears many striking similarities to Wilson's artwork (or the Canot engraving) and reveals a remarkable setting, one full of rugged beauty not unlike the Yorkshire Dales. Alice Vernon (née Ibbotson), later the Countess of Shipbrook, displayed her Wilson-inspired *View of the new bridge over the Taaff in the County of Glamorgan* at the Society of Artists in 1771 and again in 1774. At least four more examples by other artists were exhibited at the Royal Academy between 1778 and 1798. Pride of place in the collections at Pontypridd Museum is given to Julius Caesar Ibbotson's *Bridge of Beauty* from 1790, which not only rendered the bridge accurately (where plenty of eighteenth-century artists had failed to that) but also set it in the distance, with the viewer's interest captured first by hills and second by approaching cattle drovers.

Finally, there's the story of Josiah Wedgwood copying Wilson's 'Great Bridge' on to a part of the nine-hundred-and-fifty-two-piece Imperial Russian Dinner Service which had been ordered from Wedgwood's Staffordshire factory by Catherine the Great. It was once claimed that the Empress had requested – and received (for there's a copy of it in the National Library) – a miniature portrait of William Edwards to see for herself the face of the man who had designed this modern wonder of the world, the Old Bridge at Pontypridd. This is surely a legend because in St Petersburg the bridge graced nothing more extravagant than a tureen lid.

6.

Where artists went, writers inevitably followed. Lord Lyttleton, statesman, patron of the arts, and friend of poet Alexander Pope and novelist Henry Fielding, arrived in Pontypridd in the summer of 1774. 'The sylvan ride,' he recalled of his journey through the

Glamorgan countryside, 'form[ed] a pleasing picture.' Richard Twiss, on his way from London for a tour of Ireland in 1775, stopped off in town especially to cross over the 'celebrated bridge'. George William Manby, sailor and inventor of the fire extinguisher, was so impressed with what he saw that the description in his book of tours taken from his home in Clifton came close to adjectival orgasm. This is the scene from the banks of the River Taff:

> The beautiful structure of Pont-y-Pridd bursts on the sight, placed in such a situation as to be completely concealed until a very near approach, when the delight and surprize to see so light and beautiful a structure bending over so immense a stream, makes language too poor for its description; the torrent is seen stealing from behind a fertile and well cultivated hill, pleasingly diversified with wood [with] all the delight of these contrasting scenes, the eye was scarcely allowed leisure to gaze by the elegant structure which was striding across a furious stream.

John Thomas Barber Beaumont, insurance agent and amateur artist, went even further into splurging flights of fancy, telling readers of his *Tour Throughout South Wales and Monmouthshire*, that the Old Bridge looked like 'a magic bow thrown across by the hands of fairies'.

It is easy to forget when reading these accounts that the Old Bridge was erected for money. It was a rational product of a stonemason's mind and put up on commission. Searching the archives for more information reveals exactly this earthly materialism. At the Royal Institute of British Architects, for example, there is a plan of the Old Bridge as drawn by the Cambridge architect and bridge builder James Essex in 1762. At the Royal Society, there is a similar picture by the civil engineer and associate of the Lunar Society, John Smeaton, who described it as 'being the South prospect of the New Bridge over the River Taaf in Glamorgan Shire.' Although undated, the plan was evidently made sometime before the artist's death in 1792 and reflected his interest in bridge design and construction. Both plans are marked with dimensions and other architectural details.

Most eighteenth-century readers would have been familiar with the anonymous plan published in the *Gentleman's Magazine* in 1764. It accompanied an article by a writer identified there only as T. M. His real name was Thomas Morgan, and he was a Welsh nonconformist minister then living and working in Morley in West Yorkshire. Morgan possessed detailed knowledge not only of the bridge's technical specifications but also of Edwards himself. The two ministers must have known each other. Incidentally, Thomas Morgan gives the date of construction as 1756, so the advocates of 1755 are wrong. Soon afterwards the article and plan were reprinted in Edinburgh, by the *Scots Magazine*, and on the continent, where they were both included by the compilers of the French *Dictionnaire Raisonné des Sciences, des Arts et des Métiers* (a volume published in Amsterdam and Paris) and by the editors of various German magazines, thus adding to the crossing's renown.

The standout admirer of the Old Bridge was King George III, who added Morgan's plan to a collection of prints gathered by the royal library from the 1760s until the 1790s. Together they form part of a vast compendium of maps and plans compiled by the monarch in pursuit of enlightened and scientific understanding. The entire collection was donated to the nation by George IV in 1828, and so they are now housed in the British Library. Not bad going for a place shown in those drawings as not much more than a hamlet or, as Mr Beaumont put it in 1803, a little village in the hillsides.

In fact, Pontypridd was already antique when William Edwards built his New Bridge. Establishing just how old requires a detour.

The name Pontypridd – or Pont-y-ty-pridd in full – means 'the bridge by the earthen house'. You will have noticed already that the bridge (pont) is often understood to be Edwards' crossing. This is an understandable mistake but a mistake all the same. The trouble is no one in the past could agree on orthographic standards, so in the present we can be easily confused. In the eighteenth century there was considerable variety of spelling, often phonetic, and so we have:

Pontytypraid and Pontytypridd,
Pontypridd and Pontyprid,
Ponty-pridd and Pont-y-prydd,
Ponteprieth and Pont tu te'Pryth.

The further back we go, the more variants emerge from the records. My search for the first incarnation of Ponty takes me to the 1690s and to a letter sent to the Oxford antiquarian Edward Lhwyd. This tells me that the:

Taaf river washes the north and east side of the parish [of Llantwit Fardre] to Pentirch from Ponty y Ty Pridd and Pont Newidd where the Rhonddi runs into the Taaf.

Lhwyd received other letters at this time, following a series of parochial queries he had made of local clergy, and these confirm the existence of a bridge-cum-crossing place near the confluence of the rivers Rhondda and Taff at Ynysangharad and that it was called, with only minor variation (and to use the modern spelling), Pontypridd. There is one other corroborative reference to draw on. This one is courtesy of farmer Ieuan Jones. In his last will and testament, written in English and which he signed on his deathbed in September 1665, he bequeathed an earthen house, the ty pridd of the town's name, to his wife Katherine. Although there is no mention of a bridge in this source, it suggests nevertheless that Pontypridd is at least a century older than its famous Old Bridge.

Those who lived here in those days – in the reign of William III and Mary II, Queen Anne, and the Georges – are largely hidden from view. On occasion we glimpse their descendants because tourists wrote about some of the people they met. Edward Daniel Clark, who passed through Pontypridd in the summer of 1791, for example, tells of the owner of an alehouse in the vicinity of the Old Bridge who, 'with no small degree of cruelty', drowned an elderly mastiff in the river. The pub was probably the same one that John Beaumont called 'the village alehouse', but neither he nor Clark bothered to give it a name, so we do not know for certain.

The best description of Pontypridd as an inhabited place, and the only one we can still follow, comes from the author of the *Cambrian Directory* published in Salisbury in 1800. He saw those parts of the town that touring artists and writers often ignored: the industrial quarters. Noting that the town had been originally 'well adapted to retirement and reflection', he went on to say that this aspect was changing. Yes, he had been drawn by the bridge. Yes, he stayed at the Duke of Bridgewater's Arms at Glyntaff, rather than in the town centre. And yet he saw the Glamorganshire Canal for what it was – the herald of something new. It had been built almost a decade earlier in 1792, as our author says 'for the purpose of conveying the iron from the Myther Works [i.e. Merthyr Tydfil] to Cardiff [and] renders it [Pontypridd] a place of frequent business and confusion.'

With the opening of the Brown Lenox Chainworks at Trallwn at the end of the Napoleonic Wars, the town began to industrialise. The chainworks were never named for Pontypridd, however. Early appearances in press notices instead introduced the place as the Newbridge Iron Works or the Patent Iron Cable Works at Newbridge. From 1815, the English name got stuck. Thus, it was

Newbridge not Pontypridd that petitioned parliament for the abolition of colonial slavery in 1830, it was Newbridge not Pontypridd that was spoken of in 1839 as somewhere 'Chartism has widely spread', and it was Newbridge not Pontypridd that appeared on the tithe map of the 1840s and so gave John Calvert the name of his first colliery.

Pontypridd never went away entirely, of course. It existed alongside the other name, especially in Welsh language circles. Dr William Price's Chartist co-operative store, which operated in the early 1840s, was called the Pont-y-ty-Prydd Provision Company; Calvert's rival, John Edmunds, called his own enterprise Pontypridd Colliery; and there was the Pontypridd Literary, Scientific and Mechanics' Institution. When the latter opened its doors in 1845, full of the spirit of optimism that sprang from believing 'knowledge is the natural aliment of the mind', there was not even a debate about which placename to adopt. Newbridge was not considered. It was a sign of yet more change to come.

There is, I'm afraid, little truth to the legend that the town's Trollope-esque postmaster, Charles Bassett, made the switch all by himself in 1856 because, to quote Meic Stephens who relates the legend as history, he (Bassett) 'had grown tired of having to deal with mail intended for the many other New Bridges in Britain and Ireland.' The real turning point was during that year of revolutions, 1848. It was then that the town was afforded the right to process money orders by the Treasury and the Post Office in London referred not to Newbridge but finally and permanently to Pontypridd.

7.

You can still see something of the pre-industrial landscape if you go up onto the hillsides. It's where I am now, in fact, on the footpath running between the Graig and Treforest fighting with

some cavalier ferns and shoe-swallowing mud not far from a
long-forgotten firing range. On a clear day, you can stand and
stare out for miles from here. To the left (north) lies the Rhondda,
to the right (south) the downward slide towards Cardiff, and
ahead of me are the majestic woods of the Lan and Craig-yr-
Hesg. In the winter, with its rock denuded of foliage, the latter
looks just like the craggy brow of an ancient boxer.

I step off the footpath to search for a particular location: the
spot from which Tony Frank took the cover photograph of *From
the Heart*, Tom Jones's fourth studio album released in 1966. To
compare then and now I have a reproduction folded up in my
pocket. Eventually I find what I am looking for: there's the railway
line and the Brunel viaduct over the River Rhondda; there's the
spire of St Catherine's pointing into the sky; the riverside tennis
courts and bowling greens in the park; and the serpentine Taff
Street winding from the Old Bridge to the railway station. The
old hometown looks much the same.

I'm not the first to essay this place. Twenty years ago, in his
inaugural lecture at the University of Glamorgan, Treforest
native Meic Stephens imagined a frontier town on the boundary
between 'Blaenau and Bro Morgannwg, the upland and lowland
districts of the old county of Glamorgan.' For Graigwen native
Alun Richards, novelist and screenwriter *par excellence*, this was
a confluence town, somewhere like Pottsville in Pennsylvania,
where that American master of the short story, John O'Hara,
grew up. As for the Rhondda novelist, playwright, and broad-
caster, Gwyn Thomas, Ponty in its heyday was like the biblical
Damascus: a meeting place, a locus of culture and industry, trade
and tourism, all symbolised by a shopping bag and a scared
pedestrian. He stressed the town's pre-industrial as well as its
industrial past, a fusion that afforded a more genteel atmosphere
than the klondike gulches to the north. Ponty, after all, had a
branch of Woolworths and a Marks and Spencer.

My own view is different, partly because I have roots outside of South Wales and partly because I never knew heavy industry at first hand. It was all but gone by the time I arrived. Although I have learned what that older society was like, from hours of research in the archives and from talking to those who did grow up in the shadow of coal tips, winding gear, and colliery hooters, I am part of the first post-industrial generation. Millennial South Walians are compelled to ask – *now what*. The answers we have received so far are as precarious as they are unfulfilling, giving us a world of remarkable technological progress allied to political disengagement, rampant inequality, and social and cultural division.

As a historian I argue that Pontypridd lay at the heartland of American Wales. This was somewhere making money, self-invention, and being modern mattered a great deal. Contemporaries of that past, that World of South Wales, like the boxer Freddie Welsh or the coal owner D. A. Thomas, or the singer Tom Jones, would have agreed with me, as would our best historians. The local MP, Alfred Thomas, who was made Lord Pontypridd in 1912 for services to business (and the Liberal Party), and who was no 'American' Welshman, nevertheless recognised that this was a 'new world town'. It was modern. It was vibrant. It was exciting. Just like the United States, it drew in migrants from all over the world, occasionally even from America itself. To them all, it was a universal place, somewhere they could identify on a map without hesitation. Hence the capital-ess of South Wales. Anything less is to miss the point and to ignore the truth of the past.

8.

I make my way down from the mountain and head towards my starting point: the municipal buildings on Gelliwastad Road. Opened on 11 April 1906, twelve years after the creation of Pontypridd Urban District Council (PUDC), for whom they were to serve as headquarters until the council's abolition in 1974, this was where the town first developed ideas about itself. It was where the town's social democracy was set in motion, where Alfred Thomas thought it appropriate to tell the townspeople they were 'American' and that Cardiff, not yet a city of course, was nothing more than a Ponty suburb. It makes sense to begin at the beginning.

The architect was Henry Thomas Hare of Scarborough. By the time he received the Pontypridd commission, he had designed the town halls of Oxford and Henley-on-Thames, as well as the municipal buildings in Crewe, and would go on from here to serve as the architect for the expanding University College of North Wales in Bangor. Ponty was an attractive proposition for an architect of national significance, and not a provincial off-the-shelf job, as so often these things are nowadays.

There is a wedding party emerging as I arrive. I had hoped to get a clear view of the front of the building and of the sculpted busts of Justitia and Prudentia, but it seems I shall have to wait. To pass the time, and to avoid catching the bouquet, I round the corner and wander on towards the goods yard car park. Since I don't come this way very often, not being a driver, I take the chance to look at the indoor bowls centre; from the outside, at least, given I don't yet have enough grey hair to qualify for membership. The centre launched back in 1988. It is obvious from the brick and stone patterning of the walls that this was not a purpose-built facility, however. In fact, it was once a railway goods shed – hence the goods yard – and has the same dressed stone and yellow-brick crenelations as so much of the local housing stock. It fits neatly into an urban landscape fashioned by industry. Engines and engine drivers living in much the same way.

At this point, I decide I need a cup of tea and so head to the bus station café. It's a branch of the Café Royale over on High Street (one of our local Italians, but more on them later). The surroundings are modest, with Formica tables and bright orange but uncomfortable plastic seats fixed into the ground. On the walls are black-and-white photographs of what would have been blue and cream PUDC buses and local streets from a previous century. The air is a heady mix of fry-ups and halitosis, with cigarette smoke and diesel fumes flowing in from outside. A news ticker is running on the television screen, although the sound is off.

'Depressing isn't it,' says a fellow customer, taking a pause from devouring their all-day breakfast. A forkful of baked beans has been left dangling precariously on the edge of their plate.

'Always the same rubbish, mind,' they add, pointing at a politician who has appeared on screen. 'Always the same. And they're all the same n'all.'

They return to more important matters: a solitary hash brown, which they half consume and use the remains to soak up some of the bean sauce. I am about to turn to my tea when the café is interrupted by a loud, obviously alien voice.

''Scuse me,' it says, 'do anybody know, where to is jelly waisted road, please?'

'Over b'there, love,' comes the reply from one of the regulars. They follow it with a sage nod to the right, 'straight on you want.'

Gossip starts up as soon as the door closes, and, after several large gulps from the mug in front of me, I make certain to escape before it is my turn to contribute to the symposium.

9.

Despite all the cars, Gelliwastad Road functions as a boulevard. At one end stands the municipal buildings, at the other the mid-Victorian magnificence of St Catherine's Church, with three chapels – for the most part, ex-nonconformist chapels, St David's Presbyterian Church from 1883, the English Congregational Chapel from 1887-8, and the Wesleyan Methodist Chapel from 1895 – all standing in between.

When civic pride and public revenue was at its greatest, in the years leading up to the First World War, this was a tree-lined avenue and the workplace of the town's professional middle classes. Now, it is a traffic-laden road and the trees have long gone. If you look carefully, you will spy a few solicitor's offices and a dental practice, as well as one of those co-working spaces and a student dormitory, so I suppose at least some of the professionals have stuck around. Between the hours of nine and five, or three-thirty on Fridays, and then it's back in the car to a large house in Cardiff, Penarth, or the more luxuriant parts of the Vale of Glamorgan. Perhaps even to a holiday home or caravan in the west.

The former Wesleyan Chapel, better known as the Muni Arts Centre, is currently being refurbished ahead of its much-anticipated reopening in the summer of 2024. Sandstone lintels, ogival arches, and the recently restored spire glisten as they must have done when the building was brand new. As a product of the 1990s, the Muni marked the belated arrival of The Arts in the valleys, a cultural in-fill of the industrial vacuum. As a child I came here to see pantomime, theatre, and a few of the latest cinema releases: The *Mighty Morphin Power Rangers*, *The Lion King*, *The Mighty Ducks*, and so on. Had I been older, say a teenager, I might well have gone to see Blur in 1993 and decided that modern life is, indeed, rubbish.

In the olden days, which is to say the 1960s, the Muni was the Municipal Hall. No longer a chapel but a public arena, it opened to a fanfare on 14 November 1963. A little over two years later, on 14 January 1966, the hall secured one of its greatest hits: The Who. From that moment, with *My Generation* still fresh in the town's memory, the future was secure, although a scheduled gig by The Kinks that July was cancelled when Ray Davies fell ill. In 1967, it was the turn of Cream, with Eric Clapton on guitar, and in 1968 Duane Eddy then Status Quo rocked all over the world – Ponty included.

My dad worked with a Status Quo groupie for a while, as it happens, which meant a certain supply of stories whenever we met. Cautionary tales that can escape the confines of the tour without embarrassing anyone involved, that sort of thing. She was easily distinguished at the leisure centre, amid the legionaries in their tracksuits with damp hair and overlarge holdalls flung over their shoulder, by the array of band T-shirts she wore. The sort they sell to fans at gigs and for inflated prices. Or what seem like inflated prices in the hungover funk of the morning after, anyway. Dad has a drawerful at home, a reminder that he has been to Marillion and Fish gigs in all sorts of glamorous places. Brecon. Pontardawe. Yeovil. The list goes on. I have a few Billy Bragg ones myself.

If you look carefully at the building, now that the scaffolding has been removed, you will observe some stained glass above the main entrance. This commemorates twenty-five years of twinning between Pontypridd and Nürtingen, near Stuttgart in Germany, or rather commemorated twenty-five years when it was installed in 1993. The local bigwigs embraced the concept of twinning soon after the Second World War, tantalised by the prospect of exchanges and reconnaissance visits. Aka duty free. Early discussions were with the French mining and rugby town of Rive-de-Gier in the Loire, on the surface, an ideal candidate. Alas, the talks came to nothing.

The successful twin, Nürtingen, was famous for its textile industry and was known, affectionately, as the City of Knitwear. After some sightseeing, and with suitcases loaded on the return leg with gifts and ample supplies of West German beer, an informal agreement was signed in the autumn of 1960. This set the two towns on the path to formal twinning in July 1968. 'A real bond of friendship exists,' declared the *Pontypridd Observer* at the time. There were the usual grumbles about expenses and so on, as there always are, but nothing was going to derail Pontypridd from becoming actively European. Indeed, unique among its valley neighbours, certainly in Rhondda Cynon Taf, the town voted to Remain in the 2016 Brexit Referendum. The Mistake happened elsewhere.

Twinning's greatest legacy was in education and in the wider world of ideas and culture. As the poet Schiller put it: *Alle menschen werden Brüder*. Local schools were committed to teaching European languages as part of this wider continental civic mission. So it was that, forty years later, I studied French and German to A Level at what had once been the town's grammar school but was a mixed comprehensive in my day. One class had me reading and writing about the marriage troubles of Thérèse Desqueyroux and the existential angst of Meursault, the other about Heinrich Böll's clowns, Franz Kafka's beetles, and Wolfgang Borchert's disenchanted wartime soldiers. All in the original. There were regular exchanges of students and staff and a European Christmas, which sixth-formers put on each year for the younger students in years seven and eight. What a privilege.

At the time, I took all this for granted, nor do I imagine that I was uniquely unreflective. But it was rather unusual. French was taught in most schools, of course, but German was a rare offer, even then, and altogether rarer now. Annual GCSE and A-Level entries measure in the low hundreds. Coedylan taught German because of that earlier wave of fellowship and post-war reconciliation. This way we were exposed not only to the memories of the 1930s and 1940s in our history lessons but also to the perspectives of the French and German-speaking worlds. We did not question our ties to Europe, we knew we were part of it. We knew we belonged. I know I did.

I carry on with my walk and soon arrive at St Catherine's Church. I am tempted to refer to it as St Catz, in recall of the Oxford college. The church was designed by John Norton, a disciple of Augustus Pugin, although it lacks most of the latter's usual architectural flourishes. Indeed, one critic wrote that St Catherine's is better inside than out, the interior being 'muscular & 1860s-ish'. It is certainly richer inside than out. There are Gothic arches, Bath stone, and red and black brick patterning, a Star of David and *A* (alpha) and Ω (omega) are set into the walls. Forget puritanical churches and nonconformist chapels with their whitewash, there are plenty of those elsewhere, St Catz is full of Anglo-Catholic, Mediterranean colour. This is High Anglican camp.

Since I mostly visit religious buildings as a tourist, I am interested in what was going through the architect's mind when he (or she) came up with the design. Besides the pay packet at the end of the contract. With St Catz, it is almost as if one part of the work was done when Mr Norton was sober and the other after one glass too many: port or sherry perhaps. It is easily done. As a student, I was an occasional chorister at St Edmund Hall, Gwyn Thomas's former college, and where a friend was the organ scholar. He's now the organist at the Anglican cathedral in Copenhagen. The booze on offer after evensong was usually Bristol Cream. Rest assured, those lapis-coloured bottles lasteth not. Out we would roll from the chaplain's rooms to the dining hall, already tipsy and singing a variant of 'praise my soul, the king of heaven':

Praise my soul, the king of sherry,
To this glass my tribute bring.
Sickly sweet with hints of cherry,
Drink it ev'ry time we sing.
Raise them, raise them,
Raise them, raise them,
Raise your glass to Bristol Cream!

I wander towards the covered market, this time for something to eat. Entering from Penuel Lane, I move between stalls selling tea towels, biscuits, disposable lighters and fuel, and fruit and vegetables. The last has had a recent upgrade, so looks more like a farm shop than it once did. I pause to let a mobility scooter pass and it is in this moment that, for what seems like the first time in my life, although surely it cannot be, I notice what the stalls of miscellany are called: Melon Cauli.

My destination is the Cortile café in the central hall, where the smell of coffee, paninis, and ginger cake fills the air. This is where Italian tradition meets West Yorkshire ingenuity and all in a contemporary South Walian style. A young child is discovering the sounds of the piano in one of the two snugs and the tables are occupied by their usual mix of lanyards and pensioners. A pot of tea made with the smoky oolong of central Asian caravans arrives at my table, along with some cheese on toast. As I fumble with a sachet of brown sauce, I listen to the orders being placed at the counter. Latte after latte after latte, with the odd Americano or builder's brew thrown in. I make a mental note to ask the baristas what sort of coffee they sell most, although the answer is already obvious.

The stalls in this part of the market hall are testament to the different phases of a person's life: behind me are Linda's picture frame shop, a carpet shop, and one selling window blinds, ahead there is the darts specialist, the baby clothes specialist, the folks who can convert VHS into digital files, the traditional sweet shop selling liquorice and toffees from jars, and a second-hand bookshop out of which, every so often, someone emerges with a pile of romances, thrillers, detective stories, comics, or the occasional large-print western. I wave towards Simon and Kathy, who have kept me supplied with sweets and books for years.

Above me is a cinema: the Town Hall Cinema. Or rather, it was. Closed. That often happens, doesn't it. Neglect of a good thing. The original features are all there, still, so I am told, they are just covered in layers of dust, together with an ugly concrete render on the outside of the building that has all the charm of botched plastic surgery and a firmly locked entrance complete with rusty padlocks. Other relics of the Town Hall Cinema abound, like the ironwork in the lane (another one) leading between the Market Chambers and the Blueberry Hotel. In brilliant white it reads reserve entrance.

Enter that way now and you'll be greeted with a heady fusion of baking bread, Welsh cakes frying on the griddle, and whatever it is that makes brand-new push-bike tyres smell quite so appealing. This is the food hall, the oldest part of the market, where locals come to buy meat, eggs, vegetables, cakes, and pasties, or, if they're vegetarian, one of a range of spices and some falafel. The space has had a makeover in recent years, with some of the renovations still ongoing, but with a trained eye, it is still possible to spot aspects of what was originally called Newbridge Market.

People of a certain age will tell you this market is famous. It did once have international fame as the 'Petticoat Lane of Wales', that is true, but newspaper headlines declaring that SOON ALL OF PERSIA WILL HEAR OF OUR MARKET, which ran quite often in the 1950s and 1960s, have long since ceased to be printed. Now, I suspect, the market's renown rests more on its relationship with the town and its people than on the tourist trade, a return to the Victorian way of doing things. The nineteenth century was truly the golden age of indoor market halls, a symptom of South Wales' growing prosperity and consumer demand for an expanding range of fresh and dried produce. The process seems to have started right here in Pontypridd in 1805. Tredegar followed in 1811, Newport in 1817, Bridgend, Merthyr Tydfil, and Neath in 1837, Brynmawr in 1844, Aberdare in 1853, Maesteg in 1881, Caerphilly in 1889, and Pontypool in 1894. Cardiff and Swansea, which had eighteenth-century markets of their own, were upgraded towards the end of the nineteenth century.

Popular taste has changed a lot over the years, of course. Growing up, it was still possible to buy tripe in the food hall – my memory of the stuff is shaped by a squeamish reaction when someone explained where this white honeycomb, which we were buying for an elderly neighbour, came from – or freshly made faggots from the butcher. Mum liked those, or else the frozen ones from the aptly named Mr Brains. They're still around, faggots, but modern palates tend towards marinated chicken breasts, duck eggs, and kebab skewers. Oh, and the sausages are no longer the emulsified, high-fat offal tubes they used to be. There is one new star: an award-winning Chinese restaurant. Opened in 2019, Janet's is always full and the wisest visitors to the market slow down as they walk past, for a long breathe in of the aromas coming from the kitchen. Janet's has proven so successful that it has expanded to three times its original size and, in so doing, it has taken over the former American diner. There's a metaphor for our twenty-first-century moment.

Outside on Church Street is the local branch of Lloyd's Bank and an imposing grey stone building whose wheatsheaf emblems give away that this was once the Co-op. Not Pontypridd Co-operative Society – founded in 1899, folded in 1905, and based at No. 36, Taff Street – this was instead the headquarters of Ynysybwl Co-operative Society. With much fanfare and optimism, they unveiled this building in June 1932, cocking a snoop at the market company opposite, and marking half a century of sustained growth as a business. At its peak, Ynysybwl Co-operative had branches as far afield as Taffs Well and Whitchurch in Cardiff and pioneered self-service at their branch in Treforest. Turning back to the exterior façade of the market, I notice the various phases of construction: Georgian neoclassicism cast in dark, functional stone versus the yellow and terracotta brick of the Victorian extensions. The latter were in part an architect's reference to the coat of arms of Gilbert de Clare, the Earl of Gloucester and Marcher Lord of Glamorgan, which was a field of yellow marked with red chevrons, but they had another purpose, too.

They said, loudly and proudly, that we are prosperous, we are civic
– read: civilised – just like Manchester, Liverpool, Birmingham,
Leeds, or London.

10.

I progress on to Penuel Square. With its fountain festooned with
various slogans and dragons, sadly not the originals since they
were stolen years ago and only one was ever recovered, this is the
absolute centre of Ponty. It is to the town what the Hayes is to
Cardiff, and just like the Hayes there used to be subterranean
public conveniences. The entrance, filled in with concrete during
one phase of redevelopment, is now covered by a tree, some soft
tarmac, and set into the paving are words from the song '*Ym
Mhontypridd mae nghariad*'. Love and the Lav.

The underground loo complex is still there, as it happens.
During an eye test just before the pandemic, I discovered that the
nearby branch of Specsavers had excavated underground to
house some of their consulting rooms and optical labs. Towards
the end of the exam, the optician and I got chatting about our
mutual experiences as students, and then I explained that this
whole area stretching below Taff Street had once been a bog. I left
the variables of definition hanging as I received my prescription
for continued shortsightedness.

Above ground, as pedestrians make their way in different
directions, not always conscious of the No. 99 bus service creeping up behind them, I look around at the buildings and their
several dis/continuities. Some are Victorian, others are part of
the constant reconsideration of urban space in the last century.
Penuel Chapel, which gave the square its name, was demolished
in 1967. It had been around in that form since 1860 (with some
modifications made in 1875). An earlier chapel serving the local
Welsh methodist congregation was built on the site in 1817. Debate

about what was to come afterwards raged in the *Pontypridd Observer* through the late 1960s, with anger cast at 'outside developers'. Isn't it always? One resident told the press that 'I feel that we want more car parking facilities in the town and not more shops and offices.' Another proposed a community space because 'Pontypridd has no culture at all. It should have a museum, an art centre, or at least a live theatre.' It was 1986 before any of those ideas came to fruition. In the event, a concrete disservice to taste, officially known as Fraternal Parade, was all that was built. It's still there. The shop facing the fountain, now an American ice-cream parlour, was first taken on by Eastern Carpet Stores. It has been a pharmacy in the interim.

By the 1990s, many residents were clear that the 1960s had been a decade of good music but bad planning decisions and so had bequeathed a poor legacy to those who came after. From the vantage of the 2020s, it could have been a lot worse. Imagine the impact of a multi-storey car park in the centre of town: ever more traffic, diminished air quality, the clear and present danger of getting run over, and so on. Fraternal Parade may be ugly and architecturally redundant, like most shopping centres, but at least its stubborn resistance to change has allowed for daytime pedestrianisation of the area. For those of us with poor eyesight, that's a godsend.

I take a seat on one of the benches and lean over to retie my shoelaces. While prone, I get several offers for my future. I'll retell the story in real time. First there is Jesus, dead on the cross for my sins. I recognise Idris, the man carrying his banner. He has come down from Ynysybwl on the bus. The painted cloth celebrating the gospel is decades older than me. Soon he is replaced by athletic American missionaries in tight trousers and crisp white button-downs, they have a black and white badge on their breast pocket and are offering me the book of Mormon. Muscular Christianity has its temporary charms and for a moment they even seem encouraged by my willingness to play along, apparently unaware that my own knowledge of their faith has been framed by a Broadway musical. They eventually realise that I am an atheistic heathen and so scurry off to convert someone else. My final caller is a self-proclaimed communist:

'I dreamt I saw old Joe last night,' he says, musically. 'Alive as you and me.'

'Isn't that hill abandoned now,' I reply, showing off my knowledge of Paul Robeson's back catalogue.

'No,' he says. 'No. The Republic of the Workers is soon to be upon us. J. C. is with us again. J. C., J. C.' He trails off slightly. 'Jay Z.'

From the cavernous insides of his pull-along trolley he extracts a newspaper. I recognise the print as belonging to the *Daily Mail* but say nothing. Perhaps this is all part of some elaborate know thy enemy scheme. Enough people in their seventies and eighties have told me that their parents would buy both the *Daily Herald* and the *Daily Express* from the newsagent to suggest that it might be, though I have my sincere doubts. There is no getting around the *Mail*'s popularity, is there. According to the latest news consumption survey published by regulator Ofcom, the *Mail* has the biggest sales of any newspaper in Wales and traffic to its website outstrips that going to WalesOnline or more progressive sources like the *Guardian* and the *Daily Mirror*. The figures for the *Mail*'s audience are higher in Wales (at fifteen per cent) than they are in Scotland (at twelve per cent) or Northern Ireland (nine per cent), with the combined UK figure at thirty-six per cent of the total.

'Good paper the *Mail*,' he says eventually. 'Specially for the financials.'

'Lots of people read it around here,' I reply.

'Well, aye, I've noticed. I have to get to the paper shop early of a morning or they sell out, don't they. Used to always get the *Observer* but it's all adverts now, isn't it.'

I nod, aware that I have not read the *Pontypridd Observer* for some years myself, and so leave Red with his paper and its enclosed reports of last week's turbulence on the FTSE. With my laces newly tied, I resume my search for things that have gone. The electronics store Tandy, for example, which arrived here in 1990. Known as Radio Shack in the US, Tandy sold video games and consoles, as well as BASIC computers and their necessary peripherals.

My own memory of the place is of buying torch batteries and, in the company of my parents, a few games for my Sega Mega Drive. It is hard for a child to appreciate, or even to remember, the costs involved in the purchase of video games consoles in those days. Fortunately, someone has digitised a run of Argos catalogues from the period and placed them online, so I can check. Alright, yes, it is so I can reminisce as well; nostalgia is a powerful drug when correctly administered. In a few moments I find myself staring back at my childhood. Gameboys (£69.95), Sega Mega Drives (£127.95), the Super Nintendo (£109.99). Mario, Sonic, and Zelda. My eyes widen and are drawn to the prices. Adjusted for inflation, those 16-bit machines of the 1990s were much more reasonable than today's consoles with their life-like graphics, but there can be no doubt that Mum and Dad had to save up and go without to afford them.

Tandy is gone, there's a bargain shoe shop in its place, and I do not suppose it is mourned. Anyone with a mobile phone in their pocket holds a device more powerful, both in processing and graphics, than those old games consoles and home computers. In a few seconds, I can download the original Sonic the Hedgehog game and start playing. But it is not really the same as on a flicker-ing thirteen or fourteen-inch portable black-and-white television with a three-button controller and your sister demanding her turn and your dad telling you you're going the wrong way.

I got distracted from the fountain, didn't I. Sorry. If Penuel

Square is the centre of town, then the fountain is its heart. It has no grander title, just The Fountain. With its days as a water supply over, it now exists as a temporary shelter for pigeons or for discarded crisp packets and cigarette ends, but this remains a worthy landmark all the same. It was unveiled in October 1895 and paid for by Alfred Thomas (yes, him again). The cost of the thing was £250, the equivalent of about £27,000 today. Given its longevity, not a bad investment, but a substantive one all the same. Thomas knew what he was doing. Progressive towns on the make need public art. As he told the townspeople at the unveiling ceremony, Pontypridd 'has been designed by nature for a great town' and it was 'the first duty of those who were entrusted with the public weal to see that art might second the great opportunities that nature afforded.'

The winning design, submitted by Charles B. Fowler of Cardiff into a competition of thirty entries, was heralded at the time as being 'thoroughly Welsh in character' as well as 'filled in with ancient British ornament'. Jets of water were intended to evoke leeks, the lamps at the head of the fountain were to be supported by dragons, and various mottos, such as *Duw a Digon* (With God, Enough), were carved into the stone. All this added to the fountain's apparently Cymric virtue. As far as I can tell, the fountain was intended to be a symbol of Wales and of the Welsh at a time of cultural, political, and economic optimism but also significant change. In other words, it was to serve as a physical reminder of tradition amid rapid transformation, even Anglicisation. In this spirit, Thomas expressed himself in favour of changing the town's name from Pontypridd to something else, something that would give an 'indication as to the character or appearance of the locality, as Welsh placenames usually did'. Or so he said.

The answer was not Newbridge, as it happens, but Aber-Rhondda: the mouth of the river Rhondda. In Thomas's view, this was Ponty's 'natural name'. One too many glasses of ceremonial wine or parliamentary cognac lay at the heart of this invention. No, I'm being a little unfair. These were standard sentiments among the Liberal-supporting middle classes of the 1890s and have been around in the minds of the Cymry, if not the Welsh, ever since. Alfred Thomas would have heartily signed crankish online petitions to overturn the 'English' name for the Brecon Beacons, or Snowdonia, or even Wales itself, and may have even started them if given half the chance. Thomas's fountain contains an ironic secret, however, which I reveal with a mischievous enthusiasm of my own. Despite its 'ancient' symbolism, its dragons and its Celtic patterning, the fountain was in fact made in Cheltenham by expert English (or should that be Anglo-Saxon?) craftsmen. The stonework was undertaken by H. H. Martyn and Co. - one of the founders of Gloster Aircraft Company in 1917 - and the ornate copperwork by William Letheren and Sons. It is apt, I think, that the fountain's shallow Celticism can be scratched away to reveal a more diverse reality beneath. After all this was the essence of Penuel Square.

Among the shopkeepers who ran businesses here when the fountain was brand new were jewellers and watchmakers David Cohen, Weibert Heitzman, Morris Malitz, and Francis Xavier Tritschler. There was wallpaper specialist Morris Rubenstein as well. Not all of them were Jewish, although they were all immigrants: some from Russia, others from Germany. Italian cafés busied themselves not far away, and still do. The concentration of Jewish shops in this part of Pontypridd was no accident. In Penuel Lane, just along from the fountain and towards the entrance of the fruit and vegetable market, there is now a gap where buildings have been demolished over the years. It's sadly overgrown with buddleia and other weeds, but on this site once stood a 'cozy little synagogue' - the first non-Christian place of worship to be opened in the town, though by no means the last - the culmination of twenty-five years of settlement and assimilative integration.

Services began in the summer of 1867 with room enough inside for about fifty congregants: the common language would have been Yiddish – and in all its dialectical variations, from northern Litvish to southern Ukrainish – with Russian, Polish, German, or perhaps broken English as a second tongue. Subscriptions for upkeep and maintenance came from as far away as Birmingham and London, even Jerusalem. The senior member was David Goodman, in all probability Pontypridd's first Jewish resident. He established his watchmaking and pawnbroking business near the market in 1843, moving south from Merthyr Tydfil when he was in his early twenties. His parents came from Poland. In 1846, he married Louisa Himes (an anglicisation of Hyams), the eldest daughter of one of London's long-established Jewish families. Moreover, when Louisa's father Barnett died in 1875, at the apparent age of one hundred and one, he was described as the city's 'oldest member of the Jewish community'. Louisa's sister, Isabella, married an equally interesting individual: Yantub Levy Bensheton, a Moroccan Jew. The pair settled in Merthyr, where Yantub opened a second-hand clothes shop in Castle Street. When he died in 1878, after forty years living in that place, one local newspaper said of him that he 'was highly respected'. I have no doubt that Yantub and Isabella were seen in Ponty visiting their in-laws at a house on the corner of Bridge Street and Taff Street – where the town library now stands – for in those early years of the community, Ponty's Jews thought of themselves as an extension of Merthyr.

Once Pontypridd had its own synagogue, it became an independent centre with social extensions running into the Rhondda. News from the town flowed into the Jewish press, too. There were a mere two mentions of Ponty in the *Jewish Chronicle* prior to 1867, but hundreds in the decades afterwards, giving detail on all sorts of activities that might otherwise have gone unreported. Of this mid-Victorian Jewish milieu, nothing much survives in physical form. There is neither signpost nor plaque nor notice-board, nor is there literary evocation akin to Saul Bellow's Chicago, Paul Auster's New York, or Bernice Rubens and Dannie Abse's Cardiff. History and memory, fragile as they are, even when described as heritage, are all that are left. A record to mark the creation of a Zionist association of fifty members in 1900, census returns, the synagogue minute books, however incomplete, a small number of photographs, a match report, notices of weddings or funerals, and those picture postcards of the fountain in the background of which can be seen the sign for Rubenstein's wallpaper shop.

II.

I make my way from Penuel Square to The Prince's café. The brainchild of Dominico Gambarini, this place has been on Taff Street for three quarters of a century, perma-set in post-war art deco. Most days there is a queue to sit in, another to pick up food for takeaway, and a third just for bread and cakes. A meal in the art deco dining room is always stamped special occasion, even if your excuse is nothing more than dodging the weather. A noted local pastime, that one. I have saved up some calories over the past few weeks to justify a custard slice with my lunch. There is something wonderful about this confection of puff pastry, white fondant icing, and bright orange-yellow custard that tanta-lises and treats.

And it is not just me. Every day the shop window is filled with a fresh batch. None ever survives until tomorrow, the posher ones with a layer of blackberry jam in the puff pastry often disap-pear first. It is the same with the cannoli, the crêpes, the fruit tarts, the pasties, and the bread rolls.

My slice arrives along with an espresso, and I take a moment to consider my assault. Some adopt the divide-and-conquer method:

you cut the custard in two along the horizontal axis and dig in with a spoon. The danger with that is either the fondant icing or the custard sticks to the plate. A pyrrhic victory. Others, me included, go for the skirmish: the use of a spoon to scoop out the custard until success is assured. Only the novice slicer ever attempts the all-in-one. For that you need a bib, like the ones you get in an American or Canadian restaurant when lobster is served, and anyone around you should take a step back. Or two. Or three, just to be on the safe side. Custard ahoy.

After drinking my coffee Italian fashion (three gulps), I use my phone to research what the café was like at the beginning. WHEN IN TOWN, I read in the *Pontypridd Observer* as though it is June 1948 again, VISIT THE PRINCE'S CAFÉ-RESTAURANT ... MORNING COFFEE LUNCHES TEAS THEATRE SUPPERS. The story goes that Signor Gambarini got the idea for a café on a visit to Bournemouth. It is not difficult to imagine him being inspired by the sea or by one of those tearooms one often finds in coastal resorts and spa towns: Betty's in Harrogate, perhaps, the Grand Café in Oxford, the Georgian tearooms in Bath, or the Winter Gardens in Weston-super-Mare.

Out-of-town visitors often remark that entering The Prince's is like stepping back in time, but I disagree. It is not time that you are wading into, nor even the past, but memory. A community's shared memory, more to the point. Sit here long enough and you will see people married for fifty years flirting with each other like it is a first date; you will see children being taught about life through the medium of food by their grandparents or making faces in the shine of the giant copper coffee machine on the countertop; you will see observers like me chuckling to ourselves as we notice the way the decades collapse in on each other like the compression of an accordion's bellows. It's a scene from an Alan Bennett play, just with a valleys accent.

In fact, there has been a café in this building for a very long time. Before the Gambarini family took it over after the Second World War, the business was owned by Hopkin Morgan, the local equivalent of Brace or Hovis or Warburton. It had been Morgan's since 1888. His bakery-cum-factory was in Trallwn but this restaurant at 74 Taff Street, together with a smaller café at 5 High Street (near the train station), was the main shop front for his business. Back in the nineteenth century, his advertisements were simple and repeated one word four times:

CAKE! CAKE! CAKE! CAKE!

He later branched out with: 'When in Pontypridd, if you want a good dinner or tea served up-to-date call at Hopkin Morgan's.' I prefer the first version, with its hypnotic, sugary rhythm. Why not combine it with a chant from Sardis Road:

Oggy Oggy Oggy!
Cake, Cake, Cake!

It was not only slogans that Hopkin Morgan went in for. He also pioneered the use of commercial machine and then steam baking locally, producing an entire range not just of bread but of cakes, biscuits, and sweets.

All of this made Hopkin Morgan incredibly wealthy. At his death in 1935, he left behind more than £125,000, which in today's terms is worth more than £6 million. His wealth enabled him to enter politics and to direct local civil life. First, he served as a Liberal member of the School Board, to which he was elected in 1889, and then he was a founding member of Pontypridd Urban District Council in 1894. He remained a councillor until his death and served as chairman twice: in 1901-1902 and in 1914-15. His photograph in the newspaper in 1894 showed a dark-haired, moustachioed, thick-set but wide-eyed and alert man of almost forty years. He epitomised this new-world town on the make. There are few alive now who can remember a time before No. 74, Taff Street, was anything other than The Prince's Café. Who indeed can remember a time before custard slices and cannoli, before cappuccinos and lattes, before a fusion of Italian cuisine and British seaside tradition. Not that it matters much.

'Anything else, love,' says the cashier, as I hand over my bill.

I shake my head and explain that I'm full of a custard slice. Ahh, comes the knowing reply, say no more. I hold the door for an older couple coming into the café and take the time to observe the habits of the customers once more. There are those who have come in for a sausage roll, others who are clearly treating themselves to the richest confectionary they can get away with, and still more who come in for loaves of bread, a bag of rolls, a sweet apology for their partner, or the office lunch order. In one way or another, we're behaving exactly as Pontypriddians have always done. Some traditions don't need to be invented.

Outside on Taff Street again, another Italian name catches my eye: Carini. Ponty is blessed with some of the best fish and chip shops anywhere in the world, and with good reason. Many of the Italian families who came here in the nineteenth century were from Bardi or neighbouring villages in the upper Ceno valley south-west of Parma. They brought with them northern Italian traditions of coffee making, gelato, sweet pastries, and, of course, the Genoese method of frying lightly floured fish in olive oil. The chip came from France via Belgium, of course, but it was in South Wales, the Kingdom of the Chip, that fried strips of potato were turned from a Parisian amuse-bouche into a proletarian essential. In the hands of valleys folk, as Gwyn Thomas put it, the humble chip became 'the great culmination of human experience' and the chip shop was an 'extension of the university'.

There have been Italian cafés and restaurants in Pontypridd for more than a hundred and twenty-five years, beginning in the

1890s with Alfonso Fideli's ice-cream shop in Mill Street, Augustine Grande's fish and chip shop, which was also in Mill Street, and a branch of the Bracchi Brothers chain in the centre of Taff Street. That name, Bracchi, was so commonly associated with Italian cafés that it has become the collective name for them in this part of South Wales. In addition to the local Bracchis, there were outlets in Aberaman, Abercarn, Abercynon, Aberdare, Abertridwr, Caerphilly, Ferndale, Glynneath, Hirwaun, Mountain Ash, Newbridge, Newport, Pentre, Pontardulais, Porth, Porthcawl, Resolven, Senghenydd, Tonypandy, and Treorchy. No wonder the name stuck.

The shops developed from hand-drawn ice-cream carts, which were pulled along to wherever a queue might form – the Italian equivalent of the travelling Jewish draper. That was how Antonio Carini, the patriarch of the Carini family, set out on his career. Or so his daughter, Francesca, known to all as Fran, once told me. Her other stories of Toni (as he was known) and his business were about the cart, the churning process, and her own turn at running a café. There, she learned how to fry her chips to be just so. I have never met anyone else able to critique the quality of a strip of fried potato from five-hundred paces, and all by the look and smell. No matter the dousing of vinegar and the coating of salt, Fran always knew whether to take up the offer of a chip or to refuse it.

Armed with a notebook full of historic addresses, I make my way through the town centre to pay homage to what is and what was Ponty's Little Italy. Some of the businesses have gone but many remain open. I start at the top end of town, opposite the entrance to the park. Here is Park View Café run by the Cruci family, as their new awning declares. There is never not a queue here. It can feel like an outpost, set far apart from the rest of the chippies and cafés, but this is a modern phenomenon. Where the library now stands, there was once a row of shops containing a pharmacy and two cafés, one of which (33 Bridge Street) was run by Giuseppe Marenghi. Construction of the Taff Vale Shopping Centre in the

1960s compelled his move around the corner onto Taff Street itself. When I was a child, this second Marenghi's had become The Mighty Cod. Other names appear in my notes: Servini's Café at 26 Taff Street, Albert's Café at 24 Taff Street which was owned by the Antoniazzi family (they also had a chippy in Coedpenmaen Road), and Franchi's Restaurant at 41 Taff Street. Franchi's was another casualty of the shopping-centre development.

The one you'll hear most about, and with due reverence for its legendary quality, is John and Maria's. Situated near the railway station, it was a staple of culinary life for a generation and much missed, although different generations of the family still run the Café Royale and Zucco Juice Bar. John and Maria's restaurant was even mentioned in parliament. This is the story. It was just before the by-election in 1989, which had been prompted by the death of the town's previous MP, Labour's Brynmor John. Jocular to-and-fro about campaign visits led one parliamentarian to remark:

'I assure the honourable gentleman that there is an excellent Italian restaurant.'

The speaking voice belonged to Dafydd Elis Thomas, then Plaid Cymru MP for Dwyfor Meirionnydd and later the ennobled presiding officer of the National Assembly for Wales. His interlocuter was Richard Holt, Conservative MP for Langbaurgh in Cleveland.

'I am sure that he [Holt] will want to dine there,' Thomas continued, 'because he will have nothing else to do if he is to canvass for the Conservative candidate.'

Hansard records laughter from the opposition benches. The parliamentary stamp of approval for John and Maria's was enough to cause a frenzy and not a little jealousy among the town's other cafés and restaurants:

'A source has revealed to us that bags of fish and chips have been arriving in the Commons post from concerned takeaway owners,' wrote the *Pontypridd Observer* a few weeks later.

Kim Howells, the Labour candidate, was duly elected with a majority of more than ten thousand, although there is no record of which café was his favourite. He would serve as MP until his retirement in 2010 and still holds the record for the constituency's largest single majority – a peak of twenty-three thousand votes, which he won in the New Labour landslide of 1997.

Little Italy thrives not because of parliament privilege, though, but because it offers customers pastry, potato, and punchy espresso, all of a quality that is up there with the best of them. There is no need to travel to Birmingham or to West Yorkshire, as one might when searching for a superior curry, or to London for Georgian Khachapuri, the cheese bread with an egg in the centre that might just be the finest food (besides the fried chip) ever invented. And if anyone ever believes the view expressed from outside that working-class people do not drink lattes, well, I refer them to one of the cafés, for this town practically invented frothy coffee.

In fact, I feel strongly that the valleys should make far more of this aspect of our culinary heritage. Forget the black sludge of lava bread that they try to sell you in Swansea or the heavy, speckled lumps of bara brith that have come down from Gwynedd. Forget too about cawl and beer-infused cheese on toast, neither of which are Welsh in the first place. No, for us it is the chip. This is our food. Pontypriddians eat chips with such reverence that one could almost confuse it for an act of religious worship. So cross yourselves and repeat after me: the chip is the chip, it is life itself.

12.

At this point, you must be wondering whether we are in Wales at all, or whether this is an imagined extension either of Manhattan or Bardi, even Odesa. I am not confused myself; I know exactly where I am. Progress along Taff Street from The Prince's Café and you will find a bit of Cymru, I promise, albeit tucked away down a side street. What you're looking for is down the lane between Boots and an estate agent on the opposite corner. From the outside you can tell that the building is of nineteenth-century origin, it has that robust and rugged, some might even say rustic, character of the period. It was built as a brewery, part of the estate belonging to the Rhondda Valley Brewery Company. After 1945, following various consolidations in that trade, it became a warehouse. Then it was bought by a co-operative of like-minded individuals and turned into what it is today.

Sometimes there's a sign which reads Clwb-y-Bont: '*un lleoliad i'r gymuned gyfan.*' When it opened in 1983, this was the first functionally bilingual venue of its kind anywhere in the country, somewhere the entire community could meet (that's the meaning of the Welsh I just quoted) and all apparently without a language barrier. Whether or not that aim to be inclusive was successful, I do not know. From the outset this was known as the Welsh club – i.e. the Welsh language – an idea that became fixed in public consciousness because the executive committee was dominated by members of the nationalist party. The nickname, whether fair or not, stuck fast. For years it was all I knew about the place, and I still don't go in. I am not sure of my welcome. It's here that I feel most like a foreigner, the Englishman of my passport, an alien in my hometown.

Early on, patrons came not only to drink and listen to folk and trad music but also to learn Welsh, to lose weight, to play chess, to heckle any posse of poets who visited, and to campaign for social change. Pontypridd branch of the Anti-Apartheid Movement met inside in the 1980s, for instance, and still today you can find campaigners ready to fill your pockets with leaflets about climate change, the dangers of nuclear weapons, or, as happened in 2002, a 'festival of republican celebration'. Lesson number one: how to stuff the monarchy. In its inimical fashion, Clwb-y-Bont has revitalised an old tradition: social spaces for those movements

47

adjacent to the mainstream, usually on the political left. Some of these movements quickly shifted to the centre as they gained electoral momentum, but not all of them were attracted to power and were quite content existing on the margins.

There is a walk through the centre of Ponty that links all these old political hubs together, I realise, and so I make a note to myself as a reminder to do just that. What do they have in common? What signs of life are there, still? I make a list of those places that I can remember from earlier research on my book *Labour Country* – the Socialist Sunday School, for instance, which met at Graig-y-Wion School on Courthouse Street – and leave space in my journal to fill in those that I have forgotten or have yet to find. None, I know, will be marked by a plaque, or recalled by anyone. I may be the last to have this knowledge in my head. Historians should be realistic, not romantic. Often things are forgotten precisely because they should be. What is interesting in the past is not always significant for the present.

The biggest danger is not political so much as environmental: the River Taff itself. When the water is high, this handsome spot overlooking the park is liable to cause palpitations in patrons, chairpersons, and loss adjusters alike. In 1983, the club hadn't been opened even six months when it experienced its first flood. There have been numerous others in the decades since. The morning after Storm Dennis hit in February 2020, I walked down to Taff Street to survey the damage. Those of us who had gathered at the corner with Market Street watched as a car tried to drive through the floodwaters only to become half submerged outside Boots. It floated into another vehicle which had earlier tried to make the same run. This aquatic traffic jam was strangely absent from the evening news. Clwb-y-Bont itself was cut off: the lane I am now standing in was a muddy, smelly extension of the river. For more than two years, with the pandemic raging, the club was closed for repairs and for reconstruction work to be carried out.

But it is back to a roaring trade and certain voices mutter if you'll let them:

'Been to Clwb yet?'

'Na,' I reply.

Poking my head up against the main entrance, I can see there are some FIFA World Cup posters left over from Cymru's entry into the 2022 finals in Qatar. This is a soccer club, after all, not a rugger one. I also spy the unmistakeable red and white outline of COFIWCH DRYWERYN. This is a copy of the original graffiti painted onto the wall of a ruined cottage south of Aberystwyth by Meic Stephens in the early 1960s. It started out as a protest at the creation of a reservoir near Bala to provide drinking water for Liverpudlians but has since become something else, a kind of pop art that has found its way onto cushions, postcards, and copy-cat memorials from here to Nebraska. Meic's other graffiti, painted on a park wall in Merthyr in support of language rights in 1963, has since been forgotten. If it even still exists.

Getting to know Meic, an icon of Welsh-speaking Wales, a year or so before he died in 2018, I quickly learned that he was a local boy, born in Treforest in 1938 and educated at Pontypridd Boys' Grammar School, not, as I had imagined him to be, a mab of Machynlleth. After a short career as a schoolteacher, mainly in Ebbw Vale, he moved into the literary world and founded the magazine *Poetry Wales* in 1965. Two years later, he became assistant literary director of the Welsh Arts Council, a role which gave him considerable influence over the development of Welsh writing in English – something he retained for the rest of his life.

From the 1990s onwards, Meic was secretary of the Rhys Davies Trust, alongside Dai Smith (as chair), Sam Adams and Peter Finch, a body which used the financial legacy of its name-sake, the Rhondda novelist Rhys Davies, to stimulate short-story competitions and numerous other cultural initiatives, and he was Professor of Welsh Writing in English at the University of

Glamorgan in the early 2000s. His novel, *Yeah, Dai Dando*, appeared in 2008. The story had just enough of Pontypridd in it to tempt me into a reading back then. What I found was the kind of pastiche they love on BBC Wales: 'Hiya, I'm Dai Dando. From up the Coeca estate in Ponty. Working down year [sic] in Cardiff at the Gwalia. We do sell mortgages, see.' I never finished, the faux Wenglish was just too much for me. Sorry Meic.

Emerging from the Clwb-y-Bont courtyard, I turn left into Lower Taff Street, so called because it is at the southern end of the town centre. Developers – and hoodwinked councillors – are busy trying to install the idea of a 'Southern Gateway' (to greet our lords and masters from Cardiff who would never venture up here otherwise). The name makes me want to barf, but as ever bad taste seems to have appealed to those in power who are rushing ahead with it convinced as they are that 'regeneration' means: 'knocking stuff down and putting in some benches'. Growing up, this was the town's commercial heart: Smith's (opened 1984, gone), Woolies (opened 1921, gone), Marks and Spencer (opened 1939, gone), Burton's (opened 1926, gone), and associated banks (gone), restaurants (gone), and cafés (gone). What's left? Poundland, B&M, some phone shops, and a branch of Cortile Coffee.

Some of the retail units around here will always be something else in my mind. It is one of the tricks of memory that affects us in places we know from childhood. Take the gym just along from Boots. That place used to be a Poundstretcher. One of the kindest people I ever knew worked there: Elin. She was a close friend of my mum's. Both in their twenties with young children, they were quite mad when put together, especially when the soundtrack to the *Rocky Horror Picture Show* was put on the stereo and a few bottles of Lambrini were consumed. Whenever I hear the lyrics to 'The Time Warp' or to Mika's 'Big Girl (You Are Beautiful)', I see the two of them in my mind's eye conspiring, giggling, and enjoying life as it ought to be. Perhaps they still are dancing, somewhere.

Mum and Elin met as part of a group of volunteers running the entirely secular Friday-evening Zion Youth Club in the vestry beneath Zion Baptist Chapel in Ynysybwl. The other leaders, all older, in some cases much older, were Gill, Bruce, Pat (who collected our 20p subs in a tin marked up for different household utilities), Jean and Brian (who I later learned had been in a skiffle band in Maesycoed in the 1950s), and white-haired Mahoney Rees who ran the sweet stall. It was a unique sort of environment, a hangover from a very different time, and dedicated to teaching children simple arts and crafts skills. We put on plays (I once appeared as Dopey in *Snow White*), went on fundraising walks over the mountain to Penrhiwceiber, and had summer bus trips to Barry Island. The chapel minister, Keith John, who has since made his career in London, even acquired a ping-pong table for us, and tested his own Christian patience by teaching us how to play.

Meanwhile, the eye-catching Tudorbethan edifice next door to Costa is generating discussion. You know the sort (vocal action, physical inaction):

'It's sad to see such an old building falling apart,' says a well-meaning incomer to a companion.

I stand back and eavesdrop.

'It must be hundreds of years old, and they just let it go. Shocking.'

'Shameful.'

'I've a mind to tell them to do something about it.'

'Quite right.'

The building certainly looks venerable, but I assure you it is a fake, a folly. Formerly a chemist, a musical instrument salesroom, a political party campaign headquarters, an auctioneer's rooms, it is now a charity shop. Perceptions are key here. You're supposed

to think this is the oldest building on Taff Street, and many have
fallen for the ruse. But it is twentieth century. The buildings
either side and opposite are all older, they just happen to look
Victorian or Edwardian. This is what heritage and cultural nostalgia
does to the public's perception and reception of the past, sadly:
it creates a distortion, one that historians are professionally
compelled to correct, when they can.

A few doors up from the Tudor artifice is a three-storey-high,
five-window-wide temple to acquisition: the former Barclays
Bank. It exudes neoclassical confidence in money making. Until
it closed in November 2023, this was the largest bank in Ponty. In
fact, until NatWest closed in February 2024, this corner of Taff
Street was flanked by branches of most of the major high street
banks. Barclays and the Midland Bank (later HSBC, the first to
go in 2021) on the left, as you face the train station, NatWest on the
right. They were joined by the building societies, all named for
their place of origin: Abbey National (with its roots in London),
the Principality (Cardiff-based, of course), Nationwide (which
began as the Co-operative Permanent Building Society in 1884),
the Leeds, the Halifax, and the Bradford and Bingley. West Yorkshire again. It was an early lesson for me in English industrial
geography, much as others once drew their knowledge from the
Football League.

Building societies were designed to mutualise the acquisition
of housing and land, to make it easier, in the long run, for working people to buy homes, and so these organisations were rooted
in the towns and cities in which they were first established. Ponty
had four with titles like 'freehold land and building society',
'house property and investment company', and 'permanent
benefit building society'. None still exists. With one eye on what
happened with the right to buy during the 1980s, the Rhondda
novelist, short-story writer, and environmentalist, Ron Berry,
once called the high rates of home ownership in the South Wales

Valleys the 'conservative bloom on socialism's compost heap'. As younger generations find it increasingly difficult to buy houses of their own, even here, that history of mutualism and demutualisation takes on a fresh relevance. I suspect Ron would have choicer words for the lanyard class, the weeds on the rubbish tip, who can be overheard moaning about their experience as a small-time landlord in whatever Ponty café you choose.

13.

Crossing the road again, I find myself outside Marks and Spencer – or rather, what was. After years standing empty, the store has been knocked down to clear space for a new riverside amphitheatre. Any town with an M&S had a certain quality. Neath had a branch, opened in 1935, so did Llanelli (1937) and Cardiff, Newport, Swansea, and later Cwmbran, but nowhere else in the valleys, certainly not the Rhondda or Merthyr, Caerphilly, Tredegar, or Ebbw Vale. On the M&S Archive website, there's a photograph of the Ponty store taken just after it opened. A couple are shown, arm-in-arm, looking in the window at some nightdresses and stockings. In another large window, to the right of the store's entrance, are men's and women's shoes. A staff photograph from the Neath branch taken in 1938 tells us just a little more of what M&S was really like in those days. Everyone has their hair set just so, uniforms are pressed and ironed, and the company logo is visible on every necktie.

Turning the corner, I am suddenly in a realm of dressed stone. This is the High Street, a narrow corridor between Taff Street and the car-filled death-trap known as the Broadway. The first building on High Street – designated No. 2 by the Post Office – is an office at present but in the last ten years it has been a recruitment agency and a haberdasher's shop. No. 1 High Street, as it happens, was absorbed into Marks and Spencer during expansion of that shop in the late 1950s. So now it is gone for good. Before it disappeared, No. 1 was home to Plowman, Ponty's premier fishmongers. The family also ran a chippy on Mill Street, the aptly named Plowman's Lunch.

High Street, I confess, is better travelled in the past than the present, but I shall do my best to sell its current virtues, of which there are a few, I assure you. No. 3 has been a branch of Nationwide since 1974 and was a wallpaper shop and a butcher in earlier decades. No. 4 is the Café Royale. At No. 5 is one of those modern takes on a pawnbroker, a staple of credit supply to poorer and more vulnerable members of society. Thirty years ago, it was a catalogue bargain shop. Fifty years ago, it was a kind of furniture shop-cum-ponzi scheme which advertised false hope to those looking to make money as sellers in tough times. Has anything changed?

Nos. 6 and 7 tend to be let together. At the start of the old century, they were home to RV James's drapery shop and, by 1970, to the Welsh Dry Cleaners. More recent tenants have included a recruitment agency and a beauty parlour. No. 8 is now a barbershop, but I'm told by a passer-by that it used to be an Italian café. Next door, at No. 9, is the Trattoria, one of Ponty's more formal Italian restaurants. The building stands out from its neighbours thanks to a postmodern render which has stripped away much of the Victorian façade. Such is the extent of the change that it is not actually possible to identify the original purpose (a hotel) with the naked eye. I stop at the window to read the menu. My nose begins to imagine it can smell fresh parmesan shavings atop a properly made carbonara spaghetti or the garlic-infused steam that normally follows cutting into an arancini ball. Alas, the restaurant is closed as I pass: I'm too early for dinner. No. 10 was a Lebanese takeaway for a while, and before that the Express Café, but now the proprietors specialise in pizzas, kebabs, and burgers. Nos. 12 and 13 are also dedicated to fast food.

No. 11, now Platform 11, was formerly the Criterion Hotel, aka the Cri. If you look down, beneath the bowl window that is its calling card, you'll notice a mosaic, a modern reproduction of the unsalvageable original. It reads, in attractive cursive, Criterion. I am as certain as I can be that the mosaics were first installed by a specialist mosaic tiler. On the 1911 census there was one such artist living in Ponty, his name was Giuseppe Capoletti, one of the few Italians to escape the hospitality trade.

In its heyday, say in the late 1950s and early 1960s, the Cri was run by champion boxer and local hero Glenn Moody. Moody was born over in East Street in Trallwn, one of seven brothers, all of whom were fighters. The best known was Frank, aka The Pontypridd Puncher, who won the British and Empire middle-weight titles in 1927 and the British light-heavyweight title in 1929. Glenn followed his older brother's success soon afterwards, winning the Welsh middleweight title in 1930. On taking up the license at the Criterion in 1957, Glenn Moody was inundated with requests from parents, all keen for their sons to learn some-thing of the noble art from their focal hero. In response, he opened a gymnasium at the back of the hotel – it received a grand unveiling on 15 March 1960 – and organised the Criterion Boxing Club to train as many as fifty youngsters in a single session.

Nothing on the outside of this building tells of its connection with illustrious pugilistic heritage. More's the pity. With the demolition of the former Clarence Hotel which stood opposite, where Freddie Welsh trained for his bout with Jim Driscoll in 1910, it feels as though we have stopped commemorating our international champions. Boxers like Welsh and the Moody brothers put their hometown on the map long before rugby or soccer did; indeed, they were among the best individual indica-tions of Ponty's global aspirations. They deserve far better from us. They deserve a collective memorial at the very least.

I call in at the Royale for another coffee. This is one of the more remarkable survivors of the town's sometimes turbulent retail history. The windows of the café, which announce its foundation in 1903, serve as a visual lesson in Welsh-Italian heritage. A photograph of the Castello di Bardi serves as the centre piece. I enter, order a coffee, nod cheerfully in the direction of the owner, Marco, and take a seat near the window. Suitably ensconced, I begin searching for details of No. 8. I think the person who stopped me had in mind the Clarence Café, which was run for many years by Giovanni Cordani. He took it on from the original proprietor, Giovanni Tamburoni. I get so engrossed in these little details that it is soon time for a fresh cup, but the Royale's getting busy with the afternoon crowd, so I head down to Mill Street. That's where Marco's son, Enrico, has a café-juice bar of his own.

14.

Of all the sections of the town centre, none has experienced a postmodern renaissance quite like that of Mill Street, which in the community interest proclaims itself a Quarter. Once upon a time, this was the main road from the Rhondda into Pontypridd, a bi-directional tip of the hat to trams, motor vehicles – miniature by today's standards – and the odd horse and trap of Shanks pony vintage. You weren't far from the police station, or the infamous skating rink where soldiers were often billeted as they awaited deployment to quash riots in the rebellious valley to the north, or an indoor shopping arcade that gave the upstarts down south a run for their money.

As ever, the problem was too many cars. In the 1950s, the *Pontypridd Observer* reported an 'ever-increasing flow in[to] Pontypridd's two narrow streets', Taff Street and Mill Street. There was talk of a bypass, but two decades went by before it was built. All that's left of the old road is a subway tunnel. It is tiled with various bits of the past. There's Sir Geraint Evans as Falstaff, the triumphant Glyncoch Swingers Jazz Band (formed in 1971), male voice choirs, of course, Beverley Humphreys in full voice, and a tribute to the national anthem. Evan James and James James, the father and son who lovingly captured the Cymric spirit in song, lived in a building next door.

The plaque which tells me these things overlooks the main road, although it used to be on Mill Street and should be relocated once more. Most people seem to walk past where the plaque is now, affording little attention to things that, in other countries, would be commemorated with great columns or statues on such a holy site. Indeed, given all the overpowering monuments to icons of Scottish or Irish nationhood, William Wallace, for instance, or Daniel O'Connell, let alone Mount Rushmore in the United States or royal statues all over Britain, it says a lot about the Welsh that their national song and the people who wrote it can be so lightly treated in their birthplace.

Wales! Wales?

I arrive at Zucco, purveyor of 'the best coffee in town'. The café attracts everyone from the Clwb-y-Bont faithful to rugby professionals to artists and writers. The place is full inside and out. White espresso cups mingle with the rounder bowls serving a cappuccino or a latte.

'Macchiato, per favore,' I say, when it is my turn in the queue. I have spent a bit of time practising my Italian at home. 'And a pastel de nata.' That's a recent extension to the otherwise authentically Mediterranean menu.

'Prego.'

Enrico whips a tea towel onto his shoulder after placing the cup in front of me, and then says 'diolch.' He's been brushing up for the Eisteddfod, he says. I'm not, so I reply:

'Grazie.'

A fourth-generation Welsh Italian, Enrico is often to be seen in a Ponty RFC jersey, as befits a civic booster. With an effective team, including the ever-genial G, who has at least half the town's orders memorised, this young businessman has authenticity and the necessary charm to make this place a roaring success. The crowds are proof of that, especially on weekends when the pizza ovens are lit and cocktails flow.

The richness of my macchiato hits on the first sip. I savour it even as my head begins to buzz.

'Hiya Dar.'

Turning my head, I find a group of lads I was in school with, and Lewis is poised to tap on my shoulder. We look the same as we did when we donned the white polo and black sweater of comp five days week, twenty years ago. Oh sure, there's more grey hair, there's kids, mortgages or rental agreements, and that sort of thing, but personalities remain consistent, and they show in the drinks order that follows. Americanos, lattes, juices, and some turmeric-ginger wellness shot for the health conscious. I tried that one once and felt the kick for days afterwards.

'What are you working on?' Lewis says.

'Book edits. Making sure eyes and tees are in the right place, that sort of thing.'

I am in that mundane stage of drafting: the life of a writer is nowhere near as glamorous as Hollywood or Hemingway makes it out to be, especially as the emails fly between editor, copyeditor, publisher, and myself. At least the title is locked down: *American Wales*.

Directly opposite the café is Storyville Books. I wander over after my coffee to have a natter with the (not-at-all Bernard Black-esque) owner, Jeff. Now, I love this shop: it is not just my romantic enthusiasm for literature and the calming atmosphere that I like, though they are there in the background, there is a unique quality to *this* shop. Part of it is the fusion of different styles: the classic American book cover posters on the wall; the cards, badges, and wrapping paper hanging from a rack like a modern day Trajan's column with Paddington Bear and Charlie Bucket fighting it out in relief; the table of the latest releases in hardback; the sound of children rushing to find something to read or a surly adolescent calmly picking up a copy of something they've seen on TikTok or some manga in a section of the shop curated by Kaden, Jeff's Japanophile assistant.

'Hi guys, you alright,' Jeff says to a group that follows in behind me, with traces of his native Plymouth accent seeping in now and then. They head directly into the children's area.

Then he turns and says to me, 'Awrite.'

We get chatting and he's soon selling a masterplan for the Mill Street Quarter and making sure literature is at the heart of the town's cultural life.

'Well,' I reply affirmatively, 'we are on the left bank of the Taff. Ideal for organising *Les Philosophes de Ponty.*'

For a few seconds afterwards, I feel a pang of existential and geographical doubt. But then I remember that I have read enough of the sources to know that locals *did* flock to watch the latest Fritz Lang thriller at the Town Hall Cinema in the 1920s. They *did* absorb Sergei Eisenstein's montages in the 1930s. And yes, miners and their families really *did* read Dickens and more than a few other things besides. To my mind, this puts the matter beyond dispute. Ponty loved Tolstoy and Chekhov and Ibsen in the past. Why not philosophes, caffè, and Aperol spritz in the present.

Outside the bookshop, I'm stopped by a familiar face who pops over to say hello. This is Jayne, who taught me in primary school. Miss Coleman, as she was to me then, was fresh-out-of-training, a newly qualified teacher who landed the challenge of guiding more than forty unruly six- and seven-year-olds through Year 2, the last spent in the infants' department. We were the oldest and biggest kids on our yard, and thought we knew it all. All change as soon as we entered the Juniors, of course. These days Jayne can be found running Martha's Homestore, an Aladdin's cave of artisanal products and recovered antiques that has steadily reintroduced mid-century style, continental flavour, and circular economics. I call in for some postcards to send off to friends as unusual birthday greetings: there's one of The Prince's, one of Zucco, and another of John and Maria's.

For decades Mill Street's reputation was made by food. Near the junction with Taff Street was the Wimpy Bar, opened in 1963, which sold hamburgers and fries to those in search of a cheap replica of the American Dream. For a long time, townsfolk held out hope for a set of yellow arches, but they never arrived. The envisaged plot for that branch of Maccy D's is a supermarket now, as Max Boyce would say. For those with more adventurous palates, the places to go were either the Bombay Restaurant on the corner of Bridge Street and Taff Street, or the Gim Hong and the Pakistan Restaurant, right here on Mill Street. The former was a Chinese, of course, but the latter, at No. 37, was a curry house affectionately known as Sweaty Betty's.

Back in the 1960s, No. 37 was a Chinese restaurant called The Oriental Cellar, but memories of that place have faded in favour of the tongue-searing vindaloo served by Betty Raish and her husband Mohammad. Find a local in their fifties or sixties, mention Sweaty Betty's to them, and you'll fill the rest of the afternoon with reminiscence. I'm out of luck today, so I make do with back copies of the *Pontypridd Observer* and the *South Wales Echo* on my phone and some more tea and biscuits at Zucco. This is how I discover that Sweaty Betty's was still open in the early 1990s, a late-night eatery beloved of rugby teams and those worse for wear after a session at a local pub – that explains the noise complaints in several of the columns – but I have no memory of it, and this leaves me temporarily bewildered.

And so, I stare out across the plaza and the adjacent car park, which was created when part of the Co-op was demolished –

there's a multi-storey on the opposite side of the road, too, as if to remind us how many cars are around – and on towards St Catherine's and the grey/white wisps of cloud behind the spire. This, at least, is comfortingly familiar. My mind teases the Saturday market that filled this space once, but does no more. I am beginning to realise, as I suppose we must all do after a certain age, that part of getting older is coming to terms with loss and with gaps in our memory that cannot be filled. Some of us attempt to fill the void with myth and nostalgia or with folklore and imagination, but historians are supposed to know what really happened. Or else what is the point of us?

There is another name for the profession: remembrancer. We historians remember what others forget, either unconsciously or as a conscious act of erasure. But we are capable of amnesia as well, if we are honest. We are no better than anyone else, in this regard, despite our training. We are a part of the people but not apart from them.

Leaving Zucco and Mill Street suitably refreshed, I retrace my steps back onto Taff Street. Ahead of me is the Butcher's Arms Hotel, later the Midland Bank, later again HSBC, and now empty. This was once home to Pontypridd RFC, when the team was nick-named the 'Butcher's Arms Boys' in the 1870s and 1880s. The lane to the side of the place leads across a bridge into the park. There's no one about, only a couple of sorry-looking pigeons tapping away at some discarded refuse ruin the view. Above the entrance to the lane a green sign announces in typographically chaotic, but legally necessary, bilingual fashion:

Croeso i	Rhondda Cynon Taf	Welcome to
Parc	*Ynysangharad*	*Park*
	Coffa Rhyfel | War Memorial	

And that's where I'm off next.

15.

I spot a couple of intrepid anglers standing in the river below the bridge. Rods lean against shoulders. I pay them little attention, thinking that they are probably taking a break from catching whatever passes for pescetarian delight in the Taff. But then I notice in the corner of my eye that the two men, as they are now revealed to me to be, are making out, using their hoods and waterproofs as cover. Good for them, I mutter to myself, as I carry on into the park. It's the little acts of rebellion that make society better for us all. Why should public displays of affection be restricted to the middle-aged husband and wife, to young parents trying to keep things ticking over now that they have a child in tow, or to teenagers with no sense of decorum.

It was not so long ago that a same-sex kiss in public ran the risk of physical violence or vocal abuse. You all know the words. They were thrown at anyone who did not quite fit the stereotype of Valleys Man. Rugby playing, beer swilling, slightly rotund, misogynist towards women but a mammy's boy if anyone asked. Etcetera, etcetera, etcetera. Whether such habits have gone away entirely, I doubt. The words are said aloud often enough and local masculinity, with hands down its grey sweatpants checking on operations, remains as fragile as ever. But at least we are exposed to alternative ways of living these days, and that *has* made a difference.

Mind you, as I discovered when I wrote *A Little Gay History of Wales*, the homophobic stereotype was never quite right. Back in the early 1970s, a group of campaigners for civil rights plastered lamp posts, lavatory doors, and billboards with CHE stickers. No, not Che Guevara but the Campaign for Homosexual Equality. They'd come up from Cardiff and, with the support of students from the Polytechnic of Wales in Treforest, hoped to convince residents that gay is good. Almost no fuss was made. A journalist set out to discover why:

'Can I ask, are you shocked by the stickers?'

'No.'

'No?'

'Why would I be? It takes all sorts to make a world.'

No more than a minority expressed disgust at the campaign. And not one of those who told the journalist they were outraged wanted their name printed in the paper. In 1971 'the general reaction [to homosexuality] was one of indifference.' Within a couple of years, there was a gay pub night in Merthyr Tydfil and a branch of the Gay Liberation Front in Aberdare to go along with the open-mindedness of Pontypridd and its people. Later, during the miners' strike of 1984-5, the Southampton branch of Lesbians and Gays Support the Miners (LGSM) provided financial aid to those taking industrial action in Abercynon and on visits experienced little antagonism.

I can hear the voice of Alun Richards in my head as I write these things, asking questions. Is it true? Is it real? Or simply, is it? In his long career as a writer, he felt the constraints of stereotype and argued more than once that it revealed rather less than it ignored. He wanted his colleagues to be honest about the society and culture they were portraying in their work. He wanted them to move beyond the notion that valleys folk had the gift of the gab, that they all came up from underground, pulled on their rugby jersey, and afterwards downed half a dozen pints in the clubhouse. What about the unpoetic, the irreligious, and the ludically incompetent. Well, Richards said, Celtic Twilight blinds us all.

Repeating the boys in the *duw it's 'ard* stuff ad infinitum limits our understanding of the valleys, past, present, and future. Instead of history, we get folk tale. We get risings where there were riots. Icons are made from figures – Owain Glyndŵr, say – with tenuous links to the lived experience of common people. We are in danger of the past being turned into a world of pure imagination. Let us call it Cymru. Round and round in circles we go, never quite returning to reality. In the corner of my eye as I step off the bridge into the park is a so-called Mab stone, part of a network erected by the town council at a cost of thousands and all to celebrate the *Mabinogion* which has nothing to do with Pontypridd at all. My heart sinks. The myth makers and the fantasists have got here before me, public subsidy in hand.

All I can do is keep going, keep telling the truth and refuting fallacy. So here are a few real things that I think should be commemorated in the park instead of fable. One of them is the occasion in November 1938 when *España Libre*, the Basque boys' football team based at Cambria House in Caerleon, arrived for a match against Pontypridd Boys' Club. In the December 1938 edition of their magazine, the *Cambria House Journal*, the Basques, all aged between eleven and thirteen, wrote up their experience:

> We believed we were going to win. We left our house at half past one and we arrived there at three. We enjoyed the journey, singing and telling stories. When we got there, there were a great many Welsh people waiting for us. ... Several members of our team distinguished themselves during the game – Fedo and Antonio, who nearly succeeded in scoring a goal by hitting the ball with his head, the ball striking the cross bar – and also Gabriel and Manolo who made some fine passes. The final score was 1-0 [to Pontypridd]. Afterwards we went to the club [above Pontypridd YMCA] and played several games: ping-pong, billiards, and others, and we had a good tea.

Over the next year or so, *España Libre* and others from Cambria House, which gave shelter to children fleeing the destruction of the Spanish Civil War, visited various communities in South Wales, to play games or to perform in concerts, including Cilfynydd and Ynysybwl. 'We have been over nearly all South

Wales,' the children wrote in their magazine in July 1939, 'where we have had some very good times.'

Another bit of the past to commemorate is the experiment with Irish hurling in the 1910s and 1920s. Pontypridd Hurling Club took part in an annual championship between 1913 and 1926, one organised by the South Wales County Board of the Gaelic Athletic Association (the GAA, based in Dublin). Ponty's rivals included teams from Bargoed, Caerphilly, Cardiff, Maesteg, Merthyr Tydfil, Mountain Ash, Neath, Newport, Swansea, Treorchy, and Tonypandy. In fact, the cricket ground at Ynysangharad Park hosted the final championship match held under the auspices of the South Wales County Board. This was in the autumn of 1925, a few months prior to the General Strike and miners' lockout of 1926. The awards ceremony was itself held at the New Inn Hotel on Taff Street. Challenge matches were arranged to raise funds for the park, too, with visiting teams from Cardiff and elsewhere. But when it came time for the 1926 season, county cricket was due to arrive in Pontypridd and so the town's hurlers, Irish immigrants who mostly lived in Treforest, were told by the council to find somewhere else for their sport – since nowhere was available, the club folded. Sadly, there has never been another.

16

Come to think of it, is there any finer park in the land than this one? Roath Park has its lake and its lighthouse, to be sure, Bute Park fringes a castle, and Cyfarthfa in Merthyr Tydfil has a boating lake, miniature railway, and a museum, but there is something quite special about Ponty Park. For one thing, and I suppose from now on I had better use the official title, Ynysangharad War Memorial Park ensures that the town centre has balance. Urban development on one side of the river, a vast open space on the other.

There has been a park here for more than a century. Last summer, dignitaries gathered to mark exactly one hundred years since the visit of Viscount Allenby on 6 August 1923, the summer bank holiday, when he officially opened this memorial to the fallen of the First World War. It is often said that Allenby, the officer in charge of British forces in Palestine in that war, was conscious that his role in history was to be learned about in a museum, whereas everyone would know the exploits of Colonel Thomas Edward Lawrence. There is, after all, no David Lean film about the noble lord. Well, it is not the case in Ponty, at least, for here Allenby's name will be attached to the park forever and to the war memorial perched on the Common which he unveiled on that same summer's day.

If you had walked through on that first afternoon, knowing what the park looks like now, you might have been disorientated. Much of the fabric has changed: there was no bandstand, no lido, no statue, no war memorials either for that matter. No, in 1923 the park's appeal lay in its tree-lined avenues, its bowling greens, tennis courts, children's playground, and a large paddling pool. 'No fitter memorial could have been provided,' exclaimed the *Pontypridd Observer*, especially for a generation tired of war. This is why the park was once a memorial without a memorial. In the 1930s, 'War Memorial' was even dropped from the park's name, hence Ynysangharad Park or, more simply, Ponty Park. The bandstand was completed in 1926 and opened on 24 July by Artemus Seymour, a Labour councillor from Cilfynydd. The lido followed in 1927, a miniature golf course in 1929, and the statue to Evan James and James James in 1930. Further enhancements, including a concert pavilion and a crazy golf course, were installed after the Second World War. There was further refurbishment in the 1990s, in the wake of Storm Dennis in 2020, and ahead of the National Eisteddfod in 2024.

Before it was a park, this area of Pontypridd was known as

Ynysangharad Fields and was the residence of local industrialists, Lewis Gordon and Alice Lenox. The former ran the nearby Brown Lenox Chainworks. The Lenoxes lived at Ynysangharad House and were sufficiently benevolent to allow residents the use of parts of the grounds for sporting activities: Alice opened a series of river-side lawn tennis courts in 1892 and her husband made a similar gesture towards the town's cricket and rugby clubs, allowing use of fields in much the same location they are today. Eventually, albeit informally, the Fields became known as Ynysangharad Park, and in the 1890s, with local government now bestowed upon the town, the idea was floated that the Fields should be municipal-ised. It took thirty years for that to happen. Ynysangharad House, incidentally, became a clinic in 1931, providing maternity and child welfare services, inoculations, outpatient psychiatry, and even a pioneering birth control unit.

Having entered the park from what used to be called M&S Bridge, I now have a choice to make. Do I head to the left (i.e. to the north) towards the lido, to my right and onto the path leading alongside the river towards Treforest, or straight ahead and onto the cricket ground. If I follow the last route, I shall pass a series of sports facilities known in the trade as MUGA (Multi-Use Games Areas). These are on the right. A group of teenagers are busy playing basketball. The other view, to the left, takes in the rest of the park. There are some mature trees, whose leaves bring autumnal spectacle each year, and an open patch of land where some puppies are being trained by their owners, and younger children, evicted from the MUGA by their older siblings, are kicking a ball into the air. Then comes the sunken garden with its memorial to the miners, before a left turn takes me on to the bandstand, which has just been refurbished, the cricket pavilion, the William Goscombe John statue of Evan and James James, and the new education centre called Calon Taf.

Instead, I walk towards the lido. Outside there is a noticeboard and some wind-up speakers on posts. They look a little like the talking pipes that appear on the Teletubbies. Turn the dial and someone will start speaking their memories of the pool in past times. And what memories they can be. When I worked here as the heritage officer in 2018, one of the locals came in and told me all about the time she trod water for half an hour watching Tom Jones strut about on the poolside in his white underpants.

'Corr, love, ewe could see everything!' she says. Caught in the hot flush of desire, her hands move across her body as if she is measuring something.

'O'corse,' she adds, breaking the mood, 'he wusn't Tom Jones in those days.'

'Woodward he was,' her husband chips in from behind.

'Never forgot tha' I haven't, taught me everything about men it did see.'

She makes the measurement again, larger this time, as the pair move off for their swim. My manager, Brent, who has handled the transaction at the till, is in hysterics. As am I.

I got a lot of stories like that from people popping in to tell 'the boy who is interested in history' (me) all about goings on in the old days. Children conceived in changing boxes. Partners picked up on the sunbathing platforms or rescued from distress having ventured a bit too far into deep water. A triumphant dive from the top of the platform. The perils of the woollen bathing costumes. One of my favourite stories came from the jubilee year of 1935. The town had invested a lot in electric illuminations, putting them up everywhere it was possible for lights to go. Then Pontypridd Swimming Club had an idea. Why not hold an illuminated gala. So, in the fading light of August 1935, that's exactly what they did. The club held a further event at the lido in 1938 to mark their own tenth anniversary. An innovative lot.

I cannot pretend to be much of a swimmer, I leave that sort of thing to my sister, Katrina. She was a loyal member of Pontypridd

Swimming Club for many years, along with my dad who became one of the club's coaches, she swam in galas, won copious medals and trophies, and was always off to a training session somewhere exotic like Edwardsville or Llantrisant. Occasionally I went along but I paid little attention. I preferred to read a book instead, with my back turned to the pool.

It was working on my doctorate and then rewriting the research for my first book, Fields of Play, which was published in 2012, that I began to understand swimming pools have a history of their own. I realised that I should have been paying attention after all. These places are a quintessential part of our built heritage. But getting the history right is important. So here it is. The oldest sections of Ponty lido opened in 1927, a year after the General Strike. This part of the building is arts and crafts in design and has the usual gable trellising, which is the giveaway. A later revision to the structure in the 1930s added new sections – a café and a larger pumping station – that were always art deco in style. When the council restored the place a few years ago, to popular acclaim, they settled on a branding that was entirely art deco, but this was never the full story, just a part of it. Go through the automatic doors and there is a small ticket office right in front of you, with stadium-style turnstiles made in the north of England either side. This was the original entrance. The pool itself, the outline of which is thankfully preserved, was made from reinforced ferro-concrete and the terracotta roof tiles, which seem to evoke an Italian villa, were in fact made in the rainy climes of northern France and Belgium.

Until its renewal in the 2010s, the lido was closed for some time and visibly neglected. It was the Cinderella's Cinderella. The thinking was that it might collapse, eventually. Now, though, because it survived, more by luck than by design, it symbolises the Miners' Welfare Fund and its legacy in this part of Britain, facility from the past remade for the future. The National Lido of Wales, as it has become, is a living building, not a quaint object that happens to be used. The queues on sunny afternoons are testament to its success. But places like this are easily taken for granted. We forget how and why they were built and how and why they have survived. And so, if you ask me, I insist that this is as key a piece of Ponty's built heritage – indeed of Britain's built heritage – as the Old Bridge. Indeed, it is just as important as famous stadiums or racecourses, or the hunting lodges and castles erected by the rich, and it should be cherished as such. A historic pool, yes, but more importantly, a monument of and for the people.

I call in at the café, a modern extension to the original lido building, which I think is supposed to look like a ship and, in any case, completes the art deco theme that has been imposed upon the site. Taking a seat, I look through the windows at the water. Around the edge are the changing boxes painted in emerald, each with an identifying number in white on the outside. Several of the doors are original to 1927, although they were yellow then. On the outside wall is a blue plaque dedicated to the long-distance swimmer, M&S employee, PSC coach, and local heroine, Jenny James. Her medals and trophies are housed in a cabinet in the heritage centre upstairs. The plaque was installed to celebrate Jenny's many feats in the 1950s and 1960s: swimming across the Bristol Channel, the English Channel, the Suez Canal, the Loire, the Nile, off the coast of New Jersey's Atlantic City, and, of course, down the Taff. Along the way, she befriended holiday camp impresario Billy Butlin, Egyptian President Gamal Abdel Nasser, and was a body double for Joy Webster in the 1958 film *Stormy Crossing*.

There are too few memorials to women, fewer still to valleys women, and fewer again to working-class valleys women, and so it means a lot that there is one such plaque on so fine a building as this. It is a tribute not only to Jenny and her achievements but also to the Miners' Welfare Fund and to Pontypridd Swimming Club of which she was a loyal and prominent member for so many years. I can write these things with confidence because the wording on the plaque belongs to me, which is to say I wrote it.

Exiting the park via the same bridge by which I came in, I pay the crossing its due. I look to the other bank to see if I can make out any of the features of the fleapit Park Cinema. No such luck. After three quarters of a century, I suppose I was wasting my time. The building got merged into what used to be Woolworths and is now B&M. The bridge itself offers an interesting vantage point. Look north and you can see the flat Victoria Bridge of 1857 and the arched Old Bridge of 1756 blending as though they were one and the same. Some of the locals will tell you that the Victoria Bridge ruined Mr Edwards' creation, but I am not so sure myself, for me they have an appreciable harmony. Look south, though, and you'll see what I think of as the most important spot in all Welsh history: the confluence of the rivers Rhondda and Taff, at one time the greatest and most important industrial valleys anywhere on earth. It's quiet now but it was not always so.

Anyway, enough of that sort of thing. The first bridge from Taff Street into the park opened in the summer of 1925. It was quite a different construction from the one I'm standing on. A flat, ferroconcrete affair, in fact, with iron railings to prevent pedestrians from falling into the water below. The perfect design for a leisurely promenade, if photographs are any guide. William Edward Lowe, the council surveyor, whose work it was, seems to have had a penchant for reinforced concrete - a method imported from Belgium via Briton Ferry - and used it in several locations around town, including at the lido. Major flooding in the 1960s, similar in destructive severity to that caused by Storm Dennis in 2020, weakened the bridge's structural integrity, and shortened its lifespan. It was shut by the council in 1990 using a favoured euphemism of planners: 'temporarily'.

Such was the fuss about the loss of footfall in the shops that there was talk of writing to *Challenge Anneka* to get it all fixed. Alas, Anneka Rice's iconic blue lorry never came. Local government reform happened instead. With Taff Ely destined to be consigned to the history books, to be absorbed into Rhondda Cynon Taf County Borough, the money could be spent after all. A new metal replacement was lifted into place and life got back to normal.

17.

My pocket buzzes. A friend has texted to say that an ominous note has just gone around parliament, a sign that something – surely something sombre – is about to happen or has already.

'It can't be. Can it?' I reply as I make my way back into the park to find a bench on which to sit down.

'Reckon so.'

The faces of those who had heard that there was, as the media codebook for the day had it, concern for Her Majesty's health emerging from Balmoral Castle, were ashen and grey, shocked at the impending sadness of events. Those others who had little inkling of the news carried themselves a little lighter.

8 September 2022 was a miserable, thoroughly wet afternoon. Later, a brilliant rainbow burst across the London sky as the news was finally broadcast just after six-thirty in the evening. The bulletin relayed that 'a few moments ago, Buckingham Palace announced the death of Her Majesty Queen Elizabeth II.' An entire era was over.

In her later years, with her permed white hair, large glasses, and wrinkled smile, the very model of a national grandmother who might well keep marmalade sandwiches wrapped in greaseproof paper in her handbag (for later), I don't suppose we thought of ourselves as New Elizabethans. But they did when

Queen Elizabeth first came to the throne in the 1950s. Back then she was an echo of the past, as well as a vision of Britain's post-war future. The first of her name had come to the throne in 1558 after a long period of turbulence and religious upheaval; the second in 1952 as Britain apparently recovered from the Depression and a world war. It was hoped that the new queen would prove to be as glorious as the old one. With an empire crumbling, and Britain itself still exhausted by war, things did not work out quite that way and so the rhetoric was quietly abandoned.

The spirit of Gloriana redivivus absolutely infused Queen Elizabeth's first visit to Pontypridd in July 1953, how could it not. She was accompanied by her husband, Prince Philip, the Duke of Edinburgh, as part of their post-coronation tour. The royal couple walked through a vast assembly at the park – the prince in his naval dress uniform, the youthful regina in a brilliant white dress – and onto the bandstand, where they signed a memorial book to mark the occasion. 'The Queen,' it was said, in the deferent language of the period, 'captivated the great crowds with smiles and graceful waves.'

This is surely the reason so many of us felt sad, even upset, that evening seventy years later. We did not mourn someone we knew, someone we had met perhaps only for the briefest of moments – as I did, just once, at the Rhondda Heritage Park in Trehafod during the Golden Jubilee of 2002 – but someone who had been a constant, a figure who connected our present with the past. HMQ was a form of living history, especially as she aged, a visible link to an older way of life, another Britain.

By confession, I am a republican. I do not believe in monarchy as a system of government, even in a constitutionally limited and ceremonial way, and I look forward to the installation of a president one day. Yet on that affective afternoon, in that memorial park, I too sat under the lido veranda and listened to the national anthem. I had tears in my eyes as the choir sang 'God Save The

Queen' and the final chords faded from my headphones. Am I a Queenist, then, I asked myself. It turned out that, like almost everyone else in Britain in this moment, at the very end of her life, I was.

That evening every television and radio station was wall-to-wall either with discussion about the passing of HMQ, or the commemorative programmes they had stored up for years, and my phone screen lit up every few seconds with another message. It was all anyone could talk about. Some were nonplussed, others clearly upset, still others were busy planning trips to London to queue and to observe HMQ's coffin lying in state. None of that for me.

In truth, I thought about my Granny who died in hospital eighteen months before, on the cusp of widespread vaccination against the coronavirus. I thought about our final chat on the telephone when we'd said, 'speak to you soon.' I thought about the eulogy I wrote for her funeral and the lines I borrowed from Robert Burns. I thought, above all, about the time that was lost because of rules that drew a border between us that need never have existed, and about the politicians in Cardiff and in London who will never apologise for the damage they caused to society even when they knew better.

By coincidence, the same piece of pipe music was played at my Granny's funeral in March 2021 and HMQ's in September 2022 – the 'Skye Boat Song'. 'Sing me a song of a lass that is gone.' That was when I cried.

18.

The morning after HMQ's funeral, I found myself at the train station. An automated announcement says, '*y trên sydd nesau ar platfform dau yw* ...' The voice is refined, like the English received pronunciation that follows up with the next train on platform two. If these sounds had been programmed by Messrs Cleese, Barker, and Corbett, they would have looked down on those who know their place—those like us.

'Scuse me butt, is that the one for Cardiff,' a more familiar voice calls to me, at least I think it is to me.

I give an affirmative nod as the train screeches to a halt. The voice runs off in a hurry. This is the usual routine at Ponty Station. As a child, during the last days of British Rail, announcements were seldom made, and you knew everyone going into the city would get off at Cathays to avoid paying half the fare. An adult return was only £2 in any case (or about £4.20 today). No chance of evasion these days – automatic ticket barriers and surly 'revenue protectors' are in operation. Privatisation has taken away one of life's little privileges. Forget the myth about bad sandwiches and stewed tea, oh no... no, the great delight lay in watching the combined populations of the Rhondda, Cynon and Taff valleys pour out onto the tiny platform at Cathays and smile like they'd won the pools or the new-fangled National Lottery. (It was new back then.)

Ponty station is one of the great marvels of Edwardian engineering. It opened in the summer of 1912 after almost five years of remodelling to update and redesign the original Victorian construction installed in the 1840s. When Brunel was tasked with fashioning the Taff Vale Railway in the 1830s, Pontypridd was much less important than either Cardiff or Merthyr or even Aberdare, all because the Rhondda was still a very quiet, rural valley, where the population could still, just about, be measured in the hundreds.

Fast forward seventy years and the Rhondda was the world's major centre of steam coal and Pontypridd its gateway and its metropolis. Engineers had to make a station able to cope with quotidian passenger and goods traffic measured in the tens of thousands of people and tens of thousands of tons, and all without commercial upset. As the *South Wales Daily News* helpfully pointed out to readers in 1891: 'Railway traffic at Pontypridd is probably greater than at any station in the Principality and has been so for many years past.' Seven platforms and the longest platform island of any railway station in Europe were the belated result of trying to cope with ever-growing demand.

Across the road, at the former White Hart Hotel, most recently The Soul Suite and before that Silks, there was a different approach to meeting passenger traffic. With its red-brick upper floors and emerald-green tiles at ground level, it is obvious that this structure was designed for an age other than our own. Situated directly across from the railway station, the hotel looked instantly familiar to the beleaguered traveller. You could be in London or Birmingham, or Manchester or Bristol. An advertisement from the 1860s explains that 'a porter meets all the trains.'

A few bits and pieces of the station's Victoriana remain, mostly in the form of the wooden roof patterning. Everything else – minus the contemporary electronics and the new platform opened in 1991 – are products of an Edwardian mindset. You get a real sense of just how important Pontypridd was to that 'American' generation. *Bradshaw's* alas offers no guide, so I follow my own instincts, not Michael Portillo's. My eye is drawn to a brand mark on one of the green railing posts near the entrance: BAYLISS LTD WOLVERHAMPTON TVR. *This is* a call back to Bayliss, Jones & Bayliss, makers of nuts, bolts, screws, gates, even wheelbarrows. Here, though, they were responsible for the railings and the ornate ironwork marked no exit and way out. I am not sure the TVR directors, who thought of the world in anarchic red and black, would have approved of the green and cream of the Great Western Railway.

Still, I move on from the railings to a sign erected by Transport for Wales declaring the latest progress on the Metro. It is, the sign tells me, the largest railway infrastructure project in these parts for a century. As they put it in 1907: 'reconstruction has been a subject of comment for years.' Many of the platform buildings are, alas, closed to the public. In their heyday, they contained refreshment rooms, waiting rooms, offices, toilets, even a bookstall. I don't think there was ever an Allen Lane vending machine of the sort one saw in Paddington or Charing Cross – known affectionately as the Penguincubator – but I can imagine one doing quite well here. Insert sixpence and out pops an orange-covered novel, purple- or yellow-covered volume of essays, or a green-covered thriller-mystery. Bliss. It is bring-your-own in the twenty-first century.

I head down to Station Square. The Clarence Theatre and the County Cinema – later Angharad's and Castle Bingo – have been demolished, the latest casualties of progress, with a green space and bus stop planned. More of that 'Southern Gateway' stuff. Earlier phases of redevelopment saw the station façade brought up to date via the same mindset that did for Euston's great arch in London. The jutting metal that serves as the frontage today doesn't really work. Rain pours through its holes. For me it speaks to a lack of pride in public transport and a *this could be anywhere* attitude: the hallmark of contemporary urbanism and planning. Off the shelf and hideous. The earlier stonework had proto-art deco flourishes, scrolled demi-columns with gargoyle heads, and the TVR's dragon herald. A row of shops, pubs and a cinema likewise once separated the station from the main road. I barely remember them since they were knocked down in the early 1990s, when the car finally defeated its more romantic opposition and Ponty was granted inner relief.

I round the corner from the station entrance, walk speedily under the dark and gloomy underpass where I get my daily dose of exhaust fumes and slip on a river of pigeon droppings, and enter The Graig.

This is one of Ponty's quirkier districts and is wedged onto the side of the mountain like some impressionist's idea of how people might survive in a place like this. The road up – the other half of High Street – is a sharp incline that affords no respite, not until one reaches the plateau at Penycoedcae. Fortunately, I know a few shortcuts to soften the workout. I've lived in this part of town for five years, although with lockdowns, heavy rain, and line closures, it feels at least twice as long even though it isn't.

First stop is Courthouse Street. Depending on who you are, you might know this as where your Mum and Dad got married, where they got divorced, or where grandad disappeared once a month with his never-to-be-opened black case. Courthouse Street is where the Masonic Lodge meets. I stop to read the blue plaque on the wall. 'Freemasons have held meetings in Pontypridd since 1876.' The hall was built ten years later. It has all the usual and mysterious symbols on the railings and in the windows, and a set of fine Corinthian columns, although these are pock-marked by age. I can't tell you any more than that since I'm not allowed inside.

I move on past the old Courthouse, which is in the process of being converted into student accommodation, stopping instead to admire the former Poor Law Union offices, lately home to the coroner's court. The date stone reads 1913, almost the exact vintage of Pontypridd Station. This could pass for a railway station façade in fact. In West Yorkshire, there would be a busy pub in one or other wings of the building and it would be known as a stop on a Sunday tour.

In contrast to the Graig proper, the housing on this street has no regularity. Those who built residences here had enough money to say this is what I want. The census tells me that there were taxidermists, wine merchants, schoolteachers, solicitors, publicans, accountants, dealers in tea, and even an artist, the Caernarfon-born William Williams ap Caledfryn, all living on this street at various points.

From Courthouse Street, I enter Albert Road and am immediately confronted with Dewi Sant Hospital, aka The Workhouse. Thanks to Charles Dickens – his investigative journalism and novels exposed some of the worst conditions imposed by the New Poor Law in England after 1834 – the workhouse has a terrible reputation, much of it deserved. Conditions were not much better for the nursing staff, as readers of Catrin Collier's affecting *Hearts of Gold* series set in and around Pontypridd will know – the novelist's grandmother, Kitty Jones, was a nurse at the workhouse between the wars.

Pontypridd Workhouse was the last resort not only of the destitute but also of the infirm and the elderly. Those who ended up here, as the official documentation records, were often disabled – living with sight loss, hearing loss, or loss of limbs – or of what would later become pensionable age. Other inmates lived with illnesses, like epilepsy or severe depression, that have since become manageable with medication and other therapies.

One entry in the 1911 census often catches my attention. The printed detail is succinct: Emily Ebley. 65. Widow. Formerly an actress. Born Cambridge. Totally blind 60 years of age. She died about six months after the return was completed. I recognise the surname. Emily's second husband, Edward, a comedian by training, owned a travelling stage company called Theatre of Varieties. With his family and his associates, he moved from valleys town to valleys town, putting on drama and music hall, often in a temporary booth erected in one spare field or other. His son, also called Edward, carried on the business, and eventually moved into cinema trade.

At the top end of Albert Road, I join Llantrisant Road. There's a fish and chip shop across the way and a sign points me back towards the town centre, via Sardis Road. Another points uphill towards Penycoedcae. That route, as unforgiving to leg muscles as it is to car engines and gear boxes, is a good test of one's aerobic capacity. The large building to my right as I begin my climb, now the estate-agent-friendly Mountainview apartment complex, used to be the Morning Star. It is one of those places with a history so gruesome, so much a location from some of the more realistic crime fiction novels, an Ian Rankin, say, or Ponty's Leslie Scase, that I have known the Graig's ironic residents to wonder whether there should be a street sign erected:

WELCOME TO THE GRAIG
MURDER-FREE SINCE [2021]

Over its long and chequered history, the Morning Star was run as a hotel, a pub, and a local authority bail hostel. In the nineteenth century, it had a reputation as a haven for sex workers and others who fell outside the law, 'similar to Whitmore Lane in Cardiff' as one newspaper wittily put it in 1863. Back then, this part of the Graig was known as Llanganna, a name whose use declined sharply, and curiously, in the 1890s, before disappearing entirely by the start of the last century. Shortly before that, the *Pontypridd Chronicle* told its readers:

> The talk is that Pontypridd is becoming somewhat notorious in the criminal world—that David Pilmore, the man just reprieved for the murder of a gamekeeper at Pontefract, escaped the eye of the police for a time, and is lodged somewhere on the Graig.

Given roving gangs, suicides, murders, and stabbings, to say nothing of harbouring criminals and allowing them to slip into the shadows, perhaps residents thought it best to engage in a spot of reinvention. I am not all that sure they were successful: throughout its history, the Graig has been the one area of Greater Ponty with more pubs than chapels.

In fact, the Half Moon Hotel, which met its end in 1989, was said to have been the most frequented bar anywhere in Wales. More than a few stag dos ended up with the groom-to-be handcuffed to the railings outside and in 1986 there was a shock when 'one fella went in with hair and came out completely bald!' The press blamed some 'pretty strong cocktails'. If that wasn't enough, goalkeeper Gordon Banks, who won the World Cup with England in 1966 and kept out Pele in 1970, was known to drop by for a pint and to challenge punters in anything from dominoes to darts.

I had better not give you the wrong impression. Despite the darker side of life on this hill, there are positives to accentuate. For instance, the Graig elected the first woman councillor in Ponty's history: Myra O'Brien. More than that, Blodwen Randell, her successor, became the first woman to chair Pontypridd Urban District Council. That was in 1950. The area is still represented in the council chamber by women: Tina Leyshon and my old English teacher and head of year, Jayne Brencher. The Graig may have been tough, but it was also progressive.

I make my way up the hill to the old Randell residence, No. 46, Llantrisant Road. It is a modest terrace house set opposite Graig Avenue. Pebble-dashing disguises the traditional stone walls and crenelated window dressings. Like all the houses on this side of the street, there are three windows upstairs, and two downstairs – one either side of the front door. I am convinced that No. 46 should have a blue plaque, for women's history was made there and it should be commemorated.

The last house, situated just beyond the road signs welcoming travellers from Penycoedcae to the Graig, is No. 1, Dan-y-Coedcae Road, a detached cottage with views: wooded hills and valleys. The residents on the street seem to agree that they have bought a nice spot since most of them have bay windows to take advantage of the meadowed prospect. At the far end of the street, the view is even better. From here you have an unspoiled glimpse of Lan

Wood, Craig-yr-Hesg, and the entire Taff Valley as it bends towards Abercynon. City folks would only be jealous if they knew.

Taking the slip off Illtyd Street, I end up in Graig Avenue. Turning right towards the play area, I follow the footpath onto the mountain and away from the rest of the houses, they mostly look the same anyway. It is a track at first, leading past a large home built with the pleasant view in mind. Thereafter the trail becomes more typical of hillwalking, there are worn patches of ground indicative of decades of use. The paths lead on towards Treforest, but I shall leave that trip for another day. Instead, I make my way off the mountainside via Graig Street and on into Rickards Street, from where it's a dodgem dash across High Street and I'm almost home. Just in time for the match.

19.

During the season you can hear the announcements and singing from Sardis Road stadium, home of Pontypridd RFC, from most parts of town. I live close enough these days to be able to experience matches even when I am not on the terraces or in the grandstand decked out in my black and white bobble hat and scarf. Ponty is the finest rugby team that ever there was – apart from Bath RFC, my other allegiance – but then I am biased.

Besides, we're all connected one way or another to the rugby club. I was driven to school each day on the bus by Roger Jenkins. His son, the ginger-haired fly half Neil, not only invented the ground's nickname, the House of Pain, but was the first player in international rugby history to kick over one thousand points. Paul John was my physical education teacher at Coedylan – a misera-ble task given my dyspraxic co-ordination – and those of us from Ynysybwl knew exactly where to find Dale Macintosh aka 'The Chief' to ask him for tips on how to be better footballers. Even Parthian's Richard Davies, running personal risks as a Neath boy, played for us (Ponty) and not them (Neath) right here at Sardis.

My first visit to the ground was in 1991, when Argentina played Western Samoa in the Rugby World Cup. I was five years old, and I didn't really understand what was going on, but Dad was keen to induct me into the game my grandfather, Fred, and great-uncle, John, took as their religion. Back in the 1950s, Fred played for Somerset Police and John was a star fullback for Taunton. Dad preferred basketball and chess, although I know not to ring him when the match is on.

As for my own football career, to the surprise of no one, least of all my parents, it turned out that I was a not-especially-good second row forward. I played for Ynysybwl Under-10s and Under-11s and for the Trerobart Primary School XV but stopped long before I had to take the sport seriously. My bones remain unshattered. Some team photographs, a newspaper clipping, my training top, and a sweater commemorating a tour to Rhyl and Prestatyn in 1997, these things are all that remain of that time of my life. I have mostly forgotten my experiences on the field, but as a spectator in the stands, well, let me tell you it was truly remarkable and will never be repeated.

In perfect conditions, Pontypridd RFC was enjoying a golden age – ironic that it should have occurred in last throes of the amateur era – one which was to culminate in the 1996 SWALEC Cup Final against our arch-rivals, the all-blacks of Neath. What seemed like Ponty's entire population travelled down to Cardiff Arms Park on that glorious afternoon in early May, gone away to witness triumph or a repeat of the previous year's tragedy.

Final score: Pontypridd 29, Neath 22.

I'll say that again because it's my favourite line: Pontypridd 29, Neath 22.

The Taff swelled with tears of joy as they gushed from the elated eyes of the Ponty faithful, first as Derek Bevan, the man in official green, blew the final whistle, and then at the instant Nigel

Bezani lifted the trophy high into the air. We were standing on the pitch by then, all staring up at our heroes in black and white in the Royal Box and singing:

Olé! Olé, Olé, Olé!
Ponty! Ponty!

The greatest rugby game of all time – forget Llanelli and the New Zealand All Blacks, forget the shaggy-haired and sideburns-ed 1970s internationals entirely, in fact – this was the 1990s, this was Ponty, and I was there.

One reason rugby was able to retain its hold over my generation, the much-confused Millennials of the 1980s and 1990s, is that its stars – especially, though not entirely uniquely, in Wales – were run of the mill. Ordinary people. They really did live around the corner. You could meet them in the supermarket – I met Rupert Moon in the bread aisle of Ponty Tesco once – or in the village newsagents or in the street. Their glamour came from what they did on the pitch, not from the rest of what now passes for celebrity: cars, clothes, and sponsorship endorsements.

It's easy to romanticise and how often it is we say that when imagination meets hard-boiled fact. Stars like Ponty's Tommy David switched codes because playing rugby union in the era before professionalism was not a route to financial security. There was, after all, a cost to being an amateur idol. 'Tom the Bomb', hero of Ponty and Llanelli, as well as a capped Wales international, joined Cardiff Rugby League Football Club, the so-called Blue Dragons, or 'the biggest gamble in Welsh sport', as journalists insisted, in July 1981. The reason he gave to the press was straightforward: 'security for my wife and family.' And who could argue with that?

My favourite player, Garin Jenkins, a Bwl boy like me, made his name playing for and captaining the All-Whites of Swansea. He was the last miner to pull on the three feathers jersey and the final link between the amateur fields of praise and the professional's paybook. Whenever he could be, he was there on a Sunday morning as the Ynysybwl Minis took to the field in our scarlet and green stripes. He wanted to encourage us and to show that one day we could play for Wales (or England, said I) – and so follow in his footsteps and those of the village's other rugby international, Staff Jones – if that was what we wanted.

There can't be many people from Ynysybwl who have made the pages of Debrett's, even if it is in their other directory, *People of Today*. But Garin is one of them, as well as one of us. There it says he'd been a miner, a labourer, a timber mill worker in New Zealand, and a schools development officer for his chosen sport. Nowadays you can hear him commentating on the radio, lending his unique and uniquely experienced voice to coverage of the Six Nations, league championships, challenge cups, and the autumn internationals; or you'll spot him walking the dog in Taff Street with his wife Helen. For those who remember him from his playing days, when, like so many front-row forwards, he proved as capable of throwing punches as balls into a lineout, or when he came close to losing his eyes during a horrific on-field gouging incident, his transformation into a zen sage of the microphone is remarkable.

He wasn't the first to travel this road, mind you. Sardis is laid out on the site of what was once Pwllgwaun Colliery, better known as Dan's Muck Hole. Dan – Daniel Thomas – started life as a bare-knuckle fighter before he experienced a religious awakening and became a penitent coal owner instead.

20.

One part of Ponty that seems quite impervious to change is Graigwen. In an interview with the *Western Mail*, someone recently described the area as where yuppies are to be found and they have a point. I can feel my aitches being restored as I walk up the hill. Some of the houses even have plastic grass I notice, as I wander around. Perhaps this is to assuage their monthly payments to Friends of the Earth or to balance their membership of the Green Party. Or is it the other way around?

Once upon a time, this was all fields interrupted by an occasional farmhouse. Somewhere between Whiterock Avenue and Nuns Crescent was Gelli-Fynaches-Uchaf, a late-eighteenth-century house that attracted the attention of the Royal Commission on the Ancient and Historical Monuments of Wales in the 1960s. Investigators sketched a plan of the structure before it was demolished to make way for the present estate. A bit further up the hill there's Lan Farm and the house that gave this entire area its name. You can get a sense of its age from the slightly jagged gable end facing the road, even if environmental necessity has prompted the application of a smooth render everywhere else. There's a coat of attractive peach paint, too. It is almost Mediterranean.

At the bottom of the hill, I am about to turn into Tyfica Road once again when it dawns on me that the villa on the other side of the street, called Bryn Gwyn, is where Alun Richards grew up. There's no blue plaque on the wall to say so, although there should be. He writes about this part of town, the Kingdom of Tyfica as he calls it, with substantial houses cast in Rhondda Baronial (his invention), in his memoir called *Days of Absence*, parts of which were reprinted in the Library of Wales as *Dai Country*. 'Here,' Richards says, 'lived the people who mattered, who *were* Pontypridd.' There were men like his grandfather, Tom Jeremy, who ran a grocer's shop on Mill Street, or his uncle Tudor who was once president of the town's Chamber of Trade. Not much has changed. The people I know who have had houses on this street either got elected to parliament, ran English-language programmes for the BBC, or are senior executives for Transport for Wales.

I shall always regret not meeting Alun Richards. I was in sixth form when he died of a heart attack in 2004, aged seventy-four, and no one had ever mentioned him. We were told that Ponty had produced writers but only Elaine Morgan and Catrin Collier. It took the Library of Wales to bring Richards to my attention. Reading his work regularly as I do now, I realise I know him quite well. He thinks like me – or rather, I think like he did – and about lots of things that matter, from history to literature to the way things are. We have causes in common, it turns out, as Ponty boys who do not quite fit in.

At the far end of Tyfica Road, past the junction with Thomas Street, is the school Alun Richards and I both went to. He knew it as Pontypridd Boys' Grammar, to me it was the lower site of Coedylan Comprehensive. The building is full of flats now. They've called it, unimaginatively, Pontypridd House. It was almost designated Ty Ponty, I have no doubt. Every so often, one of the places inside comes up for sale and I am tempted by the idea of living in the classroom wherein I learned history or geography, maths, or religious studies. That's a sentiment I call Taffalgia. My appetite fortunately never lasts. The primary school next door, the infant's department of which served as a Red Cross hospital at the tail end of the First World War, is still very much a hive of activity. I see my sister talking to one of her colleagues on yard duty and wave, but she doesn't see me.

Wandering up here during the lockdown of 2020, I was glad to see that there was one building they had yet to do anything about: the p-shaped music block. They will knock it down eventually and I shall be sad when they do. I spent hours in there, learning to play the violin, to compose music, rehearsing in orchestra and choir. This was a refuge from the more oppressive aspects of school life, a place to figure things out, where there were no bullies. My violin playing grew serious only after Mum died. I suppose there was a connection between music and grief

– it was apparent in the pieces I chose to learn, such as the *Theme from Schindler's List* – but at the time I did not consider one, I just needed something to occupy my mind, to distract from a pain I learned not to talk about.

It was from Mum that I had inherited my musical facility. She had perfect pitch, which made the early years of the violin quite a challenge – for us both! Eventually, I was sufficiently accomplished to win a place on the county youth orchestra, which rehearsed in the dining hall at Coedylan on Saturday mornings; then I joined the Four Counties Youth Orchestra (which brought together musicians from Bridgend, Caerphilly, Merthyr, and Rhondda Cynon Taff under the baton of Derek Holvey), which met once a term at the residential camp at Ogmore-by-Sea; and finally I played with the Rhondda Symphony Orchestra, the oldest amateur ensemble in South Wales.

My favourite rehearsals were those taken by Jeff Lloyd on Thursday evenings. Jeff was a veteran violinist who looked to me, with his bald head and greyed moustache, to be as old as a wizard and just as wise. He was one of those who had founded RSO back in 1968 along with the stalwart of my section, the architect Sheila Nurse. Jeff was a storyteller at heart and would break off from guiding us through tricky sections of Tchaikovsky or Brahms or Shostakovich with a tale about how he had played this one in an auspicious concert hall somewhere, usually in London, so of course we could manage it in Dai's Hall or the local chapel or wherever it was the next concert was to be held. It was magic and it was a privilege: to be fifteen, sixteen or seventeen and tackling some of the greatest symphonies and concertos of the Western classical tradition.

As it's a nice day and I have no demands on my time, I promenade aimlessly as the flâneur of Ponty. At one point I find myself in Pencerrig Street, where the view along the valley is second to none. There was a house here once, more of a mansion really. It was the home of the Seaton family. They were prominent members of the town's Conservative Association. Keen to show their pride in the imperial mission, they named their house Jacobsdal after the first town captured by the British army during the Boer War. The same spirit led them to throw open their doors to Belgian Refugees in 1914 and during the Second World War the house was designated an emergency hostel for children evacuated from London – they moved in after a public reception held at Ynysangharad Park. That's another event to commemorate instead of the *Mabinogion*, if you ask me. In 1946, the house was bought by Hugo Schwab, a Jewish refugee from Mannheim, who had escaped the Nazis in the 1930s. He came first to Cardiff, and then to Pontypridd, to run the Precision Screw and Tool Manufacturing Company on the Treforest Industrial Estate. When he retired to Berkshire in 1952, Jacobsdal fell silent and empty. Demolition was followed by the construction of the District Club, the site's present occupant.

Crossing a bridge over the railway line, I am near St Catherine's again. I can see the former vicarage, and behind me, the large villas that make up the Kingdom of Tyfica stand like chessmen preparing for battle. But my quest has brought me to the old library building, which stands on the aptly named Library Road, a quiet side street disturbed only by a funeral parlour and a former council office turned student residence block. The familiar bust of Shakespeare over the main entrance is still there, as is the stained glass upstairs, although the building is used by the university now. The doors are closed, so there's no chance of poking my head around the door to see if anything has changed inside, although I am doubtful.

The bardic chairs awarded in eisteddfods past, which were kept in the reference department on the upper floor, and the slate plaques erected by the Rhys Davies Trust in memory of Alun Richards and Elaine Morgan, have been removed to the new library, along with other relics like a two-hundred-year-old bible. I am assured they are kept safe in boxes, but the plaques are too heavy to put up on modern walls and so have not been seen since the move.

Pontypridd Free Public Library, as it was, and as it still says on the side of the building, exuded civic intent. On the day it opened, 27 November 1890, just four years after the town committed itself to a public library system, it had twelve thousand volumes on commodious shelves, as well as room for a school of art and a mineralogical museum (which remained open until 1939). In total, the library cost £2,000 to build – almost £250,000 in today's terms – and yet more money to furnish with all those books. 'I think we all will be able to congratulate ourselves,' someone said at the time. I wholeheartedly agree.

The library flourished for more than one hundred and twenty years and launched many a local writer on their way, from Elaine Morgan and Alun Richards right up to and including the present one. Still more have come to visit: the poet Dannie Abse, the novelist Glyn Jones, the historians Dai Smith, Glanmor Williams, Gwyn A. Williams, and more recently Gareth Williams and Chris Williams. As with school instrumental lessons (given for free), I'm not sure where else, at least as a teenager with no money of my own, I might have encountered such foundations of historiography as Fernand Braudel's *The Identity of France*, Asa Briggs' essays on nineteenth-century cities, or Eric Hobsbawm's *Age of* quartet: Revolutions, Capital, Empire, and Extremes. My childhood editions of *The Odyssey* and *The Iliad*, simplified and illustrated, which my parents had bought through a book club, were supplemented by unabridged versions along with a copy of *The Aeneid*, which I found lurking on the library shelves.

Reading those books at an impressionable but improbable and precocious age, along with novels by Cervantes, Dickens, Dostoevsky, Flaubert, Pushkin, Steinbeck, Tolkien, and Tolstoy, made me think for a time that I might study Classics or comparative literature at university instead of history. In fact, that was my first approach to Oxford at the age of thirteen or fourteen: could I study Classics there as someone without access to Greek or Latin and what did I need to know beforehand. Yes, they said, but it is useful to have a modern language, too. That this was not a far-fetched idea has much to do with my parents and with the library, which in those days made world literature freely available, without deference to stereotypes of class or culture, just as its founders had envisaged. It is something to be proud of, and we don't speak of our pride often enough in Pontypridd.

Part 2

SOUTHERN BORDER

I.

Autumn with its mellow fruitfulness has always been my favourite season. It marks the beginning of the school year, of course, there's the harvest and the changing of the leaves, and the drinks with their doses of cinnamon, ginger, and pumpkin spice, all of which I enjoy. But what I value most of all about this time of year is light. In the valley of my childhood, the months of September and October saw the bracken on the hillsides flare bright orange and copper before winter decay set in. By its warming glow I could forget the creeping darkness of my north-facing bedroom and the absence of the sun for months at a time. Many cultures have festivals of light at this point: Hindus and Sikhs celebrate Diwali with fireworks and lanterns, Jews light a candle to mark Rosh Hashanah and the passage of the new year, and Christians celebrate Advent with candles of their own. Four in all: one for each Sunday leading up to Christmas.

As often as I can, I travel south at this time of year, either physically or through music and literature, and so it is, in the autumn of 2023, that I find myself mulling over the southern end of the valleys metropolis. But where does it end? To find out, I've caught the bus to the Tesco superstore at Gellihirion and from there plan to follow the Taff Trail to a point at which I no longer feel like I am in Ponty.

The contours of this footpath-cum-cycleway are unmistakably those of Victorian engineering, for this was once the route of the Pontypridd-Caerphilly-Newport Railway, which ran through to Newport's Alexandra Dock. The lines are true, the gradients are kept to a minimum, and the occasional overhead crossings, bridges and so forth, stand at a uniform height, one suited to steam locomotives best of all. No trains have run along here since the 1960s, however, and passenger travel ceased long before.

The supermarket and its car park are built on land that was once part of Gellihirion farm, a wedge of agricultural production set between the Glamorganshire Canal downhill to the west and the railway uphill to the east. The farm was never wealthy and consisted only of a few buildings and associated fields, even at its height. But here it is, still, preserved in metal and ink on a road sign and in the name of a minor industrial estate.

Almost two hundred years ago, the resident occupier was a tenant farmer called William Morgan. He paid rent to an absentee landlord: Robert Henry Clive, a Conservative politician and grandson of the infamous Clive of India.

The Clive family's subcontinental fortune, enhanced by Robert Henry's marriage to Harriet Windsor, daughter of the Earl of Plymouth, enabled vast land acquisition in South Wales just before steam coal deposits were discovered in the valleys to the north of here. The family swapped their mission abroad for that of domestic business and commerce. Money never stopped rolling in; that is, into the pockets of the Windsor-Clives. Harriet used her own wealth to develop Penarth Dock to break the monopoly of the Marquess of Bute's haven at Cardiff. Penarth itself was developed as an estate village, as were Radyr and St Fagans. To be fair to them, the family did sink some of their money into housing (rented out, of course, for this was no social enterprise), into coal mines, into the railways, and gave other sums away as philanthropic gestures towards the public realm, but there was always more profit to be had and they were never in danger of spending it all on us.

The imperial legacy of the Clives (and the later, Windsor-Clives) is heavily disguised at Gellihirion and by a quirk of preservation: Welsh-language placenames remain in use. Here, at least, the family made no effort to impose themselves, as they did in coal villages like Ynysybwl (where many of the streets are named after family members), and the municipal housing estates constructed between the two world wars paid homage to other things. Between Powis Castle, Penarth, St Fagans, Grangetown in Cardiff, and parliament, to which the Windsor-Clives were frequently elected (usually for seats in Shropshire), there was no further need to aggrandise: the money was quite enough. And so, Gellihirion survived and Rhydyfelin survived, although both were fated in the end to be villages bypassed by the motorcar.

Few travellers pay attention to communities that lie either side of their route, whether they are in a car, a bus, or a train. Furtive glances are exchanged and that is that. The rationalised rail network races from TAFFS WELL to TREFOREST and PONTYPRIDD, with occasional halts at TREFOREST INDUSTRIAL ESTATE. Road signs on the A470, which the locals adventurously refer to as the motorway, do point to Upper Boat and Gellihirion, Hawthorn and Rhydyfelin, but they are hardly tourist destinations. Unless you are a pedestrian.

It takes me a few minutes to walk to Rhydyfelin from the supermarket. When planners sat down after the First World War, keen to modernise Ponty's ageing housing stock and to stamp a municipal identity on the area, these formerly green fields were chosen as their garden suburb. Nature was to be recalled by streets named after trees: sycamore, chestnut, poplar, willow, oak, holly, cedar, and elm. Housing was low density, semi-detached for the most part, and each unit had enough private green space that tenants could enjoy the twin hobbies of gardening and keeping an allotment. Ah, the good life.

Before the war, this had been an altogether quite different place. The only houses here were terraces, all set directly across the river from the Treforest Tinplate Works, which was owned and operated by the Crawshays of Merthyr Tydfil. At least one row of houses had been constructed by the former Pontypridd Urban District Council, an Edwardian experiment in public provision. The Ordnance Survey map, which I call up on my phone, announces COUNCIL STREET rather proudly, although these days it is more wistfully known as YNYS TERRACE. You can tell that the Edwardian administrators who planned these houses had no intention of reinventing the town and its prevailing image: the terrace is uniform, two up two down, with a direct doorway onto the street and a long, narrow back garden. The only difference between these homes and those built by private speculators was the rent went to the council collector not to the Estate and its big house at St Fagans.

But I am getting ahead of myself. What I'm looking for as I wander around is another housing experiment, or the site of it at least: the Round House, which stood on Dyffryn Road from 1834 until its demolition in 1938. It was built as the result of a competition between Francis Crawshay, owner-operator of the Treforest Tinplate Works, and the Chartist, co-operator, surgeon, and cremation pioneer, Dr William Price. Their wager: to discover who could build the greatest number of houses on the smallest possible site. Price conceived of a design inspired by the eight points of the compass and a barrel.

A single, round building was erected, with eight segments- cum-houses, each of four storeys. There were internal spiral staircases and chimneys that raised from the roof and recalled – or perhaps mimicked – given Price's predilections – an ancient henge. The entrance to the site was via a stone arch, another imitation of imagined Celtic prehistory. It is a pity that the museum at St Fagans came into existence too late, this would have been an ideal submission to its anti-industrial fantasia.

Demolition of Price's prize-winning construction was necessary because the fields to the rear, now a housing estate, were destined to become the site of Pontypridd Junior Technical School – predecessor to Pontypridd College of Further Education, later Coleg Morgannwg – which opened to students in January 1943. Teenagers learned those skills regarded as suitable for the post-war world, one in which the commercial modernism of the industrial estate would triumph over the old-fashioned routine of going underground. I am reminded of a passage in Gwyn Thomas's satirical novel, *The Thinker and the Thrush*, which was published posthumously in 1988 but written in this post-war moment. One of the everyman characters reflects that 'I could have gone to the Technical School when I was twelve and done well as a draughtsman or fitter down at the Bandy Lane Trading estate' but instead he (the character) preferred to 'make quiet fun of the inefficiency' of managers and their assistants, as if in anticipation of similar behaviour by the more famous rebels of the late-1950s and 1960s, Alan Sillitoe's Arthur Seaton and David Storey's Frank Machin.

The only hint that either a school or a college was ever here is the street sign which declares this to be COLLEGE WAY. In fact, it's just a small portion of Cardiff Road renamed to memorialise what was once here, otherwise this housing estate is as anonymous as any other. There's a HEOL GRUFFYDD and PARC Y DYFFRYN and I wonder whether I have been momentarily transplanted to Rhydyfelin in Aberystwyth. There is a computerised ugliness to both estates but at least in Ceredigion they are reflexive enough to accept postmodernity, having skipped industrialised modernity almost entirely. Here in Ponty, someone has decided to take the window brickwork of a terraced house and slap it on haphazardly like a child learning to use makeup. The result is a mess, I am afraid to say. Half identikit, half an attempt to fit in with a past that is just that: the past. The estate hasn't been here very long, and it is already aged. It almost makes you nostalgic for the concrete squares of the old college building, although they won no prize for aesthetics.

As a historian, this palimpsest of erasure cannot fail to fascinate. Farmland gave way to housing, housing gave way to education, education gave way to housing, and each time the development was called progress. The thing is, usually only historians as remembrancers are aware of what was present in each phase: who lived in the segments of the Round House, who studied and taught at the technical school, and so on. We all have our blind spots, though, even me. For in 1962, a revolution in education began on what remained of the playing fields behind the technical school. This was the site of South Wales' first Welsh-medium comprehensive: Ysgol Gyfun Rhydfelen.

I don't remember it much because I only went in the place once and that was for a music competition. My memory is of display boards with a history of Wales that I did not recognise and words that seemed more like slogans from cultural movements than the work of pedagogy: *ymlaen* and *Cofiwch Dryweryn*, and so forth. It felt much more political than my school on the other side of town, and the atmosphere was uncomfortable – at least for me, I felt foreign – which did nothing for my playing. From eighty pupils in that first term in the autumn of 1962, Rhydfelen grew to a substantial school within a decade – there were almost one thousand pupils on the roll by 1973. Alumni include actors Ioan Gruffudd and Richard Harrington and the poet Gwyneth Lewis.

Finding the site of the Round House is easy enough. A row of old cottages on Dyffryn Road gives it away. The old map I have been following tells me that they were, conveniently, once called

Dyffryn Row, although that name disappeared by the 1920s. Nothing else in my immediate view compares with the cartography. These homes are wider than a traditional valleys terrace, not quite as tall, and are entered through a middle doorway, not one set to the right or left of the ground-floor window. The overall effect is distinctive, giving the front façade four windows, not the usual three, a genuine luxury.

Such is the out-of-time character possessed by these mid-Victorian survivors that I permit myself a momentary lapse into historical imagination. The original inhabitants would have looked out across fields and the busy workings of the Glamorganshire Canal: there were no railways and steam locomotives adding their noise until near the end of Victoria's reign. I ask myself if the residents of Dyffryn Row ever felt nimbyish about the estates that came to surround their tranquil idyll before concluding that they had only the choice to put up with progress or move on. Time then that I did the same.

At the top of the hill, the bus stop sign tells me that I have crossed a hidden line demarcating Dyffryn Road and Masefield Way. The houses have changed too, these ones are more distinctly 1960s, the result of a council scheme to develop land surrounding Glyntaff Farm. The homes are so far up the hillside that I would not be surprised if tenants are issued with climbing gear when they move in. Certainly, there was a recognition, even when the scheme began in 1965, that residents would require a motorcar to live up here: in Shelley Walk, each dwelling has a built-in garage. The added benefit is a nice balcony area to take advantage of the views, but the car also meant planners could get away without any of the facilities that would make an estate a community: shops, a library, a park, or a school. There are more cars now than houses, metal boxes as the knotweed of human invention.

What I am looking for is the cut back to the Taff Trail. I spot an entrance via Tennyson Close. The signpost tells me that

Pontypridd is a mile and a half away, with Cardiff lying ten miles in the other direction. I munch on a toffee or two as I make up my mind and decide to scrap my original plan of scoping border country and to aim for the mountain road up to Eglwysilan instead. The flâneur regenerates into the hiker.

It's a tough slog but with the sun high in the sky and nary a cloud to be seen, today's the day for it. As ever, the hillsides afford incredible views of the valley. This is a landscape for the poet, for the writer who sees and hears, for the composer attracted by birdsong, for the photographer drawn to light (mostly) uninterrupted by human activity. Wordsworth would have enjoyed this sort of place.

After an hour's climb, at the very least, I emerge puffing and panting onto Eglwysilan Road. As I look around and catch my breath, I begin to feel as though I am on top of the world. In the far distance, appearing as mere specks on the horizon, are the buildings of the university campus and the surrounding terraces of Treforest. A few farm vehicles have passed me on the road on the way up. I saw the drivers mouthing 'awrite butt' as they do, sometimes raising their hand off the steering wheel in a demi-wave. I waved back but remained mute. In any case, it isn't long before I finally reach the hamlet.

It's a typical uplands kind of place this, at least in Glamorgan: a pub on one side of the road, a church on the other. The pub's called the Rose and Crown and the church is St Ilan's. Oh, and there's also a Victorian post-box. It's built into the wall of the churchyard. I do wonder how much demand there is for the services of the Royal Mail up here in the wilderness.

I enter the churchyard and start looking for the memorial to William Edwards, which I know is here. It's a double tomb, square, and made of local stone. Given the significance of Edwards and his bridge to Ponty's identity, I thought it might be more distinctive than it proves to be, but alas not. It is difficult to appreciate, if you come this way by car, just how remote this church would once have been. There is no town, as there is in Llantrisant, no castle for that matter either. Just the church, the pub, the hills, and a few farms with sheep in the fields. I am reminded of *The Canterbury Tales* and of the prologue wherein Geoffrey Chaucer tells of the country folk who long to go on their pilgrimages to the city and its great cathedral. Merely going downhill to Caerphilly or across the valley to Llantrisant would have been quite a trek when this medieval church of St Ilan was built, let alone any further afield—say to the cathedral at Llandaff. But for centuries that is exactly what happened. People walked for miles without giving it a second thought.

In the church there is a slab of sandstone with a carved figure, believed to be a knight. It was found during a routine grave dig in 1904 and reckoned as having been made well before 1000 AD/ CE. Perhaps it is this stone that brings tourists up here these days. Perhaps it is the many graves dedicated to those who lost their lives in Senghenydd in 1913 that does so instead. Perhaps, as I do, they come up here for moments of solitude and artistic contemplation, to slow down their world just a little.

After a while, I follow the mountain road back towards Ponty. The verges soon give way to open fields and the sheep look up at me confused and baa. I baa at them and carry on. They run away so I must have been impolite, or they have decided I have nothing on me to eat that improves on fresh grass. But for the sunshine, it would be bleak up here; not unlike the Yorkshire Moors as the mist descends, beautiful in its own way but also quite dangerous. I feel exposed on the descent as the road narrows around me. My senses heighten. There is no space to dive out of the way of a passing car. After yet another hour of walking, I am greeted by a welcome sign: PONTYPRIDD GOLF CLUB. A few minutes more and I'll be on the Common and back into urban civilisation. My pilgrimages are at last complete.

2.

It's a couple of days after my impromptu excursion to St Ilan's and I'm on the 132 bus out to Hawthorn, one of the more affluent suburbs, to resume my southern tour. There's drizzle in the air, so it's not ideal weather for hillwalking. I get off opposite the Hawthorn Inn. As the bus pulls away, following its route towards Cardiff via Taffs Well and Tongwynlais, I sit on a low wall and orient myself.

Now, where am I? Oh yes.

The pub and its adjacent row of houses, Spencer Place, all built in the mid-nineteenth century, are among the oldest parts of what was, then, a standalone village. The terrace has none of the architectural character of a mining one – Hawthorn is not coal country, per se. I make my way towards the park. When I get there, I am caught up in a memory. I am ten years old and running, with little enthusiasm and somewhat windlessly, after a rugby ball. Already I desire other (indoor) pursuits, but Dad's not yet ready to give up on me. Selectors are standing on the touchline; dark tracksuits and fraying clipboards are the sole indication of their authority over us. They are all schoolteachers, all men in middle age wearing tracksuits that don't fit, with red faces and a temper that is quick to flare.

This is the Dog Track. The name is mysterious, at least to us, but the Chosen who will turn out for Pontypridd Schools Representative XV for 1996-7 are no surprise to anyone. I have been put in the possibles, everyone else I know is in the probables. Neither word is accurate. I am as likely to win a place on the team as I am to solve Fermat's Last Theorem. Mum has promised that this is one last go to prove that I am not very good at sport after all and that I can stick to books and musical instruments from now on.

Jump cut to today, a quarter of a century later. One thing has changed. The sign announcing the fixtures of the local rugby team has gone, nowadays it is the local soccer club that plays here at the Dog Track. The clubhouse, freshly painted in a brilliant white, announces WELCOME in red capitals. Welcome, that is, to the HOME OF RHYDYFELIN AFC. I step through the fence and stare at the field that augured the end of my rugby career.

I am looking for the remnants of the interwar greyhound track, which is the reason this patch of green exists at all. I wrote about its social history for an article published some years ago, about how the residents were annoyed by their loss of power while the floodlights and totalisator machine at the dog track ran without interruption. There are a few tell-tale signs of that former purpose: bits of banking, the long straights which have served the rival footballing codes well, that sort of thing. But aerial photography is more revealing of the past.

Hawthorn Greyhound Track opened in 1932, part of a craze that resulted in hundreds of similar tracks all over the country. Ponty, in fact, had two. There was another three miles away at Porth, which gave Gwyn Thomas ample material for his fiction. Tens of millions went through the turnstiles at dog tracks each year. Some fans, including Aneurin Bevan, welcomed the sport as Ascot for the Common Man partly because it brought employment and economic investment to areas like the South Wales Valleys suffering from the downturn of the Slump, and partly because they genuinely enjoyed the excitement of the race.

Keen to do their bit in those days, proprietors even held benefit races with profits donated to the local cottage hospital. Come for the race, go home with your place on the surgeon's list. But such charity was just a gloss, the real attraction for everyone who came to the tracks of an evening was gambling: in the depths of the 1930s, a few pennies on Dame Fortune or Adonis or Evergreen could turn into a week's wages, if there were any wages coming in, and all at the speed of the totalisator machine's whirring electric-powered dials.

Across the street is something else I want to pull out of the historical ether. The building that is there now, Hawthorn Leisure Centre, opened 1 December 1975 at a cost of £300,000 (about £2.3m today), or so I read in the archives, with its inspiring stock photographs of athletic ambition and faux-brick cladding, is interesting to a degree as a symbol of former investment in public health. But the ground below was once the site of Pontypridd Miners' Hostel, temporary residence of wartime Bevin Boys, as well as, briefly, the Rhondda novelist Ron Berry. In old issues of the *Pontypridd Observer* kept at Pontypridd Library, you can find small ads with addresses like 'Bed 78, Miners' Hostel', which shows just how much space these men had to call home.

The camp came into its own after the Second World War when it was the temporary home of several waves of refugees and migrant workers from Eastern Europe and the Balkans. There were Polish miners in residence by 1947, attracted by the offers of work from the National Coal Board, which was suffering from a serious labour shortage. Jan Zarzeski of the BBC's Polish Section, which had developed during the war, visited Pontypridd to interview some of the men and was told that they were 'happy here'. There were soon to be Czech and Yugoslav workers at the hostel, too, with some moving out to more permanent accommodation in Treforest and Cilfynydd as that became available.

In 1956, Ponty rallied to provide material support for those fleeing the Hungarian Uprising and the subsequent Soviet invasion – an aid committee, which drew on the memory of the Aid to Spain Committee of the 1930s, raised well over a thousand pounds that year. As many as fifty refugees were then billeted at the miners' hostel during 1957, including the so-called 'Junior Hercules of Hungary', Bela Papai. He'd escaped across the Hungarian border into Austria and from there made his way to Britain. At twenty-eight years old, this former circus performer was recruited by the NCB and sent to South Wales for training and for English lessons. It's clear those who met him were impressed with this muscle man who could sing and dance and play Romani folk tunes on the violin, although his party trick was lying on a bed of nails with two fifty-six-pound weights resting on his chest. He eventually moved away from the town and lived the rest of his life in Bromley, South London.

Most Hungarian refugees, like their Czechoslovak counterparts, who arrived in the wake of the Prague Spring and another Soviet invasion in 1968, followed Papai into coal mining, often under-ground at the Albion in Cilfynydd or the Cwm at Ty Nant, but a plucky few were employed by Rediffusion to install televisions in the homes of Ponty's affluent. Whenever I see a concrete cover with the Rediffusion name stamped into it, I think about that quirky connection and how, following more recent invasions in Eastern Europe, of Russia into Ukraine since 2014, history rhymes. In the 1950s, the recall was of Greek refugees who camped on the Common in 1897, arriving there after the outbreak of the Greco-Turkish War. 'There were no warmer sympathisers with the outraged Greeks during the recent [conflict] than the fervent-hearted people of Pontypridd,' remarked the *South Wales Daily News* at the time.

The town council bought the miners' hostel site in 1960 and flattened the dormitories turning the area into a large playground. All that survives of the hostel is just off Fairfield Close. The Green Hut, its name for decades, hardly looks much, you could easily ignore it when walking past and would never notice if you are in a car. The Hut has a corrugated roof and wooden sides, and that is it. But the truth is tangible and only a little bit of knowledge about what the building was gives it its present-day poignancy. On the surface Hawthorn is genteel, perhaps even bourgeois by the stan-dards of other parts of Ponty, but even here you're never far from the great forces that have shaped the societies we live in – and still do.

Which reminds me, there's one building I have always been intrigued by: the hexagonal St Luke's Church, just off Cardiff Road. This early 1960s replacement for an Edwardian mission, one that was altogether rectangular and made of corrugated iron, is unlike most religious buildings. It is a proto-postmodern refashioning of the ocean-liner style, complete with suitably sharp edges. It might even be said to be neo-Byzantine, although ships make much more sense in this part of the world. There is a light-filled tranquillity inside that belies the next-door neighbours: Hawthorn Ambulance Station.

As I contemplate the appeal of 1960s revivalism in the church foyer and recall reading about the televangelist Billy Graham and his several visits to Ponty in the 1940s and 1950s, there's a deafening peal of the blues and twos. In a moment it passes into the distance: direction A470. I make my way to the bus stop. A few minutes later, the 132 pulls up. I get on, wave my ticket at the driver, and we head in the direction of Broadway.

3.

One of my fellow passengers is trying desperately to convince me of the latest online conspiracy: the legal name fraud.

'Ever been to court, butt?' he says. His stomach, little contained by a stained turquoise polo shirt that is several sizes too small, bounces and jiggles each time we run over a pothole. Then a reddened, jowly face turns to look me up and down. I stare back blankly and push my glasses up to the bridge of my nose. Code for: leave me be. To end the otherwise awkward silence, I say:

'No. I can't say that I have.' And so, I'm reeled in.

'Well, next time you're in court, tell them that you don't recognise their authority and that whatever they say is your legal name, you are a flesh and blood individual and that it is not your real name.'

'I see.'

'So,' he carries on, oblivious to my already loud scepticism, 'if they say your legal name is John Jones.'

'Uh-huh.'

'Right. Then you say in court that no it isn't, my name is John of the Family Jones, see.'

'I do.'

'And because the court can only do its business – do you see what I'm saying, butt?'

'I think so.'

'And because the court can only do its business with the legal person and you refuse to be the legal person, they have to let you go.'

'Uh-huh.'

'Try that next time the judge is on to you, butt. Worked for me. Got out last week I did.'

The face turns away. I stare ahead.

My intended stop is just outside the World of Groggs. For those unaware, the Grogg was invented in 1965 by artist and sculptor John Hughes. At the time he was looking to escape the rat race, as the shop's website puts it, and so gave up corporate life for that of creation. The first statuettes were made in a garden shed but by 1971 production had moved into the former Dan-y-Graig Arms, where work continues. This new studio, christened the John Hughes Gallery, was later renamed The Grogg Shop. Here Hughes spent time creating portraits of rugby stars, as well as mythical creatures and other so-called 'uglies', and these helped the business take off. Soon, anyone with an ounce of Welshness in them was after a Grogg as a present. There's even a Max Boyce song about them: 'The Boy Who Climbed a Mountain'.

If you go back through all those autobiographies written by rugby players since the 1970s – or ghosted, at any rate – you'll find talk about a date with destiny. No, not running out onto the field at the Arms Park, or Murrayfield, or Lansdowne Road, or Twickenham, but the day they were presented with their likeness as a Grogg.

'You haven't made the grade,' writes former Wales international and Trallwn resident, Rupert Moon, 'unless John [Hughes] has immortalised your features.' Neil Jenkins went one step further. 'To be selected,' he said in an interview with *The Times* in 1999, is an 'honour somewhere between a knighthood and an appearance on Desert Island Discs.' Alas, no one has yet chosen a Grogg to take to the island as their luxury item. It's surely a matter of time.

If, as the historian Simon Schama suggests in his book *The Power of Art*, 'art doesn't so much duplicate the familiarity of the seen world as replace it with a reality of its own,' then the Grogg is art. It is Ponty's singular, high-kitsch contribution to that form of culture, drawing on well-established influences and techniques. There is nothing of the stiff formality of European high art, of course, but no more than there is in a painting of a Coca-Cola bottle or a Campbell's soup can by Andy Warhol.

There is a direct line between a Hughes statue and those of Frenchman Jean-Pierre Dantan, the father of sculptural caricature, who in the nineteenth century created proto-Groggs of composers and writers and politicians. The Duke of Wellington, for instance. What I mean is, the Grogg symbolises the merging of statuary, portraiture, caricature, and Pop Art, all in ceramic form and with a playful nod to the richness and vitality of a society, our society, that can sustain creative endeavour – if it so wishes.

But I have a confession to make. Until today, I had never been into the World of Groggs. Besides, they haven't a roster of the truest uglies: historians. Wisely, I might add. It's bad enough having our photograph taken!

As I enter the famous doors and step inside the shop, I cannot help but gasp. I feel like Charlie Bucket entering the Wonka Factory for the first time or Obelix falling into the magic potion and absorbing its power all at once. There are cabinets here full not just of every Hughesian statuette ever made but of sporting memorabilia that any Hall of Fame would be jealous to possess. I manoeuvre cautiously, fearful of an accident with my rucksack, which would be just my type of misfortune, and look around for those sporting stars and celebrities whom I know and those whom I admire most, rugby players like Garin Jenkins for instance.

After a chat with the owners, I am ushered into the museum via a door to the right of the main desk. I leave my bag with them for safe keeping. I'm keen to find an example of the Grogg my grandfather once owned: a burly, black curly-haired rugby forward of 1970s vintage. Some of the statuettes I see are substantial and I do not just mean the almost life-size impression of Luciano Pavarotti's stomach. It fills a large part of one case. There are knee-high portraits of Gareth Edwards and Mervyn Davies and a surly-looking dragon that I imagine is saying 'are you talkin' to me?' in a Welsh-Italian New York accent.

My favourite of the displays has nothing to do with the Groggs, though, but rather it is the one that details John Hughes's early career as a ceramicist. These pieces show his talent for the Gothic, a talent that would not be out of place in a Tim Burton animation of *The Nutcracker*, Hans Christian Andersen's *Snow Queen*, or an adaptation by the director of a tale by the Brothers Grimm. The drummer boy, with his dark cobalt-blue glaze, draws my attention. There are similarities with early Groggs, that much is clear to me, especially in the manufacture of the eyes. These were made from dimpling the clay, rather than painted on as they might have been in another's hands. It is no exaggeration to suggest an echo of the work of Bristol animators and creators of Wallace and Gromit: Aardman.

In all, the museum charts the artistic transformation of the

Grogg, from the deliberate caricatures of the 1970s to the more realistic figurines of the twenty-first century. This says something about sport, as well. We have moved on from the pot bellies of beer-swilling amateurs with their thick moustaches, bandaged ears, and out-of-control hair, to the sleek, professional athleticism of stars like Leigh Halfpenny, George North, or Louis Rees-Zammit, whose sixpack abdominal muscles burst through their red shirts. Props, of course, still look like props – the last of the sporting uglies. The historians of the football field.

Before I leave, having emerged from the museum wide-eyed and overwhelmed by what I have seen, the owners tell me a bit more about the building. Their most recent discovery is that the Dan-y-Graig Arms was first known as the Griffin Inn. Then it occurs to me: the Griffin isn't a bad emblem for a legendary place like The Grogg Shop. The body of an eagle, the legs of a lion, and a unique ferocity, those are the animal's characteristics. A guide to medieval heraldry and bestiary tells me something else that I find apt: the Griffin was known for digging gold from the mines underground. Isn't that what John Hughes did, through art, all those years ago?

4.

There's yet more art to be found in Treforest. Arriving at the University of South Wales campus, I take the steps up towards the front of Ty Crawshay, the original home of the South Wales and Monmouthshire School of Mines which opened there in 1913. On lawns to the left of me, as I approach, is some sculpture and a Victorian steam engine which has stood here for more than a hundred years. It was forged for use at the Newbridge Colliery and installed there by its owner, John Calvert, in 1845, but rescued from subsequent disuse and brought to Treforest in

1920. I have come to the university to explore its art gallery, Oriel y Bont, which recently celebrated its fortieth anniversary.

There is a notable and sizeable collection of paintings by the Rhondda artist Ernest Zobole, including a self-portrait, a realist still life of a kitchen table, and the more abstract landscapes of his native valley for which he is, rightly, famous. I spot other names I recognise and admire, too, including Abergwynfi's David Carpanini, Rhondda's Charles Burton, and the Swansea painter Valerie Ganz.

The university authorities spent a lot of money in the 2010s – when there was still money in the higher education sector – to establish a new identity (as USW) and to compete effectively in an overgrown and overheated student marketplace. Some of the buildings at the front of the campus, which were of 1970s vintage and had outlived their purpose, were demolished or remodelled, work which had the effect of bringing Ty Crawshay into view once more. I make my way through the busy and lively campus towards the library, or the learning resource centre as it is called. The doors slide open and closed with welcome regularity.

This whole site was once owned by Francis Crawshay. Mr Frank, as he was known to his workforce, came under the (what I think of as sadly malign) influence of Dr William Price and began to follow some of the older man's more outlandishly druidic affectations. For example: inside Forest House, Crawshay installed a hidden compartment with a stone altar for ceremonial purposes; if you ask nicely at the desk in Ty Crawshay they can show you because it still exists. In the grounds, he had two circles of standing stones erected. The longest surviving of these so-called Druids Stones, or Crawshay's Grove, was demolished in the mid-1950s when the Glamorgan Technical College (as the Polytechnic was then known) began to expand. The other set, situated on the opposite side of Brook Street, disappeared when the villas on lower New Park Terrace were erected in the Edwardian period.

Crawshay's Grove was captured from the air by passing Aerofilms photographers in the 1930s. From their point of view, it must have looked like a semi-ancient henge, like its more famous cousin near Salisbury, rather than something of relatively recent construction and used by a cult of middle-class eccentrics and cultural fabricators.

Shortly before demolition, a set of photographs was taken at ground level. They are now in the care of the town library. What they show is that the stones were curiously notched using a regular system, one not unlike that present on early-medieval ogham stones, which probably served as the inspiration. The central plinth, however, contained a carved stone plaque on which was marked the names of successive generations of Francis Crawshay's family together with the year in which they were born. The list was as follows, with Francis' uncles placed at the bottom and out of date order:

W^m	Crawshay	1650
W^m	Crawshay	1713
R^d	Crawshay	1739
W^m	Crawshay	1764
W^m	Crawshay	1788
W^m	Crawshay	1810
F^s	Crawshay	1811
H^y	Crawshay	1813
R^t	Crawshay	1817
R^d	Crawshay	1786
G^e	Crawshay	1791

There was a weight on Crawshay's shoulders, a set of paternal expectations which he always struggled to meet, as most of us would have done. The Treforest Tinplate Works were meant to be his contribution to the family fortune, but they never made any money, and he was dismissed by his father, the iron magnate, William, as lazy, overgenerous to his staff, and incompetent, although his brothers were more forgiving.

In a letter to fellow industrialist Walter Coffin, sent in 1831, William Crawshay complained that 'Frank is spending my money at a devil of a pace.' Certainly, the younger Crawshay preferred the lighter side of life, but he also maintained a closer-than-usual relationship with his workforce, a paternalism which his father never managed at Cyfarthfa – and which few other industrialists in South Wales achieved. The nearest comparators were members of the Evans-Bevan family in Neath, coal owners and brewers, who used their money for philanthropic effect in that town.

Recently, at the National Museum in Cardiff, I came face to face with some of Francis Crawshay's employees. John Llewellyn, the foreman smith, for instance, in his top hat and polka-dotted neckerchief, or John Davies, the manager, bald with sideburns and a marvellous mustard-yellow waistcoat and black bowtie. My favourite of the Crawshay Workers, as the set of sixteen portraits have come to be known, is David Williams, a carpenter. He looks, to me, with his hat, waistcoat, wide eyes, and tools, every bit a man who took pride in his work and posed for the artist with a quizzical curiosity. A century later, his descendants would adopt similar looks for the motion-picture camera operators as they captured life as it really was in the streets of Britain's industrial towns and cities. I am drawn to Williams for personal reasons, too. Several branches of my family were carpenters. Whether they lived in Scotland, in Somerset and Devon, or near Hereford and Worcester, this was their trade. Since there are no photographs of my relatives, Mr Williams, pulled out of history by conceptions of art and so placed in a gallery, stands in not only for them but the many thousands like them from the past.

In the end, it was not the druids and their *barddas* rituals that mattered most to Francis Crawshay, nor was it the pursuit of money, which had given his father and grandfather their purpose in life, but rather Mr Frank was exercised by a desire to find his place. A place which he could occupy in an ancestry that otherwise included some of the richest people who had, up to that point, ever lived. He made Treforest and parts of Rhydyfelin his memorial. The streets took the names of his family: Laura (his wife and his daughter), Francis (himself and his son), De Barri, Owen, and Tudor (his other sons), Lionel, Mervyn, and Gwilym (his grandsons). When his daughters Laura and Isabel married the sons of Treforest industrialist Rowland Fothergill, so Fothergill Street was brought into the family fold as well. This empire of the placename proved that Mr Frank was a Crawshay after all.

5.

I make my way from the university campus towards Fothergill Street. There is no escaping the fact that Treforest is the most challenged part of Pontypridd. This is studentsville, after all, and the nearest one gets to a modern-day slum. It is not their fault, the students I mean, the responsibility for this neglect lies, as it did then, with absentee landlords and the property holding companies, those who profit directly from the compaction of human existence, from the mould- and damp-infested walls, and who face few penalties when things go seriously wrong. The law, in fact, is on their side.

Life finds a way of surviving, though, and the students themselves have created a lively, occasionally rambunctious, milieu quite unlike anything else in town. There are independent cafés like Olive's Attic, sandwich bars, and a few great pubs in which to pass the time. For the religiously minded, St Dyfrig's Roman Catholic Church continues to thrive, as does the Cornerstone

Pentecostal Church which has taken over the former Mount Libanus Baptist Chapel on Fothergill Street, built 1841 and rebuilt in 1896. Libanus: well, that's Welsh for Lebanon. Standing in front of the former Cecil Cinema, a listed gem of Edwardian architecture, it occurs to me that Treforest is somewhere that would benefit from what literary scholars call a 'close reading', or as anthropologists have it, 'thick description'. On the surface, this is an ugly but lovely part of Ponty.

I swing left up the hill to the rear of the Cecil and make my way onto Old Park Terrace. The remnants of the former Bridge Hotel are not much to look at, now, but there are stories waiting to be discovered. Take the life of rugby player Frank Hawkins. Born in Wiveliscombe near Taunton in Somerset in 1885, he began his working life as an apprentice blacksmith before migrating to the coalfield to work as a policeman, which was a better prospect. When he left the force in 1908, he entered the pub trade as licensee of the Tynewydd Hotel in Porth. At the same time, he was appointed treasurer of Pontypridd RFC. By now he was an established fixture on the field (as a forward), as well as in the boardroom, and would go on to serve as club captain. Then, in March 1912, he was selected to play for Wales in their fixture against France. The *Pontypridd Observer* exclaimed: 'all football Pontypriddians hail with delight [this] inclusion... The Welsh Union recognise merit after all.'

During the First World War, Hawkins served as an officer in the Welsh Regiment and was at the bloody battle of Mametz Wood on the Somme 1916. There he sustained serious injuries to his legs and was gassed at one point as well. He returned home with the military cross, a promotion from lieutenant to captain, and threw his energies into developing his beloved rugby club. He organised testimonial games to support injured soldiers, too, including Jack Jones of Cwmbran who had been disabled in the fighting at Gallipoli. After the war, and until his death in 1960,

Hawkins was landlord of various pubs including the Bridge Hotel.

I round the corner and dip into a side street where I am met with the imposing but decaying edifice of one of Ponty's oldest chapels: Saron. It's shut up and there's a for sale sign, which I look up online and by chance I can explore a 3-D model of the inside. Saron was built by the Welsh Methodists in 1832 and redeveloped several times in the nineteenth century. The internal layout is as you would expect. A ground floor where the pews would once have been, an upstairs gallery, and a ceiling made up of some beautiful roses. The pulpit is apparent, and one can almost imagine the preacher full of *hwyl* delivering a sermon; now though, the paint is peeling from the walls and years of discarded waste fills every nook and cranny.

Back on the main road and a few yards further on from the Bridge Hotel, I come face to face with a long, narrow, and modest building that seems, in the absence of any plaster rendering, to be very old. This is St Dubritius Roman Catholic Chapel, which opened on 14 May 1857. The *Catholic Directory* for the following year, which gives me the date, also tells me that there were about eight hundred Catholics living in the area at the time, all of them labourers and mostly employed at the Taff Vale Iron Works owned by Fothergill or Crawshay's Forest Tinplate Works. Welcome to Ponty's Little Ireland – over on Long Row, the single-storey houses with their high-pitched roofs even look as though they have been imported from Cork and erected here in South Wales.

On the corner of this quiet side street (Old Park Terrace) stands another of the area's hidden historic gems: the former Oddfellows Hall, built in the late 1840s. The building has a date stone set into its front façade but that only tells part of the story. In the 1850s, Oddfellowship, with its roots in Manchester, was a major force in Treforest providing mutual aid, health insurance, funeral care, and other social services that were then absent from the state. The local lodge had been formed in 1834, two years prior to its sister 'Newbridge Lodge', which met in the Butcher's Arms on Taff Street. But whereas the Catholic Church could claim that its members all worked for living, mostly at the tinplate works owned by Mr Frank, the Oddfellows had a broader social spectrum. The lodge secretary for much of the Victorian period was auctioneer, builder, and undertaker, Moses Cule. He left behind an estate worth more than £15,000 in 1888, that's the equivalent of almost £1.5m in today's terms. His was a rich man's world.

Turning into Duke Street then into Kingsland Terrace, a familiar tune emerges from my headphones and my head starts bouncing back and forth to its rhythm. The houses here look much as they do in any other of the Glamorgan valleys, save for the bay windows which reveal them to be of a *fin-de-siècle* vintage, the highwater mark of Ponty's prosperity.

Standing on the pavement opposite No. 57, I recall that, on 7 June 1940, a young boy was born in this house. His name was Tommy Woodward. There is no blue plaque, no markings, not even a house number, but this anonymous terrace, with weeds growing from the steps leading up to the front door, is it. The Birthplace. Sir Tom's real backyard, however, is a short walk away from here at No. 44, Laura Street. The Growing-Up Place. There's no blue plaque there either, just a view across the valley. For a few minutes I pay homage by listening to some of his greatest hits and then I scribble some notes into my journal with a stubby pencil that is nearing the end of its useful life. He'll be glad, I think, to know that the old house is standing and that the paint is cracked and dried only in a few places.

I notice later that I have scribbled some alternative lyrics for 'Georgia On My Mind'. I assure myself that this was all quite by chance, rather than any channelling of the holy spirit:

Ponty, Ponty
The whole day through
Just an old sweet song
Keeps Ponty on my mind.

There is one last place to visit on this trip through Sir Tom's early life, No. 3, Cliff Terrace, to which he moved with his wife, Linda, in 1957. He remained in residence until 1964 when his singing career took off. Cliff Terrace is really an alleyway, inconspicuous, and easily missed. The house itself is unremarkable, small, unimposing. Again, there is no blue plaque.

But it seems to me that Cliff Terrace left more than one mark on the life of Sir Tom. The American repertoire, which the singer has very much made his own, provides a clue: 'My Yiddishe Momme', an unusual Vaudeville hit from the 1920s written by Jack Yellen and Lew Pollack. In his autobiography, Sir Tom recalls learning the song from his father, but in an article published in the *Jewish Chronicle* in 2010, it was speculated whether Jones had picked it up somewhere else. 'When he was a boy', the newspaper noted of Sir Tom, 'he used to be a Shabbes goy' – a non-Jewish errand runner, someone given tasks on the Sabbath that orthodox Jews could not undertake, just like his friend, Elvis Presley. As I walk, I listen to the song. I find it a striking arrangement, barely two minutes long, which begins with solo voice and guitar, with Wurlitzer organ, strings, and clarinets to follow. Once over, the player switches immediately into the tense, attacking opening chords of 'Delilah'. I guess I also saw the light.

6.

The building at the town end of Cliff Terrace recalls a Congregational chapel. Its brickwork, once a kiln-fresh pale terracotta, has been painted an appealing shade of crimson and the dressed stone has been cleaned and brought back to something close to its original glory. High above, the building declares itself PONTY-PRIDD SYNAGOGUE. On the memorial stones closer to ground level are, or were, as two of the five are badly weathered, the names of those families and notable individuals who were either central to Jewish life here in the nineteenth and twentieth centuries or were among its most enthusiastic gentile supporters. Those names that I can still read are these:

THIS STONE WAS PLACED HERE
IN MEMORY OF THE LATE
GEORGE GOODMAN, Esq.
THE FOUNDER
OF THIS CONGREGATION.

THIS STONE WAS LAID
BY
DAVID LEYSHON, Esq. C. C.
PONTYPRIDD

The other memorials, according to a contemporary press account, were laid in the names of Colonel Albert Goldsmid, Jacob Marks, and William Thomas Leyshon. The first of these men founded the Jewish Lads Brigade and, as the colonel-in-command of the Welch Regiment, was the highest-ranking Jewish officer in the British Army at that time. The second, a leading member of Swansea's Jewish community, was one of the building's principal subscribers alongside Lord Rothschild and Colonel Goldsmid. The last was a Pontypridd solicitor and the son and heir of David Leyshon. George Goodman was the brother of David Goodman and had similarly moved south from Merthyr Tydfil, where he was born in 1827. He arrived in Pontypridd to set up a pawnbroking, clothing and jewellery business in 1849 and remained in the town until his retirement in the 1890s. Then he removed to Swansea where he died in 1896.

Pontypridd Synagogue was unveiled by the Chief Rabbi, Dr Hermann Adler, in October 1895. It remained in active use until 1978, when the congregation disbanded. The sacred Torah scrolls, together with the paper records of the local Jewish community, which was almost one hundred and fifty years old by that stage, were removed to Israel for permanent safe keeping. There they remain, housed in the Central Archives for the History of the Jewish People at the National Library in Jerusalem. The synagogue building was converted into flats, which explains all the bins I can see outside.

From the pages of the *Jewish Yearbook*, digitised copies of which I can pull up on my phone with ease, I can establish who served as rabbi at Pontypridd from 1891 through until the 1950s, together with the synagogue's officers. There was David Jacobs, Abraham Rosenberg (who was in office in 1895), Maurice David Hersham (who then transferred to Newport), S. D. Cohen, Abraham Kraut, Woolf Jacobs, Elimelech/Emanuel Berry, Abraham Warshawsky (who arrived from France), Harris Bergin, Maurice Schwartz, Isaac Chaitowitz (who came to Pontypridd from Brynmawr), and Emmanuel Morris. Others known to have ministered here included Simon Marks, Solomon Turtledove (who also ministered in Aberdare), and David Caplan (who moved on to Abertillery).

The presence of a Jewish community in Pontypridd made a difference as to how the town's other residents responded to events overseas. That was the view of one observer in 1947, anyway. 'At Pontypridd,' they said, 'more tolerance [is] shown to the Jewish community than in any other part of Wales.' Others may disagree, those in Merthyr Tydfil most especially, but I think it was broadly true. One of those lucky few who made it onto the

Kindertransport in 1938, for example, was sponsored from Ponty, and there were protests here at anti-Jewish activities in Germany within a few months of the Nazi Party coming to power in January 1933.

I recently found a sermon preached by Rabbi Isaac Chaitowitz at the synagogue at the end of that fateful year, 1933. Outside his workplace, I read it back to myself using the notes I have entered in my copybook. Here is the beginning of what he said:

> We meet this day under the shadow of a dark cloud which looms overhead. Today we pray not only for ourselves but also for the thousands of our fellow Jews who have fallen victims of the cruel and bestial brutality of Nazism in Germany.

Five years later, in the summer and in the aftermath of Kristallnacht in the autumn of 1938, the doors of the synagogue were again opened for people to gather and to reflect on the continued 'attack on religion and human freedom', the very words that were used at the time. By then German and Czech Jews were busy developing the Treforest Industrial Estate, which was a refuge of its own in an age of existential crisis.

This is powerful evidence not only because we know what happened in the twelve years between that first speech at the synagogue in 1933 and the liberation of Europe by the Allies in 1945. This is powerful because Pontypriddians sensed, even then, what sort of threat had been unleashed by people thought entirely reasonable by plenty of Britons, including the Barry-born journalist Gareth Jones. While he was busy praising Joseph Goebbels in a series of diary entries as someone who reminded him of a Welsh miner, that is someone with a keen enthusiasm for debate, those same miners were acting otherwise by protesting and opposing fascism at home and abroad.

Jones is a complicated figure about whom I have mixed feelings, personally and professionally. He is now celebrated for his role in unveiling Stalin's enforced famine in Ukraine in 1933 – the Holodomor – which saw vital food supplies redirected to urban centres in Russia, notably Leningrad and Moscow. Urban Russians were able to survive at the expense of rural Ukrainians who starved and died in their millions in the depths of winter or were reduced to eating tree bark and human remains. 'I walked along through villages and twelve collective farms,' Jones famously wrote of what he saw, 'everywhere was the cry *there is no bread, we are dying.*' But Jones was not the first to raise the alarm, that honour goes to Rhea Clyman, a Polish-born Jewish-Canadian journalist who was expelled from the Soviet Union for reporting 'false news' in 1932.

Consistently anti-Soviet and, given his on-the-record enthusiasm for the German language and culture, Jones was regarded by the Nazis as 'one of us'. Late in 1933, about the same time as the public meeting at the Pontypridd Synagogue which denounced Nazism and warned of the dangers of anti-Semitism, Jones appeared at Sardis Chapel to give a lecture called 'Hitler and Germany'. This was based on his experiences travelling with Hitler during the election campaign that February, and articles published in the *Western Mail* at that time. There Jones wrote of 'a great Hitler', a politician who had 'stirred Germany to an awakening'. He would subsequently note the arrival of fascism and dictatorship and the absolute decline of democracy, concluding that,

I do not believe that any nation can long be happy, prosperous, or peaceful under a dictatorship which denies freedom, lauds militarism, and seeks to cut itself off from the rest of the world.

Here was his liberalism coming to the fore, as it would in his second address before a Pontypridd audience in February 1934, this time at the Liberal Institute on Taff Street. His theme on that occasion was the decline of freedom in Europe. He cast Hitler's dictatorship as being in tandem with the dictatorship of the proletariat in the Soviet Union and warned of the consequences for the system of international relations that had prevailed since the end of the First World War. All of this we can accommodate, if we accept a certain naivety on Jones's part early in 1933, and he was not alone in that.

In a sympathetic reading of his politics and reportage, Jones was like Kazuo Ishiguro's Lord Darlington, the misguided employer of Mr Stevens the butler in *The Remains of the Day*. But given Jones was hostile towards Franklin Delano Roosevelt, the American president, and warned that the New Deal and the various new federal agencies established to ameliorate the Depression might lead to a democratic dictatorship in the United States, I am loath to be sympathetic. He was wrong, of course, about FDR, as he had been wrong about Goebbels, but this is precisely why my own feelings about him are mixed and why I am not certain that Jones deserves the accolades he has posthumously received.

As I walk along Cliff Terrace, past Calvary English Baptist Church, then past the junction onto Wood Road - that's the street on which the swimmer Jenny James grew up - I consider the many families who worshipped at the synagogue and where their families have now ended up. Some, I know, took advantage of the law of return, and emigrated to Israel after the Second World War. Others moved on to bigger Jewish communities elsewhere in Britain - mostly to London, but also to Birmingham, Leeds, and Manchester. But a few, like the optician Bernard Elkan, who, as a child living in Ralph Street in Trallwn, had helped his father, Sender, to keep the clocks at St Catherine's Church in running order, stayed and maintained the community right until the end. He died in February 1978, weeks before Pontypridd Synagogue closed for the last time.

The most famous descendants of Pontypridd's Jews are the comedian Sacha Baron Cohen and his brother, the Cambridge psychologist Sir Simon Baron-Cohen. Their grandfather, Moses (or Moishe) Cohen, who was born in 1900, was the son of Hyman (or Chaim) and Martha Cohen of Middle Street, Trallwn. The Cohens had arrived in the valleys from Eastern Europe and settled in Pontypridd to run a jewellery business. Eventually, of course, they moved away, first to Cardiff and then to London. But the ties to South Wales were never entirely forgotten. Hyman's son Gerald, who was born and educated in London, would go on to run a very successful menswear company, Calders, with its large retail units in Cardiff city centre.

It was this perpetuality that the Nazis and their homegrown allies in the occupied countries of the continent could not eradicate from history. Jewish life survived in Europe because branches of families from Poland, Lithuania, Latvia, Belarus, Germany, Austria, France, the Netherlands, Belgium, and, of course, Ukraine, moved away during earlier waves of violence, those frequent pogroms that engulfed the Russian Empire, for instance, and so found safety and security in unlikely places like Pontypridd, Porth, Tonypandy, Aberdare, and Merthyr Tydfil, as well as the more likely ones in London and New York.

It was in that American metropolis that Ponty's most famous sporting son, the boxer Freddie Welsh, born Frederick Hall Thomas in 1886, married a Jewish emigree from Odesa. They had met in a Manhattan gymnasium. Journalists may have muddled up her name when she visited with her husband in 1913 and was wined and dined at the Bunch of Grapes, calling her Fannie Weston instead of Fannie Weinstein (although her Hebrew name was Brahna). But that was a small, typographical error, the result of a misunderstanding or a bad transcription or perhaps increased Germanophobia. To add to the confusion, or was it a Freddie-style reinvention, Fannie was turned from a working-class daughter of a

Brooklyn confectioner into the apparent heiress of a wealthy, all-American dynasty. No matter her identity, I'd like to think that Freddie took a moment on that trip, however brief, to show his wife the synagogue of his hometown. I'd like to think that Fannie caught a smattering of Ukrainian-accented Yiddish carried on the Ponty air. I'd like to think that she thought of this as her hometown, too. This shtetl of greater safety nestled in the hills.

7.

From Cliff Terrace, I take a short footpath that leads under the railway line onto the long, wide boulevard running from the centre of Treforest to the edge of Ponty's shopping district in Taff Street. The first building, to my right, is a brick and tiled pissoir, not somewhere to evoke glamour but a bit of history all the same. It has the misfortune of being overlooked by the railway. To the Victorians this was the Tram Road, but I much prefer the Edwardian-American re-appellation: Broadway.

I make my way towards Taff Vale Park. It is not exactly a looker, not anymore anyway, just a patch of green hidden behind Parc Lewis Primary School. But what if I told you that almost twenty-five thousand people packed into this place to watch Wales versus England in the rugby. You might shrug and think that a small crowd. What if I told you those thousands of instant Christians were, in fact, rugby league fans. Now I have your attention, don't I? You see, Taff Vale Park was Ponty's commercial sporting hub for much of the early twentieth century. Powderhall races on foot, speedway on motorbikes, bicycle races, boxing, baseball, soccer, and rugby league, you name it, Taff Vale Park sold it. And sold it big.

I have a soft spot myself for the short-lived Pontypridd Rugby League Football Club, which made Taff Vale Park its home between 1926 and 1927. It was an unlikely team born in the middle of the industrial turbulence of a miners' lockout and the after-math of the General Strike. But it was warmly welcomed by local fans, a thousand of whom established a Supporters Club to prove their loyalty and turned up week after week even when the management of Rugby League, based in the north of England, lost faith in the project. Some local rugby union players even sacrificed their careers in the amateur game and switched codes; they would eventually go north when their Welsh prospects dwindled. D. L. Davies, Ponty's MP, a former rugby player him-self, in the amateur code, of course, was all in favour, and agreed to be the guest of honour when Taff Vale Park was opened as a rugby league ground at the start of the 1926-7 season. Sadly, the experiment in professional rugby ended abruptly when the ground was sold to a greyhound syndicate at the end of the season and Pontypridd RLFC was made homeless. The club resigned from the Rugby Football League in late October 1927.

That was a mistake because it deprived Ponty of a vibrant alternative to more traditional sporting practices, but in the late 1920s, greyhound racing was an unstoppable force and Taff Vale Park fell under its spell. Speedway, or dirt track racing, soon followed. It was the illuminations, the petrol-head mechanics, the totalisator gambling machines, that made all the difference. Fish and chip shops in Treforest cashed in by advertising directly to patrons of the dogs and the dirt track. Crowds were large and stars were made of the riders: Syd Parsons from Australia, Walter Charles 'Nobby' Key from London, Ronnie 'Whirlwind' Baker from Merthyr Tydfil, and even James Lloyd 'Sprouts' Elder from California, all appeared. The local hero was Tom Lougher, then a teenager from Coedpenmaen, who went on to race for the West Ham Hammers.

It is easy to look at Taff Vale Park today, given its vibrant history, which came to a sudden halt when the ground was bought by the council in 1931, and fall into a lachrymal pessimism. That is not the lesson I take. I am drawn to the story of Taff Vale Park, of Pontypridd RLFC, of the greyhounds and the speedway riders, because that story says something about Ponty's optimism in the face of the all-too-real adversity of the 1920s and 1930s. Tom Lougher returned from West Ham in 1932, he settled down to the family business (butchery), and married his sweetheart, Elsie, at St Mark's Church in Pwllgwaun. He continued racing throughout the 1930s, joining the Cardiff team on their travels around Britain, before the Second World War brought all that to a close.

I emerge from Taff Vale Park and make my way back onto Broadway. In the distance I can see the recently opened Mosque at No. 144, which caters for the town's growing Muslim population, and the older Spiritualist Church around the corner on Cyrch-y-Gwas Road. The spiritualists have had a presence here for a long time: their activities, including seances and communion with the dead, were encouraged by the physical toll taken by heavy industry and by the violence of the First World War. An earlier spiritualist meeting place was situated in River Street, where speakers came to deliver talks and hold trances. Visitors included local leaders Richard Rollo Rostron (Graig), a factory worker, and the church president Arthur Jacob Essery (Maesycoed), a coal miner turned herbalist. Regional figures included the Oxford don turned Cardiff MP, Ernest Bennett, who frequently visited haunted houses in search of the paranormal. And on the national scale there was Sherlock Holmes creator, Sir Arthur Conan Doyle.

As a young doctor, Doyle had attended seances and wrote about his experiences for various spiritualist newspapers. In 1893, he joined the British Society for Psychical Research (BSPR), a body that aimed to study spiritualism from a scientific standpoint and began to conduct experiments to prove the existence of lines of communication between the living and the dead. Other members of the BSPR included the Welsh naturalist Alfred Russell Wallace, the aforementioned Bennett, and the Conservative prime minister Arthur Balfour. But the trauma of losing his son and other relatives during the First World War amplified Doyle's belief and he wrote extensively on the subject, producing as many as twenty books before his death in 1930.

I make my way past the social club, down Windsor Road, and onto James Street. It's a circuitous route but I am on a mission. For this part of my perambulation, I've been joined by Edwina, a Hartlepudlian recently retired as the town's librarian. She wants to show me a particular house but won't give away the reason, except to say that this, and another house on Broadway which we'll get to shortly, resulted in her appearing on the Qatari news channel, Al Jazeera. When we're outside the house, she says one word:

'Mubarak.'

What, I begin to wonder, had the former president/dictator of Egypt, who died in 2020 after being deposed during the revolution of 2011, got to do with a side street in Treforest? I cast Edwina a quizzical glance.

'Mubarak's mother-in-law,' she says, at a pace that maintains the mystery for as long as possible. 'She was born in Ponty.'

My eyebrows lift at the revelation.

'And his wife lived here, too,' she continues, 'and she went to Parc Lewis School.'

Over a working lunch at the Otley Arms, the details begin to flow. Suzanne Mubarak's mother, Lily May, a hospital nurse, was the daughter of Charles Henry Palmer, a coal miner of English descent, and his wife Lilly Parry. Lily May had met and, after eloping to London in 1934, married an Egyptian medical student called Saleh Moustafa Sabet, who was studying at Cardiff. The pair left for Egypt – not, Edwina assures me, in either Nile Street or Egypt Street (Treforest) – in 1936. Suzanne was born five years later. She met and then married Hosni Mubarak at the end of the 1950s, becoming First Lady of Egypt when her husband assumed the presidency in 1981.

I promise to watch the documentary on YouTube when I get home. It's called *The Family*, a self-described tale of politics, power, and greed first broadcast in 2012. I spot my late friend Brian, the town's former museum curator, who pops up as a talking head part of the way through to explain what life would have been like for Lily and her husband. Edwina valiantly tackles diversity in the town's historic population – a topic that had not yet found its champion when the documentary was made. Nor were there many sources available to help. One thing is certain, there were very few Arabs or those of Muslim faith living in the town when Lily May was a child. The situation is quite different these days. One reason for opening the mosque on Broadway, inside a former chapel no less, was the community had outgrown the prayer rooms on the university campus.

Another friend, Lynne, has given me *The Yacoubian Building* to read, with a warning about a sad ending. In the evening, after the documentary has finished, I make a start on the novel. This is post-war Egypt as ruled by Nasser, Sadat, and Mubarak. The author, Alaa Al-Aswany is scathing about the regime and warm about the people. He unveils an unexpected romance amid the horrors of living cheek by jowl with violence and prejudice. By coincidence, I find another copy of the novel, this time in hard-back, at Simon's stall in the market the following weekend. It's only £1, so I buy it and flick through the pages looking for anything that might tell me who else has been spending time in this fictional Cairo. Alas, I find nothing, not even marginalia.

8.

It's mid-October as I write this and I'm walking past the bus stops on Catherine Street when the 404 pulls in. It will take me through to Llantrisant and since I'm up early and have no appointments, I join the queue, *The Yacoubian Building* still in hand. Or rather, in my rucksack. We head towards the Graig, up Llantrisant Road, and are soon in Penycoedcae: the hilltop village that feels just a little bit out of the way. No, isolated. On the way, I look out for what remains of Fawlty Towers, a genuine late-1970s/1980s motel – calling it a hotel crosses the line of copyright, but it was absolutely inspired by the famous television series. There is nothing left, alas: a nursing home complex has erased all trace.

The motel itself closed just before Christmas 1991 having outlasted its television counterpart by more than a decade, so I cannot remember it myself. All I have to hand are the whispers passed down. But in all that time, its greatest claim to fame was the year 1978, when a visiting Scottish rugby team got snowed in for two whole days. 'Fawlty Towers didn't run short of whisky,' reported the *Pontypridd Observer* dutifully, once the ordeal was over, 'the Scots drank beer and lager mostly.' There's no risk of snow today, just the ever-present rain.

Pen-y-coedcae, per the road sign, or *Pencoeca* in the vernacular, and Penycoedcae to me, is the sort of out-of-the-way community that you pass through. I can see the attraction of the place to the people who live here: incredible views and a rural lifestyle quite out of synch with the post-industrial valley floor. There is a familiar terrace here, still, a subtle reminder that you are indeed in The Valleys and industry was never far away. Built in the early part of the twentieth century, the houses on Tonyrefail Road provided homes primarily for quarry workers and colliers, as well as their families. There's the Queen's Head pub, of course, and, in the corner of my eye, I notice the belfry of what was once the church mission room; now converted to residential use.

As the bus makes its way through the hilltop country lanes, I delve into the natural history of the area on my phone, although signal is intermittent. *Coedcae*, the dictionary tells me, means 'land enclosed with a hedge'. More accurately, a hedge of living trees. As I scroll through the various definitions over the centuries, the one I instinctively prefer is from the seventeenth century 'a park or enclosed place for wild beasts'. The Panthers of Penycoedcae.

These steep hillsides surrounding Ponty and the valleys to the north were once among the most heavily wooded parts of Britain. When medieval armies came on campaign, they not only needed wagon trains of food but entire companies of wood-fellers, often snaffled or press-ganged from the Forest of Dean, who were specialists in the art of clearing pathways through the trees. The woodland survived almost intact until the end of the nineteenth century, when intensive exploitation of the vast steam coal deposits finally led to its large-scale but incomplete destruction.

'The woods that now survive,' wrote the doyen of this subject, Oliver Rackham, in his celebrated study *Trees and Woodland in the British Landscape*, 'are ones that escaped.' Thereby evading the demands of industry and widespread manipulation of the uplands by the Victorians, who transposed woodland for moorland and arable or pastureland. The effects of these processes of development are easy to spot. Some of the hedgerows are trees and a little way down the hillside, in either direction, are excellent examples of the surviving broadleaf woodlands.

If you have the time, following the outlines of these hedgerows makes for a fulfilling ramble. I join the footpath just along from the Penycoedcae playground. After about half an hour or so, I reach Darren Deusant (The Cliff of the Two Saints). According to those in the know, this is a Celtic fertility shrine. Some must have believed in its powers because there are carved faces in the stonework all around here; some of them are hundreds of years old. They're like the faces in Tolkien's Dead Marshes, themselves based on the writer's memories of the Western Front and the bodies trapped in the flooded shell holes of no man's land. A bit creepy if you ask me.

The other landmark on this ramble is Castellau Independent Chapel. This is an 1877 rebuild of an 1843 original: a turreted Gothic and gable-ended edifice, with a graveyard to the front and farmland to the rear. I can't go inside because the doors are locked. Across the road is the only neighbour: a very fine house. Its origins are as a nineteenth-century pub: the Lamb and Flag Inn. It was one of those rural pubs that you might go to for Sunday lunch or stop off at partway through a walk to parch your athletic thirst. But it is no more. The pub was severely damaged by fire in December 1998 and turned into a home after renovation.

Back on the bus, we're in Beddau (pronounced, locally and therefore properly, as *bay-thuh*). There's no easy way around the name, even though it sounds a smidge more romantic in Welsh. Simply put, Beddau means graves. It is a curious thing to call a place, although since Gravesend exists it is not a unique idea. But this one is even more curious because the local farm, the colliery, the village pub, and the comprehensive school all take their name from something else: Celynog (Holly Grove). Legend has it that the village takes its name from Croes Heol-y-Beddau or Crossroad of the Graves in English. The junction is easy to spot, although it's now punctuated by a roundabout with a clock in the middle. This marks the meeting point of four old roads, those leading to Castellau to the west, Penycoedcae to the north, Llantrisant to the south-west, and Gwaunmiskin to the south-east. Before the clock and the roundabout there was a large beech tree. One of its branches was used as gallows. Thieves were hanged and then buried in the soil nearby so that anyone using these four roads would quite literally walk across the final resting place of the condemned. It is at least a fine story.

I get off the bus at the next stop. Walking around, it soon becomes apparent that Beddau and neighbouring Ty Nant experienced its period of rapid growth not in the nineteenth century but in the twentieth. This means that it escaped the long stone terraces with their classic three-window façades, two up and one down. Anyone writing a dissertation on the provision of housing in Britain in the last century could take the village as a case study and they would never have to go anywhere else. It is all here, every phase: the good, the bad, and the ugly.

Ty Nant is home to the local library, a product of mid-1960s optimism, a post office, and one of the buildings that I have come out this way to see: Cwm and Llantwit Welfare Hall. It dates to the early 1930s: the grand opening took place on 21 October 1933 with Captain Charles S. Mason of the Miners' Welfare Fund doing the honours and cutting the ribbon. I must confess, even as I look at it in broad daylight, it is not the most impressive example of the welfare halls. It lacks the concrete Sovietism of post-war Onllwyn, which took its inspiration from visits by NUM officials to Donetsk and Moscow, or the gigantic insistence of Victorian Blaenavon and the Park and Dare in Treorchy.

The present, rather dismal, paint job makes it seem even less inviting. A pity. For some reason they have even covered over the trellising of the roof gable, reducing but not entirely erasing the arts-and-crafts style of the original building. A lot of the rest has been mangled by extensions and additions which have detracted from what was once a reasonably handsome construction. Still, it has survived where the industry from which it was spawned has not. As has one of the foundation stones, which reads:

LAID BY

D.L. DAVIES, ESQUIRE MP

11 AUGUST 1932

The other stone, laid by A. G. Brown, agent of the Cwm Colliery and the representative of Powell Duffryn, the former proprietors, has long since faded. Exactly as it should be.

9.

Another bus carries me away from Ty Nant and on towards Llantwit Fardre, Church Village, and Tonteg. At last, I'm nearing Ponty's southern border. The trip reminds me of a conversation I once had in school:

'You know how Llantwit Fardre is called Llanilltud Faerdref in Welsh?'

'Yes.'

'And Llan means the Church of so-and-so, in this case Church of St Illtud.'

'Yes.'

'Does that mean St Illtud means St Twit in English?'

I shall leave you to make up your own minds.

Illtud was a sixth-century saint, although details that far back are patchy at best. One relies as much on faith as on written evidence. His associates included Tyfodwg and Gwynno, who gave their names to the parishes that once made up the Rhondda and much of the Cynon Valley. We know a little bit about Illtud because he appears in an eighth-century hagiography of one of his other pupils, St Simon, and because he was the subject of a later hagiography of his own: the *Vita Sancti Iltuti* which was written in Pembrokeshire in the twelfth century. These books present Illtud as one of the wisest and most learned men in Britain, a cousin of King Arthur, and even as one of the three knights tasked with guarding the Holy Grail.

I have never forgiven Llantwit Fardre for the theft of my lunch-box. Someone, somewhere, got a marvellously plastic construction stickered with *Real Ghostbusters* characters and full inside of stale crusts and the crumbs of chocolate biscuits. But still, they took it. I had been at the hospital for an eye examination, a regular after-school trip in my childhood that was no one's favourite activity. East Glam was notorious for its car thieves, bored young men who preyed on the vulnerable: sick children, cancer patients, and those who had drunk a bit much the night before and broken their arm in a fall. Back then, Dad had swapped his Kawasaki motorcycle, which took him back and forth to work, for a sporty version of a Ford Escort, the XR3i. I imagine it was bought in response to turning thirty. He also had an XR2i, the Fiesta, so perhaps he just liked them. Boy racer, I hear you say. Not with an eight-year-old to drag to the consultant ophthalmologist every month or two.

In the hour or so we were at the clinic, the thieves struck. They took the car, the lunchbox, and my copy of *Fantastic Mr Fox*. I was gutted, Dad devastated, and Mum secretly glad, I think, that we might now have a normal car. A Vauxhall Cavalier, say. Once it had been established that the magic machine had, in fact, been nicked, we faced the long walk to the local police station. This was a survivor of the old way of policing an out-of-town neighbour-hood: a stationhouse. The officer on the desk was genuine but as soon as Dad said, 'the hospital', in response to the question about where the car had been taken from, we all knew it was a lost cause. 'Probably taken for a joyride,' the man said, his grey hair complementary to his navy-blue tunic and light-blue shirt, 'we might find it, but you're best off ringing your insurer.'

After that, we always took the bus. Three decades later, give or take, I am conveyed to the area by the Edwards bus company, I've paid by card, and the hospital, police station, and offending car park are all gone. St David's Avenue still leads up the same hill, so for a few minutes I am on familiar territory. But the roundabout, which was not here when I was a child, hints at the changes that have taken place. There are houses now, the ponds and fountains have gone, though it is still obvious where they were, and the streets are all named for healthcare icons of the past. There is Aneurin Bevan Drive, Fleming Walk, Jenner Walk,

Lister Close, Pasteur Grove, Barnard Way, and, almost where the main entrance used to be, Nightingale Gardens.

I'm done reminiscing as we cross into Church Village. It's a busy place but one that disguises its history with a roadside façade of 'don't bother, you've seen it all before.' Only, you haven't. St Illtud's Church, the standout feature of the place, is a mixture of fourteenth- and sixteenth-century development. Oliver Cromwell would admire the whitewash applied to the outer walls of the seventeenth-century bell tower. Nevertheless, you can get a very good sense from this place what religion meant to the people of early modern Wales and what churches in this part of Glamorgan looked like before the Victorians decided they knew more about medieval design than anyone else in history.

They did get to work here, in the 1870s, as indicated on some of the ironwork outside, but it isn't as bad as elsewhere. The 1970s extension, by the Cardiff architect John Rodney Wallis, is as sympathetic as anything that that decade might otherwise have achieved. A stained-glass window, titled *Christ in Majesty*, by the artist Frank Roper was installed in the nave in 1974. Roper's glasswork is trippy. Christ in purples, blues, and a pinkish red, with green and aquamarine bellows of smoke rising behind him; apparently the colours were influenced by Roper's wife, Nora. There's a healthy borrowing from Henri Matisse, too, I think, especially from the Chapelle du Rosaire in Vence. Here Christ stands on tiptoes, palms out, as if about to greet the viewer in a bear hug. His face. Well, that brings to my mind the visage of the 1960s singer Arthur Wilton Brown. We can leave the burning horned helmet aside, that might not be the right attire for a church – one or two allusions that could get mistaken. But there's an echo of him, I am sure of it.

At Tonteg, I squint out of the bus window at the plaque for John Hughes, composer of *Cwm Rhondda*. The house is called Tregarth, a modest semi-detached opposite a car dealership.

Although born in Dowlais, Hughes made a career for himself as a clerk with the Great Western Colliery Company and so was able to afford a nice house in what was then a quiet and still largely rural village. Not anymore, I'm afraid. And yet, Tonteg is what it has always been: a suburb of somewhere else. Once it served Pontypridd, now there is another master: Cardiff.

What you cannot see from the thoroughfare is an unusual mound known, to the locals, as the 'Monkey Tump'. It is all that remains of a Norman Motte, probably nothing more than a watch tower or outpost, which was erected here around nine hundred years ago to keep control of the natives or to stamp authority on the surrounding landscape. The Welsh name for this piece of contested terrain, which lies now in the middle of a roundabout in a housing estate, is *Tomen y Clawdd*. So, there we are, King Tommen first of his name, one of the few honest and decent characters George R. R. Martin's *Song of Ice and Fire*, started out as a tump near Ponty.

The Victorians, ever inventive about the past, especially when they had no evidence, believed that *Tomen y Clawdd* was part of a much larger castle complex, something called *Caer Odyn*. Odin's Fort. Unfortunately, excavations have proved that theory entirely incorrect not turning up even so much as a sniff of an accompanying bailey, let alone real fortifications. The actual purpose of this tuft of land was instead the base of a watch tower or outpost, nothing so grand as to warrant designation as a fort. I suppose if you want to picture the scene about nine hundred years ago, you can think of a couple of lads entirely bored waiting for the locals to get a bit restless so they could alert the castles at Llantrisant and Caerphilly, like one of the outposts on Martin's fictional ice wall in the north.

10.

All that remains of my southern excursion is the industrial estate, so I get off the bus in Upper Boat and make my way there as a pedestrian. The village is one of the more historic parts of Ponty-pridd, where canal boatmen, lock-keepers, and their families, all used to live, in the days when the Glamorganshire Canal was the main highway linking Merthyr Tydfil to Cardiff Docks, but there isn't much to see anymore. Most people drive past paying little heed and walkers are rare. I'm aiming for the bridge across the Taff which leads towards a section of the industrial estate full of car dealerships and a Greggs outlet. I'm tempted by a sausage roll but decide to treat myself on the way back.

Admittedly, this is an unlikely tourist destination and there is nothing much to recommend. No authority on earth is going to designate this an Area of Outstanding Natural Beauty, not even with the Taff in broad flow. No, this part of Ponty has all the character of someone shouting, 'move along please, move along'. So why am I here? Well, there's the ghost of the power station, built 1902, decommissioned 1972, demolished 1976; one of those buildings destined to be known only in black and white, only from certain angles, and only when historians decide to write about it. There is a meta-phor to be recovered from this absent feat of engineering, it seems to me. A metaphor about energy, about self-reliance, about civic-mindedness, but perhaps those things seem themselves a little black and white and stuck in the past.

The same might be said about the industrial estate, or the Treforest Trading Estate as it was known when the first sod was cut back in December 1936. Guided by a political desire to rein-vigorate the local economy, by now blighted by the collapse of the coal- mining industry and the onset of the Depression, the estate provided new units for light industry, manufacturing, and commerce. Only there was a problem. Most British business-people simply weren't interested: wrong area of the country.

Fortunately, Jewish refugees from Europe were willing to take a chance, they had nothing else to lose, and so, by May 1940, Treforest Trading Estate was home to dozens of Jewish-owned businesses and a workforce of almost two thousand people. Some of the employees were refugees as well, including Harry Weinberger, who had escaped via the Kindertransport. During the war, the estate expanded so rapidly that by 1945 it had more than one hundred and thirty units, seventy separate companies, and a workforce measured in the tens of thousands. It had become a city of industry.

It's no longer straightforward to find examples of the original factory buildings on what is now a sprawling and modern estate: most of the units have been demolished either to make way for later expansions (and contractions) or for different businesses entirely. What remains is the legacy of that earlier time and the singular contribution made to local economic recovery and to the war effort by those who opened businesses and by those men and women who staffed them, whether they made cigarette papers so essential for military morale or the leather seat covers that went into aeroplanes.

Ponty's post-war prosperity was staked on Treforest Industrial Estate and on a turn from the decline of coal mining in the north to the growing potential of factories in the south. The Janus-face held out for as long as possible, but in the end, and is obvious today, only one direction would win: we have all been drawn to meridional light. It's encapsulated over at the multiplex cinema. I look up the address online. The website proudly proclaims that this is not Pontypridd but Cardiff. I've crossed the southern border after all.

Part 3
COAL COMPANY

I.

THERE ARE MINES all over Pontypridd. They are covered over now, of course, but hardly forgotten, and their waste tips perch precariously still on mountaintops awaiting the chance to slide. How best to summarise this world in whose winter shadows we live, I wonder. To list everything, even with the cubist brush-strokes of a historian's prose, well, that would take up too much of our time. In any case, what is a colliery if not a place of work and a business for owners and shareholders alike. A mundane thing, then, if it is reduced to its essence: employment and the generation of wealth. And yet what else but those productive and valuable holes in the ground could cause communities to mushroom and memories to linger a generation on.

My own ancestors were never coal miners, at least not in those parts of my family tree that I can decipher. On Dad's side, I trace my lineage to Devonshire farmhands, Highland crofters, Somerset railwaymen, Herefordshire carpenters, Renfrewshire thread mill workers, and an occasionally wealthier element from Worcester-shire or Ireland. On Mum's side, made more complex by her adoption, and by the adoption of my 'grandmother', there are Rhondda miners as well as Monmouthshire railwaymen, but since I share no direct relation, I cannot claim them. Those miners moved north from Dorset and settled in Treherbert, Treorchy, and Ton Pentre. My 'great-grandparents', Albert and Lilleth, left the Rhondda in the 1930s to settle in Mangotsfield near Bristol, but their siblings remained and so rose through the ranks of the mining industry. By the outbreak of the Second World War, Albert's brother, Evan, was the undermanager at the Bute Colliery in Treherbert, where he had started underground in 1911. He would go on to manage that same colliery before transferring to manage the Dare Colliery in Cwmparc in 1941 and then the Cambrian Navigation No. 4 in Clydach Vale after nationalisation in 1947.

There's a picture of Evan in the NCB's staff magazine, *Coal*, which I call up online over breakfast. It's from his retirement do in 1959. He is a small man, white-haired, with spectacles. Part of him is obscured by a vase of daffodils. In his hand is a gold wristwatch, a retirement gift from the workers at the Cambrian Colliery. He is the very model of a certain generation of South Walian, whose early years were shaped by Edwardian progress. On the few occasions I have met his descendants, at my grandparents' ruby wedding anniversary, for instance, they have turned up wearing blazers with sewn-on badges for a rugby club or a male voice choir, and their voices could be used to train others in how to speak like voters in the valleys. We live a few miles apart from each other, but we exist entirely in different worlds.

After porridge made according to my Scottish Granny's recipe – salt and water, nothing else, certainly nothing sweet – I set out from home to survey the legacy of coal. I've planned a route to carry me from Maesycoed through the Rhondda ward, then out along Berw Road and over to Cilfynydd, before returning via Coedpenmaen and the Llanover Arms. It is before dawn on what promises to be the sunniest – well, driest – day for weeks. Better make the most of these gaps in the cloud.

I cross Sardis Road car park, stopping briefly to admire the new charging stations they've installed for electric cars. They've taken the place of the mobile Covid-testing station that was here, adjacent to the Salvation Army collection bin, through most of 2020 and 2021. I took my first test here, sticking a swab up my nose and down the back of my throat, all while sat on a plastic barrel in an equally plastic tent. I'd say it was undignified, but almost everyone else had to do it sat in their car, the attendant hovering nearby, as if to say, 'are you done yet', so at least I had a bit of privacy as the gag reflex kicked in.

Maesycoed, which lies across the road, is an area of Ponty that estate agents like to call up and coming. Lots of the people I was in school with live here and their children go to the local primary: English on the brow of the hill, Welsh at the bottom. The first landmark I reach is Hermon Chapel, a pleasant enough building in arts-and-crafts style, which opened on 30 September 1914 as a Sunday school and a branch of the more famous (but no longer) Penuel Chapel. The date stone is in Welsh but the more modern signage to the right, which tells me services run twice on Sundays, is in English. I follow Woodland Terrace back towards Sardis Road because I want to see an altogether different sign.

It's not long before I spot it, a blue upright – yes, blue; you thought it would be red, eh – that reads NATIONAL UNION OF MINEWORKERS SOUTH WALES AREA. Pontypridd has been the home of the NUM in South Wales since the 1970s; the union moved to the town from their old offices in St Andrews Crescent, Cardiff. First to Sardis House, where the South Wales NUM tried to prevent sequestration of union funds by the government at the height of the 1984-5 miners' strike by occupying the building, barricading the doors, running barbed wire across the stairwells, and ultimately destroying documents. Large demonstrations took place on the road outside. But these days, with not much coal being mined and the union's activities mostly restricted to welfare, pensions, and compensation for injury, rather than existential industrial action, they are in this more modest setting. You get a better view from the front, although your eye is likely to be distracted by the pit wheel which rests in retirement. Its sheer size is a reminder of just how big the industry was, in all its aspects. This is all that remains, above ground anyway, of the Maritime Colliery.

At the far end of Woodland Terrace, I discover a more surprising memorial. I had forgotten all about its existence until Jeff at the bookshop mentioned it to me a few weeks ago. This is a standing stone on which is carved the words of 'Miners' by the war poet Wilfred Owen. Exactly why it is here is all a bit of a mystery. The known facts are these: it was commissioned by Mid Glamorgan County Council, probably in the early 1980s and located here shortly afterwards, after brief consideration that it might go elsewhere. Regardless, the stone affords a poignant reminder not only of the battlefield sacrifices of the First World War but also those who served the war effort underground, at sea, or in hospital. Standing in front of this memorial stone, aware that the building to my left functions as centre for community mental health services, I am reminded of the poet's treatment at Craiglockhart War Hospital in Edinburgh in 1917.

We like to think that we have advanced in our methods from that time, abandoning electric shock therapy, for instance, and innovating with drugs or talking therapies. But some things are difficult to treat and impossible to overcome, at least to fully overcome. Owen wrote 'Miners' in January 1918, a few weeks after being discharged from Craiglockhart. He was then in Scarborough, reunited with his unit, and awaiting his return to active duty in France. In his diary, he wrote of mixing up his artistic response to a mining disaster with memories of the trenches. How else to understand the poignant final stanza of the poem, which speaks of those unfortunates who are left lying in the ground:

The centuries will burn rich loads
   With which we groaned,
Whose warmth shall lull their dreaming lids,
   While songs are crooned;
But they will not dream of us poor lads
   Lost in the ground.

I carry on to the junction, and turn into Gelliwion Road, which takes me up hill to Maesycoed Primary School. Where I am now feels more like a mining village than an integral part of a town. I am back among the voters of the terraces. Some of the properties are very grand indeed, there is still more Rhondda Baronial to be discovered. This is the case on the Bryn Eglwys cul-de-sac. The street name means Church Hill but there was neither a church here nor is the landscape particularly undulating. It is an estate agent's conjuring trick. This site was once the Victoria Works, a factory making sanitary pipes, bricks, tiles, and other clay-fired products essential for sewage treatment and water supply. Perhaps Sanitation Avenue would have negatively impacted on house prices.

It is not long before I am on a footpath laid over the route of the former Barry railway; it leads directly into the Rhondda, but I don't intend going that far, only to the cricket ground. There is a short amble to the Great Western Fields, home of Hopkinstown Cricket Club, a venerable and successful institution founded in 1953 by a group of local enthusiasts. The fine clubhouse is a testament to their achievement on and off the wicket. In fact, they've been playing cricket here for well over a century, with church teams and colliery clubs filling in for the rest of the time. The ground takes its name from the nearby Great Western Colliery and survived as a patch of green space wedged between the railway and the River Rhondda and was at one time flanked by the Lan Colliery, a quarry, and a rifle range. Since it is mid-week and early morning, the only people around are dog walkers, who nod as I pass. Their pets run up for a sniff but soon find their own toys more enjoyable.

As I edge around the ground, I turn off in the direction of the Western Bridge and the main road. In front of me, as I cross the river, and on its hilltop perch, stands the Hetty, the surviving engine house of the Great Western Colliery, as fine a piece of late-Victorian engineering as can be found anywhere in Pontypridd. High on the southern face of the building is the date stone. It reads 1875. Inside is a working steam engine, lovingly restored by an active group of volunteers who meet here every Sunday, which drives the pithead gear. At the core of the group was Brian Davies, former curator of the town museum and of Big Pit in Blaenavon, who dreamed of turning the Hetty into Wales' foremost museum of science and technology, thus turning the historic exploitation of coal into technical education for future generations. Following Brian's untimely death in December 2023, it is up to us to ensure his vision becomes a reality.

Moving on from the Hetty, I arrive in Hopkinstown, home to St David's Church and to the venerable Capel Rhondda. A plaque on the wall of the latter tells me that this was where John Hughes' hymn '*Cwm Rhondda*', aka 'Bread of Heaven', a staple of valleys' cultural life, was first performed in 1907. Above me, a date stone gives a little bit more of the chapel's English history. It reads:

Rhondda Baptist Chapel
Built AD 1852. Rebuilt 1885

The annexe tells another story, for its memorials are all in Welsh:

Ysgoldy Capel Rhondda.
Helaethwyd 1905.

That is: Capel Rhondda schoolhouse, built 1905.

This addition to the chapel was put up during the great religious revival led by Evan Roberts and his brother Dan, and quite a few chapels in the area were rebuilt, expanded, or gained extra facilities. Dan Roberts arrived in February 1905, having been booked to spend a week preaching at Coedpenmaen. But such was his reception that he decided to stay for quite a bit longer – well into March, in fact, working with other religious evangelists in the area like Edith Jones of Ynysybwl and Ponty's Robert Davies. Roberts stayed with Davies, a greengrocer and revivalist preacher, at his house-cum-shop at 25 Taff Street. They would be shocked (outraged, even, and thrown into prayer) to find out that this is now The Patriot, an all-day drinkers' pub locally better known as The Wonky Bar.

Around the corner from Capel Rhondda is Telelkebir Road. Named for a nineteenth-century battle in Egypt, this terrace contains the childhood home of one of Pontypridd's greatest wordsmiths: Elaine Morgan. Sadly, there is again no blue plaque on the house to say that this was where it all began way back in 1920. When I wrote my biography, published to mark the screenwriter's centenary in November 2020, one of the things I wanted to re-establish was her deep roots in Pontypridd, to move away from the popular assumption that she was *from* Mountain Ash – an assumption reinforced by the erection of a statue in that place in March 2022. She may have lived much of her life in the Cynon Valley, but it was here in Ponty that she was born, went to school, in her spare time read the library books that fired her imagination and led her to write her first short stories, and later was awarded her doctorate.

I met her once, not long before she died. I'd written her a letter asking a few questions about her husband, Morien, who came from Ynysybwl and had fought in the International Brigades in Spain in the 1930s. She was kind and encouraging and did little to deflect me from my chosen path, nor did she seek to introduce her own, far more important, career into our discussion. She described what she could, and I went away satisfied that I had learned something. When her memoir was published in 2012 and, shortly after her death in 2013, a set of papers arrived at Pontypridd Museum, which I was asked to sort through and to suggest an appropriate location for permanent deposit (Swansea University), I realised that I had asked entirely the wrong set of questions, that she was far more significant than her husband, and so my biography began there, with a desire to correct my own mistake.

Elaine Morgan was the finest screenwriter Wales produced in the twentieth century, no matter the reviews, or what anyone else thinks of that fact, which is saying something given her rivals for the accolade: Gwyn Thomas, Alun Richards, Eynon Evans, Terry Nation, and Philip Burton. She was in almost at the beginning of the medium and so shaped the development of television drama over three decades from the 1950s to the 1980s. In fact, her work helped to establish the screenwriter as a viable, independent career in the arts, not just as a crossover from the theatre. Unlike Alun Richards, Gwyn Thomas, or Terry Nation, her talents were not shared with literature and the stage. Unlike Eynon Evans, she was never tempted to go in front of the camera. Unlike Burton, whose darker instincts surely disqualify him from promotion of any kind, her preference was for television rather than radio. And yet, one moment that sticks in my mind from the several years of research I did on Elaine's life comes from a morning at the BBC Archives in Reading.

I went there to look through her contributor's files and contracts, which were voluminous. Some had been read by others, but for the most part I was the first researcher to use them for research and they reinforced my belief that screenwriting, not her dedication to the spurious aquatic ape theory, deserved most attention. Once I was finished with the files, the archivist assigned to guide me suggested that I try the microfilm script library to see what might have survived. I did so and it was by this method that I found Elaine's very first radio script, which she wrote as a young mother in the early 1950s. It was all about her father, Billy, a colliery pumpsman who died during Elaine's first term at Lady Margaret Hall, Oxford, in the autumn of 1939. At that moment she faced the prospect of returning home and giving up on her education but her mother, Olive, said no, you must continue.

Parental sacrifice - Olive took in lodgers to make ends meet - enabled Elaine to make the most of her time in Oxford. She was active in student societies, wrote for magazines, and fell in love with a poet: Drummond Allison. He was killed fighting in Italy, a loss she always mourned. Her memories of the university shaped her great lost work: *A Matter of Degree*. Broadcast on the BBC in 1960, it was a counterpoint to the *Brideshead Revisited* image of the dreaming spires and a story about social and cultural change, class, and gender, and brought Elaine into contact with Dennis Potter for the first time. He was busy working on his first book, *The Glittering Coffin*, a study of social change since 1945, and his debut television documentary for the BBC, 'Between Two Rivers'. In her introduction to *The Dark Philosophers* for the Library of Wales, Elaine compared her enjoyment of Oxford with the disgust felt by Gwyn Thomas, who went up eight years before and was bullied by those who thought Mr Hitler was not so bad. The scripts for *A Matter of Degree* tell a different story, one that better aligns with Gwyn's experiences and with mine. The *Daily Herald*'s television critic complained in 1960 that when Elaine's heroine arrived at Oxford, the writing lost some of its lustre. 'What boring caricatures the University types are,' the journalist wrote, 'compared with her home folk.' But they were not distortions, they were rather close to the truth in fact, as I was to discover when I went up to Oxford almost half a century later.

2.

Crossing under Ty Mawr Bridge, with a Rhondda train passing overhead, I move from Hopkinstown into Pantygraigwen. The best route from here to Berw Road, on foot at least, is via Tyfica Road, through the railway underpass at its northern edge, and down into Pontypridd Bus Station. There's nothing new to report, so you'll forgive me if I don't add to my earlier description of this bourgeois bohemia. At the bus station café, I call in for a takeaway coffee: it's the frothy, milky kind, what else. I proceed fully aware that one false step and I shall either scald my mouth or look like I've had an unfortunate and very public bladder failure. It's mid-morning now and the pass-wielding pigeons are busy queuing for their trips north to Merthyr (Marks and Sparks), south to Cardiff, or over the mountain to the Royal Glam in response to a clinical call.

In Welsh *berw* means much the same as its anagram in English: a brew. A bubbling turbulence of water, or some other liquid, if you prefer, one which produces a heady froth. The reference is to a fall in the Taff, the sort which then drew Romantic artists and now provides a little sport for the kayaking novice. There are metaphorical meanings appended to *berw* in the dictionary, words like bustle, babble, commotion, and whim, which I suppose have some relevance to the river's history, but today it is calm and there is no need for those thesaural alternatives. The sun is poking through the cloud and the air has gained a little heat after a long wintery absence.

This is a pleasant stroll with the river to my right and a park to my left. The latter, which was once intended as the site of the cottage hospital, is unremarkable save for a drinking fountain in the southeast corner, a remnant of civic benevolence. There are grand houses on Berw Road, villas set on perches, which were evidently built for the well-to-do. A business class, perhaps, or those who worked in the professions. The middling sort. Someone like the photographer Thomas Forrest, who moved to here from Worcestershire in the 1860s and lived at No. 46. The Cambrian Studio in Market Street made him rich from the profits of studio portraits, landscapes, and picture postcards.

Looking up at the house, I notice whoever designed it took inspiration from classical as well as Gothic architecture. After Forrest's death in 1898, the property was sold to fancy goods retailer Solomon Cline. A prominent member of Ponty's Jewry, Solly, as he was often known, came from the Latvian capital, Riga, together with his brother, Barnett, who was a stationer. Solly's wife, Ada (née Bernstein), came from Kaunus in Lithuania, although she would have known it as Kovno. Their neighbours included the manager of the local branch of Singer Sewing Machines, the editor of the *Glamorgan Free Press* newspaper, an Anglo-Indian doctor, and a record salesman: Meyer Hoffman. He was an American citizen but had been born in Poland, and so spoke Yiddish just like the Clines and the Bernsteins. Passing their old houses, I try to imagine the sound of those languages, Yiddish, differently accented English, and Welsh, of course, filling the air in this part of town: the Upper East Side of American Wales.

It takes about twenty minutes to reach the bridge over the railway line and the short incline which signals the northern edge of Pontypridd town. I pause at the White Bridge (officially, Berw Bridge). It does not look much, admittedly, even in its newly restored splendour, but when this crossing opened in January 1909, it was the longest single-span reinforced ferroconcrete arch bridge anywhere in Britain. The design belonged chiefly to Louis Gustav Mouchel & Partners of Briton Ferry, now the Mouchel Group, whose other work included the lido in Ynysangharad Park, the stands for Liverpool and Manchester City football clubs, and the cooling towers at Battersea Power Station. In fact, by 1910, the company boasted a portfolio of two hundred ferro-concrete bridges across Britain and Ireland, from Merthyr to Reading to Waterford, with the White Bridge as one of their great achievements.

The bridge serves pedestrians like me as a viewing platform, a spot from where it is possible to imagine a landscape without much urban intervention. To the south, you look across the tree-lined Taff. To the north, there is a similar view, only this time the sky is punctuated with hills and another bridge – Ponty has a bridge obsession, as by now you'll have noticed. This one is a railway engineer's attempt at crossing the river. Stone pillars rise into the air topped by a long-since abandoned platform, part of a railway branch line running towards Cilfynydd and the Albion Colliery. One of stone caps proclaims proudly: TVR. Taff Vale Railway.

I move onto the opposing bank. Ahead of me are grand houses with terraced gardens and a street sign that reads: The Parade.

3.

As ever, I have two choices. Turn right along The Parade and towards Trallwn, or left, up a short incline and into Bonvilston Road, Coedpenmaen. I decide on the former and wander off in search of the boundary between the two communities that make up this part of town. Somewhere in a maze of streets and cross-road junctions the border exists, invisible but known by instinct. The valleys are full of this sort of thing: who can precisely tell, for instance, where Blaenclydach ends and Tonypandy begins or Ferndale and Tylorstown? Knowing is a measure of the local, a measure of belonging. The poet, novelist and former University of Glamorgan English professor, Christopher Meredith, has observed, with characteristic insight, that *ffin* (border in Welsh) appears in *diffiniad* and its English translation, definition. Place determines and defines so much of our personal identity, we care about it, we are nostalgic for things as they used to be, we get annoyed when things go wrong, or when our square mile is injured or abused by an outsider.

Trallwn derives from Cae Trallwng, a once-boggy field owned by the Llanover Estate and rented by them to the Brown Lenox Chainworks for housing development. The field lay between the river to the west and the Glamorganshire Canal to the east, and it is still possible to beat the bounds, albeit with the canal replaced by the A470. The field's northern edge has been paved over, too, but compare any modern map with the tithe one of the 1840s and it can be found with little difficulty. This is where it is: halfway between South Street and Ralph Street there is an irregularly shaped lane, one whose abnormality derives from the shape of the field. Everything else in this part of Pontypridd, at least according to the rules of land ownership, is Coedpenmaen.

The latter community was laid out on fields once belonging to the Bassett family and which were part of the eponymous Coedpenmaen Farm. The farmhouse and hay croft were situated approximately where today Dorothy Street meets Ralph Street. But land and everyday human habit do not always cohere and so borders move or they dissolve through their malleability. The street names tell another story. Ralph and Thurston, for example, taken from the forenames of Ralph Thurston Bassett, the son of landowners Richard and Ann Bassett and heir to the Bonvilston Estate in the Vale of Glamorgan. Ralph's eldest daughter, memorialised in a street name of her own, was called Dorothy. She went on to marry Frederick George Morgan, the Fifth Baron Tredegar. Proper social climbing.

I emerge from beating the bounds of Cae Trallwng in Bakers Wharf, named in honour of Hopkin Morgan, the baker, who had his bread factory in this part of town. It's a housing estate now, with semi-detached properties of a late-twentieth-century vintage.

From here it's back onto familiar terraced territory in East Street. With Middle Street and West Street completing this densely packed district. The residents of Trallwn have always reflected Pontypridd's wider population: a diverse mix of locals and immigrants (mostly from other parts of Wales and all over England). If Berw Road can reasonably be described as the historic Upper East Side of American Wales, then this, on the opposite bank of the river, is the Lower East Side. Terraces face each other on either side of the street and a mix of languages emerges from within.

Most of those who lived here worked either at the nearby Brown Lenox Chainworks, for Hopkin Morgan, or on the railway, an occupational fusion which gave the area a proletarian complexion and strong links to the labour movement. The most prominent politician to emerge from Trallwn and the chainworks was Arthur Pearson, the town's member of parliament from 1938 until 1970, who lived as a confirmed bachelor at No. 24, The Avenue. He had grown up in Ynysangharad Road. Prior to parliament, he was a district and county councillor, served as chairman of the urban district council in 1937, and was secretary of the Pontypridd Labour Party for many years; a status reflective of the chainworks' importance. During the General Strike he put his manifest organisational skills to use as the co-ordinating secretary of the Pontypridd Strike Committee, becoming quite literally the man in charge during those nine days of early May 1926.

It is often said, chiefly because the Trallwn council ward has had a Liberal or Liberal Democrat representative for decades, including former council chair, Mary Murphy, that the area does not have a Labour tradition, but this is not the case – it is a myth. Indeed, one of Pearson's parliamentary colleagues, railwayman David Thomas Jones, was also from Trallwn. He lived at No. 41, Llanover Road, represented the ward on Pontypridd Urban District Council alongside Pearson and left the area only when he was elected MP for The Hartlepools in 1945. Jones' wife,

Annie, herself a prominent member of the Labour Party's women's section as well as the Co-operative Women's Guild, was elected to the council in his place – only the third woman ever voted onto that body and the first not from the Graig ward.

The families who stand out in the census records for West, Middle and East streets are, of course, those who came from furthest afield, mostly from Ireland, Scotland, the Channel Islands, or the former Russian Empire. Aaron King, for example, who lived at No. 50 Middle Street with his wife, Rachel, and worked as a glazier. Or the Barnett, Bernstein, Cline, Cohen, Hoffman, and Nevies families who were their neighbours. In West Street lived Harris and Abraham Latner, who ran a pawn-broking business in the late 1890s, and dentist Isaac Whipman and Rabbi Abraham Kraut resided in East Street. The latter came to Pontypridd from his native Kutno, north of Łódź in central Poland, and went on to serve the Jewish communities of Black-burn, Burnley, and Newcastle, all before his death in 1931.

I pass Rabbi Kraut's former home – No. 37, East Street – on my way to Coedpenmaen Road. Once there, I am face to face with the A470, which lies atop the Glamorganshire Canal: there's a low wall separating me from the cars speeding along at the national limit. Every so often, I catch a glimpse of Craig-yr-Hesg mountain to my left. On sunny afternoons or in the red glow of the gloaming as so often happens in the autumn or the first days of spring, it is genuinely and movingly beautiful. Either side of the junction with Ralph Street are two buildings that draw my attention away from nature: the first is Coedpenmaen Community Church, originally Coedpenmaen English Baptist Church, a gable-ended construc-tion put up in 1887, which is most remarkable for the size of its windows. They run almost the entire length of the façade.

But I confess my secular enthusiasms are encouraged more by the building opposite the church, easily the best-preserved example of an early-twentieth-century garage anywhere in the town centre. One for St Fagans, if the owners ever decide to part with it. You can almost imagine Toad or Bertie Wooster in their driving goggles and billowing muffler speeding out of the gates. It is part of a property called Coedpenmaen House, which was once home to Ivor William Thomas, sub-postmaster for the town, greengrocer, magistrate, and member of the Board of Guardians. He was chair of that body during the miners' lockouts of 1921 and 1926, overseeing the local state's response to poverty and hardship – the only Pontypriddian ever to hold the title – and so cast as Arthur Pearson's bitter rival.

Carrying on along Coedpenmaen Road, I pass Aspen House nursing home, and on until another building catches my eye. It looks to me like an old workmen's hall or institute: space for a name plaque runs underneath the first-storey window, but alas it has been painted over, probably during the process of converting the building into flats. Subsequent research using my phone reveals that this was indeed a workmen's free library and institute, sometimes known as the Coedpenmaen Library and Reading Rooms or, as *Kelly's* trades directory has it in the 1920 edition, the Albion Colliery Workmen's Library and Reading Rooms. It became the first home of Trallwn Workmen's Club in 1936, although their modern home is a little further on. There's that fluidity of the border once again.

Doubling back, I turn into Bonvilston Road, around the corner, and then into Thurston Road. This is the densest part of Coedpenmaen with terraces heading off in all directions. Eventually I arrive at Elim Church, part of the Elim Pentecostal Movement founded in Ireland in 1915 by Nantyffyllon-born pastor George Jeffreys. The building which, in its present form, dates to 1947, is rendered in a brilliant white. In the distance, I can see the uppermost parts of St Matthew's Church, to my left, and the former English Congregational Mission Hall, put up in the 1890s, is just around the corner to my right. As I continue along Thurston

Road, I pass Trallwn Infants School. The yard is quiet, it must be time for morning lessons. There have been pupils here since 1903, although with a total roll of around one hundred, it's far below the four hundred pupils envisaged by the Edwardian planners.

I struggle to see the rest of St Matthew's Church when I get there. Foliage has almost completely taken over the site. All that is left visible, on Dorothy Road, at least, is the entrance, which now looks like an extra set from the *Lord of the Rings* films. The building was constructed out of terracotta brick and dark stone in Gothic Early English style and at a cost of more than £5,000 in 1908 (or around £500,000 today), all to serve a stable congregation of several hundred people living in and around Coedpenmaen and Trallwn. Four chapels – there's one more to introduce – and a church, all built between the 1880s and 1910s, served a population with varied religious affiliations.

There are other denominations whose imprint has not been left on the built fabric but who met in rooms at hotels or in private houses. The Latter-day Saints, for instance, organised in Pontypridd in the 1840s, during which time they held their meetings at the White Hart and at the Half Moon Inn near the railway station. Likewise, the early Independents (or Congregationalists) met at a house called Providence, where services were conducted by Daniel Thomas, a lock-keeper who lived in Trallwn in the early 1830s.

Secularists flourished for a time, as well, taking on the challenge of turning the townspeople away from religion and towards rationalism and free thought. They held public debates at the town hall and could attract speakers of national prominence like George William Foote, editor of *The Freethinker*, but for more general business among members, the Pontypridd branch of the National Secular Society met at No. 28, Middle Street. Later, when the branch was reformed as the Rhondda and Pontypridd Secular Society, they met at the Welsh Harp Hotel on Mill Street or at John's Café on Station Square. Members were described as 'nearly all working men' and their number included an enterprising secretary, Sam Holman, a miner who had moved to the area from Frome in Somerset. Branch members took an active role in developing Pontypridd Ethical Society, as well. It met at the City Restaurant on High Street and was an attempt to blend secular ideas with political progressivism for the 'elevation of humanity', as they saw it. The society mushroomed for a short while in the aftermath of the religious revival of 1904–5 before merging with the Labour Party.

I ponder these things as I make my way over to Foundry Place and pass yet another substantial chapel on route. This one is now used as Trallwn Community Centre, but the original entrance on Bassett Street announces itself as BETHANIA (1908) METHODISTIAD CALFINIAIDD. Every other religious building in Trallwn and Coedpenmaen was English medium, but this was the cornerstone of Welsh worship, along with Capel Seion on Sion Street, overlooking the river. To save money when it was built, members of the five-hundred strong congregation volunteered their time and labour to dig the foundations. A year later the work was completed, and the chapel opened on 11 February 1909.

It's the Newbridge Arms I've come to have a look at, however. A private dwelling these days, although they have made the most of the early-Victorian façade. Before it closed a few years ago, the pub was painted in royal blue and proclaimed itself 'Ye Olde Newbridge Arms 1735'. As a date, that is twenty-one years prior to the bridge – then new, now old – which gave the town its temporary English name. It's an invented tradition: no pints were served here in the reign of George II. In fact, it took until the age of the fifth George, the twentieth century to you and me, for those two things, alcohol and 1735, to coincide.

The tithe map, produced in the 1840s, hints at the real story of Ye Olde Pub. Back then, what is today Foundry Place was, like

most of Coedpenmaen, just a field and the nearest building was
a horse stable situated a few hundred metres away. Then industry
came, and the Newbridge Arms was opened in the early 1850s to
quench the thirst of workers at the nearby Coedpenmaen Foundry or the Brown Lenox Chainworks. The first landlord was a
Bristolian, George Chilcott, who swapped chain-making for
pulling pints alongside his wife Ann. When they left, the business
was taken on by another Englishman, William Wilkins, the son
of a cabinet maker and a trained carpenter in his own right.

On Wilkins' retirement, towards the end of the 1880s, the
license was taken over by William and Caroline Clode, a husband-
and-wife team who moved up from Cardiff and not long afterwards moved back. By the time the National Eisteddfod rolled up
in 1893, the Newbridge Arms was being run by Richard and
Susanna Jones. They carried it into the twentieth century before
handing it over to David Lewis not long before Census Day in
1911. Then, in the mid-1920s, the Newbridge Arms got a makeover.
A new landlady arrived, Rose Ann Saunders of the Fox and
Hounds in Llantrisant, and it was she who began to forge a myth-
ology. The pub was henceforth to be known as 'Ye Olde Newbridge
Arms'. As a name, it suited the post-war age with its cultural
recoils from industrialised slaughter in the trenches and anti-modern appeals to a lost age of chivalry and romance. Mrs Saunders
was just a little ahead of her time, that's all.

4.

It's lunchtime, at last, which can only mean one thing: a visit to
the Central Fish Bar, one of the finest in the Kingdom of the Chip.

'Hiya love, what can I get you?'

'Large chips, please.'

The lady behind the counter serves with an automatic routine.

A metal scoop slides into her hand and produces just enough chips from the fryer to be contained in a white serving bag, which is ripped open, dead centre, when it is laid upon some wrapping paper, and a second then a third scoop of chips lands on top.

'Salt and vinegar?'

'Oh yes.'

'Hiya Sian, the usual.'

She's talking to the next customer. As she does, an acetic storm and granules of saline hail fall from the sky. I'm already salivating at the prospect of the first mouthful. I pick a wooden spoon from the box in front of me. It has a brightly coloured label affixed with Blu-Tack which says: 'help yourself, take a few.'

'Anything else, love?'

'No, that's everything.'

Leaving the bag open, I hand over some money and step outside. The first chip sears my teeth but this is life itself and so I feel no pain.

The chippy is on Central Square and is part of a row of shops opposite the Central Hotel. There's a chiropractor, a hair salon, and a post office as well. For much of the last century, the main retail unit here was a DIY shop owned by the Michaelson family. The first generation had settled in Ponty from Latvia, from Bauska some forty miles south of Riga and from Liepaja on the country's Baltic coast, to be precise, and they developed a small business empire consisting of this shop in Trallwn and another (sadly demolished) in Mill Street.

I walk along Ralph Street again towards No. 20, the house bought by the Michaelsons from their business profits. The stand-out property on this street is No. 21, which is five windows wide and has a large garage door to the right-hand side. The brickwork here is red rather than yellow, as it is lower down the hill. A century ago, this house was owned by the Corkland family. The garage door was the entrance to 'Corkland's Warehouse', a retail whole-saler owned and operated by Russian-born Abraham Corkland. At his death in 1937, having started out as a haberdasher on a modest stall at the market, he was described as 'one of the best-known businessmen in Pontypridd'.

By the time I reach Dodington Place, my chips are all eaten, and the papers scrunched up into a greasy ball in my hand. I'm whistling *Help Yourself* and rewriting lyrics as I go. 'Just help yourself to my chips.' Another boundary has been crossed, or is about to be, this time from Coedpenmaen into Pont Sion Norton, formerly Pontshonnorton or Norton Bridge. No one exactly knows who this John Norton was, the man who gave his name to the bridge over the Glamorganshire Canal and to the village which sprang up alongside it, only that it was not the John Norton who later designed St Catherine's Church – the crossing was already in existence by the time he had trained as an architect. Like the canal, Norton Bridge was sacrificed for the A470. But the name lives on and so does its mystery.

It is not always clear why certain things survive to become his-tory or heritage and why other things are forgotten, neglected even by professional remembrancers like me. John Norton is one of those who has suffered from the condescension of posterity, fading in and out of memory even as his near-contemporary and rival in the bridge-building stakes, William Edwards, is lionised. It's not for want of trying on my part, I've searched for him in as many of the records as survive, encountering booksellers, criminals, and the Sheriff of Somerset along the way, but all to no avail. This is a difficult task – where was he from. I am sure (well, as sure as I can be) that he came from England, probably from Bristol, and that fact might well have been enough to diminish his local standing.

This whole area might well have been called something else, certainly in the absence of Norton's canal crossing. Bodwenarth, perhaps, which is the name of the woods on the hillside and the farm above. Alternatively, the English translation of Pont Sion Norton might have stuck around instead: Norton Bridge. That seems to me unlikely, though, given Ponty's pioneering Welsh-medium primary school is in this part of town. Ysgol Gynradd Gymraeg Pont-Sion-Norton began life as an experiment in 1951, when two classes were established for pupils to study in Welsh, at what was otherwise then Norton Bridge School, an English-medium primary. The trial quickly took on a life of its own. By the late 1970s, such was the demand for places that there were regular complaints of overcrowding, the situation eased only with the opening of Ysgol Evan James on the other side of town in the mid-1980s.

There isn't much else to see in the village. Pont Sion Norton is one of those communities where increased connectivity by car has reduced the number of local facilities available to almost zero. Thankfully, the old Bassett Arms, which for years looked run down and rather sorry for itself, has been tastefully restored as a housing complex called Norton Court. It's a shame they failed to preserve some link to the Bassetts, the family who owned the land here in the days before industry, but the mysterious Mr Norton gets the last laugh.

Or perhaps it is the Marquess of Bute who does instead. He owned a small parcel of land on the edge of the glebe, an area once set aside to generate income for the clergy. The Bute fields marked the traditional boundary between Coedpenmaen and Pont Sion Norton. Except for a short terrace of four houses, built in the traditional estate style of a doorway and three front windows, the only building otherwise constructed on this slither of the Marquess's vast territory was a pub: the Royal Oak. It has survived to become a Chinese restaurant and the whitewashed interior betrays nothing of the building's long history. I don't suppose the Butes will mind. They made their money a long time ago.

Just past the Royal Oak is Coronation Terrace, which was built just in time for George V's coronation in June 1911 and so became the first street in Ponty named after that royal event. As terraces go, the houses here are undoubtedly quite pleasant. They have large bay windows to the front, and a small porch-like front garden which shows that the designers were not intending the usual up in two-ticks that might have been built here twenty years before. No, in an age of affluence, as that Edwardian high noon surely was, why not go one better. The view isn't bad either, straight across to Craig-yr-Hesg mountain, that is if you can ignore the traffic noise coming from the trunk road below.

From here, it's a stretch of about half a mile towards Cilfynydd, or Cil (pronounced Kill) as almost everyone around here says without meaning to convey anything ominous. On the way there, I pass Gurner's, a coal merchant. It's all shut up and possibly abandoned, with the space behind the gates full of refuse and discarded pieces of wood and empty Calor gas cannisters. But the sign, a fading blue with white lettering, speaks of a different time from the present, one whose sulphurous smell is just about alive in my memory but those younger than I am are unaware of it. Soon knowledge of burning coals' odour will have faded entirely, as even I start to forget. Was this the coalman who, when I was a child, still made his rounds with blackened hessian sacks on the back of his flatbed lorry? Perhaps it was, perhaps not.

I start to remember a story my Granny told me about my Grampa when he was a young boy living either at Llanharan or Nantyffyllon. Because my great-grandfather was a policeman, the family had a coal allowance, a valuable commodity in the 1930s, which was delivered by the coalman and left in a pile near the house. It was Grampa's task, after he came home from school, to move the coal from the street to the coal shed.

When I'm at home, later that evening, I type 'coal merchant Merthyr Road' into a database, but only one hit comes up, which tells me this was 'one of the best-known residents in the district'. It's a far cry from entering some numbers into an application on your mobile telephone once a month, an act as routine as it is impersonal. A lump of coal delivered by one worker and dug by another cannot fail to remind us of its human cost. What price today's energy turned on or off by a digital thermostat and measured by an automatic 'smart' meter?

5.

The Albion Café is a curious building half composed of stone and half of corrugated metal painted baby blue. I call in for old time's sake and order a strong cup of tea. That should set me off for the rest of the day.

'How many sugars?'

This is a test. If you don't have sugar in your tea, you're probably not from 'round here or have delusions of grandeur if you are. A friend from Middlesbrough once looked at me aghast as I drank my tea sugarless at an academic conference in Huddersfield, three spoons landed in his cup, to which I said something like 'you could have just had some cake'.

'Oh, just one,' I reply, 'I'm trying to cut down.'

'Dai-betic is it love?' says the customer next to me. 'They go' sweeteners.' A red and white plastic tub is pulled across to me, but my wrinkled nose and shake of the head leads to a drawing of the line. 'Suit yourself.'

The seats are fixed to a metal bar, so I sit near the window and look up at the photographs of Cilfynydd as it used to be. Coal mines and rugby teams. There is one of the welfare ground, too, which lies just beyond the gates of Pontypridd High School. All the usual sports made their home there, rugby and men's football among them, but Cilfynydd was one of those unusual places that sustained women's football back in the 1950s. The local sides were called the Ann Street Rockets, the Mary Street Bombshells, and the Cilfynydd Bombshells. The latter played in an occasional league against the Graig Dragons, Simmons Aero-cessories from Treforest Industrial Estate, and the Park Guild; other teams were based at Stow Hill and Brook Street in Treforest, and in Ynysybwl, and so proved that women's football could be more than a one-off charity fundraiser as it had been in the 1920s and 1930s. Those games happened, too – a visiting French side played against a Great Britain team at Ynysangharad Park in 1937, kick off was by Arthur Pearson. In fact, the earliest-known women's football team in Pontypridd was in existence by 1904.

At the Imperial War Museum, there is a recording of a 'lady footballer' made in 1976. The voice belongs to Bessie Davies, who grew up in Hopkinstown and after finishing her education at the Higher Elementary School (now Ysgol Evan James) moved to work in munitions factories in Birmingham and Coventry during the First World War. 'I used to play football at the school I went to,' she told a perplexed interviewer, who was caught off guard by Bessie's admission that she was a centre-forward. Indeed, for her, playing football was entirely natural, it was just something that was done back home in Pontypridd.

Outside the Albion Café again, I walk past the long-closed Cilfynydd Inn, which met its demise in 2011, and round the corner into Jones Street. The first shop I see is dedicated to 'aesthetics, skin & beauty'. The shutters are down, though, so I cannot investigate further. It all sounds a little ominous, but what do I know of such things? As the street stretches before me, I spot another sign: FISH AND CHIPS. It's closed, alas. If you imagine Jones Street as the y axis of a graph, there are four x axis streets running off it in parallel with each other: Richard, William, Janet, and Mary. Sounds like a folk-skiffle band.

The most interesting terrace is William Street. I pause outside

No. 55, the childhood home of opera star Sir Geraint Evans. There is a blue plaque here, hooray for that. One day the entire street will be full of them. Heol Placs Glas. Cilfynydd's stars, including tenor Stuart Burrows, fly half Glyn Davies, and Home Secretary, Northern Ireland Secretary, and Labour MP Merlyn Rees, were all born here. I cross over the road and head back to No. 9, where Rees's father, Levi Daniel, grew up. It is the more striking of the two houses, with a front porch that looks a little like a mini temple. The old Evans place is just another terrace.

At the top end of William Street, just before the junction with the aptly named Cross Street, I pass the site of one of several chapels that made up the former religious complexion of Cilfynydd: Capel Bethel. Built in the late 1880s to serve a strong Welsh-language community, with many immigrants to Cilfynydd coming from the north, Bethel was demolished several years ago, long since surplus to requirements. The main language of discourse in the village switched to English around the time of the First World War and religious activity has been in steady decline for a century. The site was turned into housing instead: Cwrt Bethel. What survived of the former chapel complex was the manse next door, a strikingly handsome building entirely distinct from the long row of terraces either side.

There's another chapel on the corner of Ann Street, a few metres away. This time, the building has survived intact. Moriah Chapel served the Congregationalists. There's a manse for this one, too, although it is not quite as affective as that for Capel Bethel. The third chapel, Beulah English Baptists, is up the very steep rise on Wood Street. Remarkably, this has been rebuilt in recent times, and so is the only one still active. It was hardly pretty to begin with but now just looks like a piled-up collection of breeze blocks. A large, white cross and the words BEULAH BAPTIST CHAPEL complete the façade.

On my way down the hill, I notice a sign on the side of the

school which reads LLYFRGELL CILFYNYDD LIBRARY. There's no library anymore, it shut during the austerity round that followed the 2008 financial crisis and has never reopened, but this is a further reminder that signage so often outlives whatever is being indicated – a ghost of the past. In fact, the present generation of Cilfynydd residents is the first not to have a library to call its own. I suppose they might call this progress. But progress which takes us back to situation not known since before industrialisation? Hardly worthy of the name. The old workmen's hall and institute, which stood on the corner of Howell Street and Cross Street from the 1890s onwards, is gone too. It was replaced with a modern community centre designed to blend in with the prevailing architecture and it is quite successful, as these things go, except that the colourful brick stands out amid the grey of the surrounding stone-built houses.

I turn to look at Richard Street, the shopping centre of the village. There is not much left of this once-thriving high street: a newsagent, a corner shop, and a chemist. But it doesn't take a degree in architecture to notice the number of businesses that have been lost, there are too many awkward renders to fill in large windows and cover up signs. You could make one of those ghosts-from-the-past composite photographs, assuming you had the skills, and bring back to life the post office, the butcher, the grocer, the wallpaper merchant, the draper, the hairdresser, the shoe shop, and the provisions merchant. Oh, and the original Carini's café.

At the bottom of the hill, I find myself outside the Commercial Hotel. During the high summer of Covid in 2020, the police raided and discovered a cannabis farm valued at more than £650,000. The sheer size of the place – three floors high and ten windows wide – allied to the neoclassical architecture, is a testament I think to the aspirations of the mid-1890s. This was being constructed just a year after the Albion Disaster. The man who built it, William Games, was a native of Newbridge-on-Wye, one of those villages in Mid Wales through which the A470 now passes.

Finally, I reach the former Richard's Hotel. It looks exactly as it should do: an old pub turned into a block of flats. Satellite dishes which fringe one corner are the giveaway. But there is more to this one than meets the eye. Back in the mid-1950s, this rather unlovely building was owned and operated by boxer Dai Dower. He was the champion flyweight of Britain, the British Empire, and Europe, titles he won in quick succession between 1954 and 1955. Sadly, there's nothing on the building to say any of this – his blue plaque is on his childhood home in Abercynon. I suppose if the flat conversion was to be carried out now that Dower has died and the council has adopted a policy of naming everything in Welsh, regardless of its historical suitability, the complex might be called Cwrt Dower or something.

6.

It was the start of every conversation at university in those first weeks of October 2004:

'And which school did you go to?' A look is cast as if to say, you're not one of us.

'You won't have heard of it.' I reply.

'Oh, go on, I know all the schools.' The voice is clipped, an upper-class English accent that takes years of training at The Schools to produce.

'No, no,' I say, 'you won't have.'

The voice is perplexed: 'How can you be so certain?'

'It has comprehensive in the title.'

Coedylan Comprehensive School, to be precise. It was known as Pontypridd High School from 2008 until 2024 and will be

Ysgol Bro Taf by the time you read this. In my day, Coedylan, its forever name as far as I am concerned, was split across two sites: the Lower School on Tyfica Road, which served Years 7 and 8 and was controlled by the watchful eye of Mr Tony Giblet (my first real history teacher), and the Upper School in Cilfynydd which housed Years 9, 10, 11, 12, and 13. Five years of my life, from the autumn of 1999 until the summer of 2004, were spent in uniform at this place.

Apart from the lower block, which they built after I left, and the name changes, pretty much everything else is the same. The road in, the terracotta bricks, even the front doors into reception. I know the internal layout has altered and classrooms have moved, and most of the staff who were at the school when I was, well, they have since retired or died, but it still feels familiar. An unscholarly word that one: feeling. I can drift around and still end up where I want to be, and then hear voices or see the ghosts of those whom I knew. Besides, I'm permanently stuck on the wall because of a prize I won when I was in my final year of sixth form: Best in Show. Others in my class were off to medical school, to drama school and so be destined to become television and film stars, or to study engineering and be useful to society, or to dream about railway locomotives anyway. But not me. I was off to read history among the Dreaming Spires, where, or so Evelyn Waugh had convinced me, students carried teddy bears called Aloysius around with them.

I realise as I walk around that I am tracking in the footsteps of my younger self. If this was an animated classic, there'd be a swishy hologram alongside me racing into the distance. I stop for a moment and imagine the teenager who walked through these aluminium doors on a Thursday morning in August twenty years ago, there to be greeted with the beaming smiles of his teachers. A roll call: Mrs Emmanuel, Mrs Thomas, Mrs Rochford, Miss Angell, Mr Powell, Mr Silezin, Mr J. Davies (History),

Mr A. Davies (History), Mr K. Davies (Music), Mrs E. Jones (French) Mrs R. Evan-Jones (Music), Mrs Hewitt (German), Miss Fowler (Geography) and Mr Raybould, the headmaster. There are others I must have forgotten. Or there were those, like Mr Rivers (Design and Technology), Mrs Rickards (Maths), Mr Axe (Biology), Mr Thomas and Mr Soper (Physics), and Mrs Cooper and Mrs L. Davies (Religious Studies), whose subjects I had surrendered long before and to mutual relief.

That day they all stood behind a trestle table with our A level results printed and stuffed into white envelopes knowing what I did not yet know: that the piece of green paper inside headed WJEC read French A, German A, History A, and that it meant I was bound for Oriel College, Oxford. I was soon ushered into Mr Raybould's office to speak to a news reporter on the telephone.

In the car park, I look around for a white Ford Fiesta, which I know to be long gone. It belonged to Mrs Hewitt. She was the one who gave me extra-curricular books to read as I was preparing for my A levels. This was how I learned about Böll, Borchert, and the rudiments of Fraktur. The coal dram and mini pit wheel are still there, as a memorial to the Albion Colliery, which dominated this site from the 1880s until the 1960s, when it closed and was demolished. Before coal, all this was farmland. Ynyscaedudwg Farm, to be precise. An unusual name. It's another of those local references, surely an invented tradition, to a mysterious sixth-century Celtic saint, in this case St Tudwg. The story goes that he was the son of St Tyvodwg of the Rhondda and a disciple of the equally difficult to trace St Cenydd, a hermit who may or may not have lent his name to Senghenydd. Cenydd's son, St Ffili, gave us Caerphilly, of course.

None of this mattered after the discovery of coal. That was the great transformation, a reset that turned riverside fields and upland woods into a modern village inhabited by thousands. I have scribbled a nice description of what happened next into my notebook; I took it from an edition of the architect's journal, *The Builder*, published in 1890. This is what it says:

> Cilfynydd, a *new* mining village, with a population that has grown within the last four years from a couple of hundred, at most, to over 2,000. Here the houses are built in rows and terraces halfway up a steep hillside.

The people behind the colliery development were the Albion Steam Coal Company, initially a group of speculators led by Ebenezer Lewis, a coal owner who already had several pits in the Rhondda in his business portfolio. In the early 1890s, with contracts to supply steam packet companies and the Italian market via Genoa, from where coal went on to power the railways and industries of Milan and Turin, the business was floated on the stock market as a limited liability company. Profits fluctuated and only occasionally was the Albion seen as a good investment for outside creditors and shareholders.

One reason for the company's undulating fortunes was what happened here one Saturday afternoon. Every mining village knew death and injury, but only a few of them – Senghenydd, Gresford, Aberfan, and Cilfynydd – knew extraordinary trauma. On 23 June 1894, the Albion Colliery exploded. Almost three hundred people were killed. At the time, it was the worst colliery disaster in the history of the South Wales Coalfield, a grim title retained for almost twenty years, until the deadliest disaster of all at Senghenydd in October 1913. That blast claimed the lives of four hundred and thirty-nine people. Only Aberfan proved more shocking.

The loss of life at the Albion was profound: every street in Cilfynydd was affected. Some of the bodies were so mutilated by the blast's destructive power that they were buried at Llanfabon Cemetery unidentified. In parliament Keir Hardie raised the stark comparison between a dedicated celebration of an infant prince – the future King Edward VIII, who was born the same day – and the government's lack of regard for a devastated community. In an article published in the *Labour Leader* on the Saturday after the disaster, Hardie was blunt. The Albion Disaster, he wrote, 'puts everything into the shade'. He continued:

> Human beings, full of strong life in the morning, [were] reduced to charred and blackened heaps of clay in the evening. The air rent with the wail of the childless mother, the widowed wife and the orphaned child… Only those who have witnessed such scenes, as I have twice over, can realise what they mean. Only those who know, as I know, that those things are preventable and solely due to man's cupidity, can understand the bitterness of feeling which they awaken. We are a nation of hypocrites. We go wild with excitement and demand vengeance when some hungry half-mad victim of our industrial system seeks to wreak his vengeance on the society which is murdering him by inches, and we piously look heavenward and murmur about a visitation of providence when [hundreds of] miners are blown to bits because society places more value on property than it does on human life. Coal must be got cheap – even if 1,200 sturdy miners are murdered yearly in the process, twelve hundred hearths made desolate.

The man who ultimately rescued the colliery from its bankrupted fate was D. A. Thomas, Lord Rhondda, who brought it under the umbrella of his Cambrian Trust. This was part of his attempt to monopolise coal production in South Wales and so reorganise the industry along American principles of rationalised competition. After Thomas's death, the Albion's fortunes declined once more. He alone seemed capable of evading South Wales' already predetermined doom.

The workings were eventually purchased by Powell Duffryn who promptly engaged in a rationalisation process of their own, sacking anyone who had been engaged in trade union activity or political radicalism. A particular target for company victimisation was the local miners' lodge chairman, Llew Jenkins of Ann Street. He was an active communist, co-organiser of the National Unemployed Workers Movement and the village unemployed club alongside his brother, Ben, a correspondent for the *Daily Worker*, a hunger marcher in 1936, and, for six years in the 1930s, a member of Pontypridd Urban District Council.

On my way back over the footbridge into the village, I think about Llew Jenkins and his fight against hunger and unemployment, against fascism and war, and what sort of signal he beams from the chaos of the past. Cilfynydd, after all, was the only place in the whole of greater Ponty ever to elect a communist to political office. There are lyrics in some of the lesser sung but still translated verses of the 'Internationale' that sum up the choices made by men like Llew Jenkins in those years of the Slump: 'we must ourselves decide our duty; we must decide and do it well.' I am reminded of the old school motto: *Ymdrech a Lwydda*. Success through hard work.

7.

With what remains of the day, I head towards the rugby club. I have set myself the task of walking up the narrow, fern-hedged lane to the Church of St Mabon and back again, out of the sheer curiosity of never having gone this way before. Hikes such as these reveal the rural character of the valley's edge. I'm only a couple of miles from the centre of Ponty, a town of tens of thousands of people, and yet here, on this road, I cannot see a house that does not belong to an old upland farm. Eventually, after what seems to be hours of walking – the map claims just two miles distance, so it is not much more than half an hour – I reach

Llanfabon. There's a pub and a church, of course. It's a mirror image of Eglwysilan and Llanwonno.

The local authority sign in the cemetery, which stands opposite the churchyard, tells me I am in Caerphilly now, and not Ponty-pridd. But since so many of the victims of the Albion Disaster are buried at Llanfabon, along with several more of those killed at Senghenydd in 1913, and even some of those who died at Aber-fan in 1966, I do not feel guilty extending the boundary lines on my map. There has been a church here since at least the eleventh century, with documents detailing that construction suggestive of a rebuild and so an even older edifice. What stands before me is a product of early-Victorian intervention, however; the handi-work of John Pritchard, the architect later tasked with renewing Llandaff Cathedral.

With the light beginning to fade, I do not linger, and head instead towards National Road, my route down off the mountain, which will bring me out next to Cilfynydd War Memorial. It is a fern-hedged single track and about two miles long. Downhill though, so that's a small victory. About two-thirds of the way, the road widens. I am parallel with the coal tips. From here I can see the terraces of Cilfynydd to my left, the housing estates at Glyn-coch and Coed-y-Cwm ahead of me, and the undulating lines of the hills. For curiosity's sake, I make my way over to the conical piles of slag and coal waste, the remains of eighty years of under-ground exploitation at the Albion. All the ground underneath my feet is industrial discard.

In a mile and a half, I've travelled from the medieval to the modern but struggle to find words to explain how I feel about my progress. What was I saying about that being unscholarly? These tips are so familiar. I saw them every day of my childhood, travel-ling to school or leaving Ynysybwl for any reason at all, in fact. From that distance they just looked like dirty hills, perhaps the blacked sides reflected exposed mud. Up close, they have a different character altogether. I realise that there is not a single shade of black, but a whole spectrum of greys, blues, and purples.

In places ferns and moss have begun to grow, they disguise much, but cannot cope with the whole job that they have been left to do. In the autumn this hillside glows with an orange hue as the ferns decay before the winter. It's a sight I most associate with the hills around here. I'm sure it happens elsewhere, too, but never quite so brilliantly. I suspect there is a mineral element to the coal tips that causes the plants to turn an extra shade on their way from emerald to copper.

I sit down on the grass, which is dewy, and rest for a few minutes. Am I supposed to find beauty here, amid these poisoned ferns. No, I am supposed to recoil from the underground nastiness which created these hillside pyramids. Ron Berry, the Rhondda novelist, often made a point about such places, that one had to learn to distinguish what was true and what was invented. What peaks behind me is a human fabrication, to be sure, but it has been there so long that nature has taken it for granted – and so, I suppose, have we.

All too often writers, especially those of us who spent our formative years in the valleys, are apt to say that we come back from journeys abroad because, as Berry put it, 'I felt *hiraeth* for mountains, for space, for green silence.' On a day like today, with the sun beginning to set, I know exactly what he means. But ask me on a day when the mist is low, the rain is beating down, and the light is thin, and I'll tell you that no amount of silence or beauty, no amount of space or solace, could ever convince me that humans should live in places like this. This is the bipolar conundrum of the valleys.

At the bottom of the hill, I reach the war memorial. It is a three-column affair unveiled on 29 October 1925. Each column represents an idea: RHYDDID (Freedom), ABERTH (Sacrifice), TEYRNGED (Duty). At the other end of Cilfynydd, on the way back to Pontypridd, there's a hand car wash in what used to be a Renault car dealership. I say hello to the folks running it, who reply with an Eastern European inflection, jet washer and sponge in hand. There are various signs dotted around for the notice of customer: commandments and values of a sort. My favourite reads:

IF YOU ARE NOT HAPPY
PLEASE TELL US

IF YOU ARE HAPPY
PLEASE TELL OTHERS

There's a thought.

8.

Merthyr Road leads me back towards town. It is a land of contrasts. On one side of the street there are traditional terraces, on the other there are small villas with two-storey bay windows and balconettes. I am never surprised when I see these sorts of things in The Valleys, because this is the reality. It has always been the reality except in the stereotypes. The closer I get to home, the more impressive the buildings become. If these were what visitors saw first, rather than the terraces of yore, I think we might all have a different reputation. Take No. 64. In 1911, this was the home of Roderick MacLean, his wife Jessie, and their four children. Roderick – Roddy, shall we say – came from Gairloch in the Highlands. He spoke both English and Gàidhlig, the latter a rarity in Edwardian Ponty, but not an exclusivity since there were Gàidhlig-speakers resident in Graigwen, as well. That's something else to add to the town's linguistic crucible. Roddy's next-door neighbour, another Roderick, was a Welsh-speaking Liverpudlian and was the manager of the local branch of the Midland Bank.

I turn off Merthyr Road at the junction with Common Road and head down the hill towards town. I decide to stop off at the Llanover Arms for a drink and to look through my notes. Unlike its old rival, the Newbridge Arms, this place really does go back more than two hundred years, and you get a waft of history as soon as you step inside. The room to my left, known to punters as the vestry, has high-backed, narrow-seated wooden benches. Rescued chapel pews, in fact. To the right is the main bar. I head in and order a pint of IPA and take a seat in one of the captain's chairs near the window. On the bar itself is a classic till, made of metal and elaborately engraved. It's a reminder of the longevity of the place. Those who drink in the Lan, as it tends to be called, are wont to tell stories. But it's also more than just pub philosophy: this place is part of the sinew of an entire historical and literary tradition. Ponty's writers have all drunk here at one time or another, and there's normally one of us standing at the bar.

I'm trying to remember the first time I consciously noticed the Lan. I suppose it must have been in the company of my parents, perhaps coming home from a holiday in Weston-super-Mare, or a day trip somewhere. I think the former because whenever we had time to travel as a family, we went back 'home' to England to visit my grandparents and great-grandparents. The reason for our migration across the Bristol Channel was straightforwardly material. Dad had got a job as a chef working for the maverick West German hotelier, Thilo Thielmann, who owned and operated De Courcey's Restaurant in Pentyrch, on the outskirts of Cardiff, together with his wife Patricia.

The Tees, as they were affectionately known among the staff and so by us, had previously worked at the city's Holiday Inn – Thilo, originally from Aachen, or was it Berlin, he claimed both, was the founding manager and oversaw the construction work as well as the grand opening – but in the autumn of 1988 he and Pat struck out on their own. They envisaged a hotel at Pentyrch with Rolls Royce-sized garages for customers and a Michelin-starred restaurant to prove that Cardiff could be a culinary destination. Dad was in at the beginning of the venture, rising from a junior position in the kitchen in his early twenties to become head chef before he was even thirty; he stayed after a devastating fire destroyed the original Scandinavian-style building, once the home of Cardiff investor, solicitor, arcades impresario, philanthropist, and cricketer, Frederick de Courcy Hamilton, in 1991.

Between the fire and the rebuilding, Dad went off to train with Michelin-starred chefs all over the country, learning new skills, and gaining fresh ideas. De Courcey's reopened in November 1992. From then on, Dad established himself as one of Wales' most promising culinary talents. He had recipes published in the press, challenged for prizes, and for titles like Welsh Chef of the Year. My elderly relatives, in their interwar humour, took to referring to De Courcey's as 'Dave's Café'. Well, at Dave's Café back in 1995, this recipe for 'grilled salmon on a crab, artichoke and chive galette with a yellow pepper vinaigrette' was one recommended for a summer dinner party – accompanied by a green salad:

Ingredients (serves 4)
4 × 4 oz salmon fillets
4 oz fresh cooked crabmeat (or tinned if unavailable)
2 artichoke hearts (diced)
2 baking potatoes (medium)
Bunch of chives (chopped)
2 yellow peppers (deseeded and chopped)
1 orange
1 egg
4 fl oz olive oil

2oz shallots or onions (chopped)
1 glass of dry white wine
2 tsp white wine vinegar
Salt and pepper, cooking oil
Black seedless grapes and diced tomatoes for garnish.

METHOD

Galette

Cook potatoes until soft. Allow to cool, peel and mash well.

Sauté artichokes in a little oil until golden brown. Add artichokes, crabmeat, chives and egg to potatoes, mix together well and season.

Shape into four flat cakes on a lightly floured board, put into fridge to chill.

Vinaigrette

Lightly sweat onions until soft and transparent, add yellow peppers and orange rind and continue to cook until soft.
Add the white wine, white wine vinegar and the juice of the orange, simmer until nearly all the liquid has gone. Stir in one teacup of water.

Place in a blender and puree, pass through a fine sieve, then whisk in 4fl oz of olive oil. Cover and keep warm, but do not reheat.

Pan-fry the potato cakes in a little oil until golden and heated through, keep warm.

Brush salmon lightly with oil, season well and cook under a medium grill.

Serve

Place galette in the centre of a warm plate. Top with the cooked salmon, lightly re-whisk the vinaigrette and pour around the galette and salmon. Garnish with grapes and tomatoes.
Oh, and feel free to open a chilled bottle of Australian chardonnay.

My time in the Lan is taken up rummaging through Dad's career as a chef in digitised back copies of the *South Wales Echo*, *Western Mail*, and *Wales on Sunday*. A second pint is accompanied by a bag of cheese and onion crisps, all to stave off dinner for a little while longer. I'm learning things I did not understand as a child: like the extent of the ambition for De Courcey's and Dad's role in making it a success. Here's some more food ideas, straight from his old recipe books:

Spinach, garlic and Parmesan ravioli with crisp vegetables.
Pan-fried fillet of beef with oxtail sauce.
Vanilla and yoghurt Charlotte with lemon cream sauce.

That last, says the *South Wales Echo*, was for the 'weight conscious'. It's a shame they never printed the recipe for Dad's signature dessert: liquorice ice cream. In those days, he cooked for celebrities, international referees (the restaurant was a favourite after-match destination of Five Nations officials), and for the nouveau riche of Thatcher's and Major's Britain. He did cookery demonstrations at the Royal Welsh and on the stage at St David's Hall. He could have been on *Ready Steady Cook* or *MasterChef*, the Loyd Grossman version with the round tables at the end, which he watched every Sunday after work, if he'd wanted to be. They were exciting times.

All the same, I wonder how things might have turned out if, in the aftermath of the fire, we had then moved on from South Wales. We were not yet fully settled. I was five and my sister was not much more than two. Perhaps we should have done. But Dad was loyal to Mr T, Mum was finding her place in the village community as a dinner lady and cleaner at the local primary school, my sister was about to start at nursery, and so we carried on *sans regret*. Only I seemed to have visible doubts, that is if the hints at disquiet present in my school reports are anything to go by. My teachers thought I ought to spend more time playing in the yard and less reading or plonking keys on the upright piano in the assembly hall; that I should try harder to fit in, to belong.

9.

The next day, with the weather holding, I visit Glyntaff. What you associate with that word depends a lot on your generation. For those glancing casually at the hillside, it is probably the round houses, yet more of Dr Price's architectural concoctions. For those of a certain age, this part of Ponty holds the memories of secondary school. Boys were sent to grammar school buildings near Lan wood, but girls - including some very famous alumni like Elaine Morgan - went to Glyntaff, to the Pontypridd Intermediate School for Girls. Later to be known as Pontypridd Girls Grammar School.

The buildings that were put up in 1913 are still in place, only they're now part of a vast, multi-community and multi-campus estate belonging to the University of South Wales. Here they teach nursing and midwifery, forensic science, geology, and natural history; all within buildings that exude Edwardian ambition and civic confidence, and that technocratic vision one instinctively associates with other red-brick institutions like Victoria University in Manchester or the University of Birmingham.

If you stand at the front entrance of the old school and face towards Treforest, two landmarks make themselves apparent. To the right stands St Mary's Church surrounded by a small but significant graveyard. Designed by the Anglo-Irish architect Thomas Henry Wyatt in the late 1830s, this is the oldest Anglican establishment in Pontypridd and as high as it is possible to get before one ascends above the perfumed clouds swung into the air by a verger. Most of us have never been inside, we leave church to births, deaths, and marriages, which can lead to confusion over what really goes on in such places. Take the story I have been told of a couple who, wanting a picture postcard ceremony, made an appointment to see a vicar about their upcoming wedding. After being shown around and feeling that this was just what they wanted, their only question was this:

'It'll be normal, won't it?' says the bride-to-be.

'We can accommodate your wishes for hymns, but it will be a church service.'

'No,' she says. 'None of that. I mean it'll be normal, won't it?'

The vicar looks quizzically at the groom-to-be, at the bride-to-be, and again at the groom. The bride-to-be prods her fiancé as if to say, you tell him. After an awkward silence, the young man says:

'What she means is, there'll be no incest or nothing.'

The vicar, trying not to lose composure, bites his lip and replies:

'We do try to discourage that sort of thing in a Christian community.'

The church itself is distinctive in its use of an Italian-Roman-esque style – there are echoes at St Mabon's Church in Llanfabon, but it is rare enough for this part of Glamorgan. The plans for St Mary's, held at Lambeth Palace Library in London, reveal the original name was simply Newbridge Church. The foundation stone, an old issue of the *Monmouthshire Merlin* tells me, was laid on 10 September 1836 at a ceremony attended by Wyatt, the contractor George Strawbridge of Bristol, and the Bishop of Llandaff, Edward Copleston, who was formerly the provost of Oriel College. Copleston returned to consecrate the church in the autumn of 1839.

It is the graveyard, though, that takes my interest. Most of the memorials here are heavily weathered, their names barely visible. There are those to the young children who died at ages we would now find shocking and distressing; the occasional widow who lived into her eighties or nineties and so witnessed almost the entire nineteenth century; and finally the wealthy industrialists like George William Lenox, the London-born co-owner of the Brown Lenox Chainworks, and his wife Rosa, who tend to get short shrift from the professional historian but enjoy a warmer embrace from amateurs. In places like this, it is possible to find that stratum of society so often absented from the history books, at least in Wales, anyway, where we privilege chapel ministers and others of bardic or Celtic pretensions. For everyone else, there's the municipal cemetery across the way. As I turn into Cemetery Road, I slow down; my pace of foot is glacial, respectful, caught in the memorial tempo of funerals past. During the pandemic, these grounds provided an ideal place for reflection, and I came here often on my circular walks.

A few facts: the cemetery was opened in 1874 and has been expanded several times since John Bradshaw, the first person buried here, was interred in the summer of 1875. There is a Jewish quarter, with its gravestones in English, Hebrew, and one in Hungarian, though none is in Welsh, which is a solemn reminder of the many faiths and cultures for whom Ponty has been a home. And a rose garden for the scattered ashes of those who are not buried, but rather cremated.

The famous crematorium, which lies at the centre of the grounds, in the original burial chapel buildings, was opened in June 1924. At the time it was the only such facility in Wales and one of only sixteen across the whole Britain, the closest of them were otherwise to be found in the West Midlands, in Birmingham or Leicester, or in parts of London like Golders Green, Newham, and West Norwood. Among the funerals held here were those for the short-story writer Dorothy Edwards, who flourished for a short while on the edges of the Bloomsbury Set, and Dylan Thomas's father, David John. The poet attended his father's cremation on 19 December 1952, less than a year before he himself died. To come to terms with his grief, still traumatised by the idea that his father's head had exploded in the oven and having begged his wife that she would not allow anything like it to happen to him, Dylan began to write an elegy. It was never finished.

10.

The walk up to the Common takes its toll on the legs but once I'm at the summit of Common Road and onto one of the footpaths criss-crossing the open ground of the plateau, I quickly recover. There is no denying that the view up here is incredible – it always pays to visit. All the valleys that converge on Pontypridd reveal themselves at once. To the north, there's the Taff and the Clydach, one leading to Merthyr Tydfil, the other to Ynysybwl. To the west, right in front of me as I stand on a rocky edge, is the Rhondda. And south, well, that leads nowhere important.

As a district, the Common has three elements: the landscape, the golf club, and the Cottage Hospital. As I step off the footpath onto Hospital Road, I am greeted by the sight of a building I cannot bring myself to enter. The street is named for hospital, of course. Opened on 16 February 1911 and supported, until the creation of the National Health Service in 1948, by a mixture of philanthropy, voluntary subscription, and fundraising events, this is now a quiet district hospital. Between 1994 and 2019, it also housed Y Bwthyn, a specialist palliative care unit and the local headquarters of the Macmillan nurses; although they have since moved out to Llantrisant. It is, in its relative simplicity, a beautiful building, constructed in the arts-and-crafts style so redolent of the Edwardian period, and looks out across the valley and upon the town which it once served.

I last went inside on 9 October 2000. I was fourteen years old.

The walk up from town, which I've just replicated, was a lonely one. I got off the school bus and was due to meet Dad and my sister, Katrina. I went up along Common Road, onto Hospital Road, and into Y Bwthyn via the front gate. The automatic doors slid back and in I went to the lobby. On the right, there was a table of mugs and a collecting box. I went straight through another set of doors into the waiting room. To the left was a cubby with a pool table but most of the room was taken up with chairs and low tables scattered with magazines. I spot one of the nurses. She is dressed in a white uniform, punctuated only with a kingfisher-blue belt across her waist and a nurse's watch hanging from a pocket.

'Hello,' she says calmly. 'Come on through, your dad is here already.'

Mum is asleep on the bed. She seems peaceful, as if at rest. But her breathing is shallow, uneven, and then slow, with that rattle that anyone who has seen death, or heard it, can recognise in an instant. She has not spoken for three days, her pain is doused now with palliative medicine that keeps her unconscious, distant from us. Dad looks exhausted, weighed down, and so takes my ten-year-old sister out of the room for a break. I am left alone with Mum.

I tell her about my new subjects, what GCSEs are going to be like, and what we're going to be doing this term. I started in Year 10 the week before. Had I been older, I could have used these final moments better. I could have told her about other things, about the sort of deep-down feelings I knew I had, and that I would never get the chance to express, and that I later held back for far too long. Instead, I hold her hand, put my head on her shoulder for a minute or two, and sit in silence until Dad comes back.

For a few hours, we circulate. I try to do some homework, play pool with my sister, and then at about eight o'clock in the evening, perhaps a little later, we go back to Mum's room to say, 'see you tomorrow'. This has been our routine for the past seven days. It takes twenty minutes to travel from the hospice to the village. Dad unlocks the front door, lets us in the house, and gets straight back into the car. I wave as the car disappears at the bottom of our hill. Inside, the telephone is ringing. I answer and the nurse asks if Dad is there, she has a quiver in her voice.

'No,' I reply, wearily. 'He's on his way back.'

'Okay, good night love.'

'Good night.'

I hang up.

The nurse did her duty, it was not her place to tell me what I knew, even then, she would have told Dad had he answered. And which I understood, anyway. Mum had slipped away, a few moments after we had ourselves turned out of the hospital gate and headed for home. She was thirty-two. None of us ever got a chance to say goodbye.

Four days earlier, Mum and Dad were married in the same room. They had always put it off, thinking themselves much too young for all that, Dad was only thirty-five, younger than I am now, but time ran out. Together with one or two of the nurses, wearing whatever it was we had on – I was in a *Star Trek Voyager* T-shirt – we gathered for a short, civil ceremony. Mum was in such pain that the morphine doses were by now quite high, and her speech lacked so much of its former strength. She forced her way through to present as much of herself as she could, and for one last time.

'I do,' she said when the registrar asked the question, 'I do.'

Upon being declared husband and wife, Mum burst out, 'I'm so happy.'

They were her final words. Almost.

For two decades, I avoided this part of town. Then on a walk to the cemetery, the morning after Queen Elizabeth delivered her 'we will meet again' address in April 2020, I came back via the Common, and so glimpsed the hospital complex I had tried so very hard to forget. On a second visit, a few days later, I paused at the rose garden near the chapel of rest, where Mum's ashes were scattered. There were not many people about that day as I stood in quiet reflection, my head bowed, thinking of Mum and about her all-too-short life. I took with me the words of the poem by Canon Henry Scott-Holland, which I read out at Mum's funeral, and which I read once more:

Death is nothing at all.
It does not count.
I have only slipped away into the next room.
Nothing has happened.

Everything remains exactly as it was.
I am I, and you are you,
And the old life that we lived so fondly together is untouched,
    unchanged.
Whatever we were to each other, that we are still.

Part 4

ROADS HOME

I.

I cannot put it off any longer. I shall have to go to Ynysybwl. But first, a springtime detour. A turn off the long road that winds north from Taff Street, along Berw Road, past the Craig-yr-Hesg quarry, and a house called St Malo, and onwards to the village of my childhood. First stop is Glyncoch. Built after the Second World War, this housing estate was meant to symbolise Labour's New Jerusalem. Bigwigs like the local MP, Arthur Pearson, got avenues and crescents named after them, as a reminder of which party was putting things right after decades of chaos under the other lot, and restoring optimism after mass unemployment and war.

Entering Glync (rhymes with clink), as the locals know it, via Grovers Close, I pass through a small community play area. A group of children is gathered around the swings. This estate has long had a reputation. Just calling it an estate brings one to mind. It started off fine, with brand-new houses, modern plumbing, and heating systems, a boon to those cleared out from dilapidated slum housing elsewhere in the town. But things soon turned sour. Some of those from Treforest and those parts of Coedpenmaen nearest the canal objected to being made to move here, others found the upheaval of their transfer disruptive – at one point in time the new residents complained 'you cannot [even] buy a stamp'.

With economic turbulence added to the mix by the 1970s, Glyncoch gained its notoriety. In 1978, twenty-five years after the first houses were completed, the estate was christened Ponty's glue-sniffing capital. After a decade of Thatcherism, the headlines grew worse: despair, vandalism, and break-ins. It was reported in the press that a state of lawlessness existed, and large parts had become 'no-go areas'. It was never meant to be this way, of course.

Front gardens separate the houses from the street. Semi-detached blocks ensure that terraces are a thing of the past. There is a conscious avoidance of old-fashioned words like street: there isn't one. In fact, if you had wandered into Pontypridd in 1955 keen to know about never having had it so good, it was to Glyncoch that you were directed by well-meaning – and often rather proud – council officials.

On a fine day, you can see why planners thought this would be a good place to live, and estate agents still do. From Cefn Lane, I observe wooded hillsides, they curve and roll. Admittedly, there are slag heaps, too, but tasteful landscaping has disguised them for the most part, and it would never stop the sale of property on this windy way. Rugged views. Much sought-after location.

The houses lining Cefn Lane between Greenmeadow Close and Derwendeg Avenue are all 1950s classics. Semi-detached, brick built, they are square and robust, they have a central chimney stack and front and rear gardens. Some owners have applied an ugly, concrete render to the upper floors over the years but, as a few of the houses in Derwendeg Avenue reveal, they would originally have been red brick from foundation to roof, with terracotta tiles to finish. Quite the contrast from the endless grey of the stone-built and slate-roofed terraces in nearby Ynysybwl.

I stop off at the Spar on Garth Avenue for a bottle of pop and a packet of cheese and onion. As I munch on my crisps, I make my way towards the community centre on Clydach Close. It's a triumph of grassroots regeneration work, this. The old centre was a run-down shack with a flat felt roof, concrete sides, and ugly corrugated cladding. The sort that did its best to say: we don't care much about the people who live here. Not this new one, though. Here we have a rather handsome building cast in terracotta and cream with a slanted roof full of solar panels. Postmodern architecture, then, but given the fate of modernism on this hillside in the last century, who can blame the decision taken to try something else? As I move on, I spot a sign encouraging residents to join the Glyncoch Community Pantry, it's a way of spreading the cost of living by pooling resources, like the co-ops and friendly societies of a previous age.

A footpath leads me onto Porcher Avenue, where I'm greeted by more shops, a pharmacy, and a marvellous piece of street art. Well, some daisies, a football, and a sunflower, to be exact. I take another swig of my pop as I stare at the mountainside. It's the views that make the valleys, especially on a sunny afternoon, and I could get used to this one. This thoroughfare is named after Leonard Porcher, the long-serving, some might say long-suffering, clerk of Pontypridd Urban District Council who retired in 1949 and died in 1960. Leonard's father, Henry, had been clerk to the stipendiary magistrate. It was a prominent enough job to attract him all the way from his birthplace: Chatteris in Cambridgeshire. After all these inclines, I am sorely tempted to go in the opposite direction, but I carry on climbing.

By now I have reached the 1970s housing stock and a separate housing development known as the Cefn Farm Estate. Near the summit sits the low-rise of a primary school. Opened on 6 March 1973, Cefn Primary School was one of the last to be built by the former Glamorgan County Council. It was designed for open-plan education, as an official brochure tells me. I have procured a scan from the archives in Cardiff. 'It is no longer enough for a child to sit passively in a desk,' proclaims the anonymous narrator, they 'must participate actively and enjoy a disciplined freedom to use and learn from the equipment and material provided in and outside the school.' Exciting stuff – proof that pedagogical principles run in cycles across the generations. Ironically, the brochure has photographs of classroom activities in which the children are sat mostly at desks. One of the images gives me a brief history lesson:

Where I Live
My home is at Glyncoch. Glyncoch is about two miles north of the town of Pontypridd. Pontypridd is well-known for its market-place. Glyncoch is built near the River Taff. The River Taff flows through Pontypridd and finally carries into the sea at Cardiff. Cardiff is the capital city of Wales and is about fourteen miles from Glyncoch.

This is written underneath a heading: 'come to the zoo.' I make no further comment.

My descent from Greenfield Avenue takes me along Garth Avenue and back onto Cefn Lane. I can hear a bus straining up the hillside, it bounces unsteadily over some traffic-calming measures. Towards the bottom of the road, I spy an empty field. I had forgotten all about the demolition of Ty Gwyn. The building started life as part of Craig-yr-Hesg County Junior School, the first of the two educational facilities to be built at Glyncoch. It opened on 13 July 1965 just as the county council began adopting open-plan learning. Already committed to building a more tradi-tional school here, they compromised on the design and so built both a two-storey structure and a low-rise one. The latter is what survives today as Craig-yr-Hesg Primary School. There are, however, plans afoot for a brand-new school on this site, bringing together Cefn and Craig-yr-Hesg, so this might all be gone by the time you read these words. You think a place will last forever, don't you, but turn away for a while and suddenly it is no longer there. That's regeneration: someone else's idea of necessary transformation.

Before I leave the estate, via the junction with Ynysybwl Road, I nip down a side street. It runs alongside Pontypridd Auctions, a building that was once a branch of the co-op. I find what I'm looking for: a single, two-storey detached house with garage. A schoolfriend lived here. I haven't seen him for years; I think he's in Scotland writing puzzle books. As I recall, Jason came into school one day, not long before he moved away, and told us he was off to join the CIA. After some moments of quizzical eyebrow raising in the sixth-form common room, he added: 'The Cumbria Institute of the Arts.'

2.

Across the main road from Glyncoch stands Coed-y-Cwm. It's a B-road but in this case the B stands for busy not backwater, so it is a good idea to use the pelican crossing. It is still beeping when I make my way onto the bridge. Below me is another railway line turned into a footpath. This time it's a TVR spur that ran from Ponty through to Ynysybwl, although passengers were evicted as far back as 1953. We can't even blame Dr Beeching for this felony, British Railways came up with the idea.

Like its neighbour, Coed-y-Cwm is a housing estate. Albeit one built by private contractors for private residents. It is, in my view, the perfect distillation of the decline of taste among the baby boomers. Until the 1970s, no one lived on this side of the mountain. It was all woodland, just as the Welsh of its name suggests. But post-war prosperity expanded the middle classes, and terraced houses, often without modern amenities, were no longer fit for the aspirations of NCB managers, ladder-climbing teachers, general practitioners, and middle-tier council executives. Socially exclusive estates like this one were born with every street name rendered in Cymraeg – always a signal of *status* around here. Hafan Heulog makes more sense, apparently, than Sun Trap, Ffordd y Bedol instead of Horseshoe Way, Bryn Aur rather than Golden Hill.

The oldest sections of Coed-y-Cwm can be found nearest the Ynysybwl road: the chalet-style housing of Clas Cwm, Bryn Awel, and Clas-Ty-Gelli, and the Dutch-inspired Heol Pen-y-Foel. The Tudor mockeries higher up the hillside came along a few years later. If I were to introduce the ghosts of the poet John Betjeman or the architectural historian Nikolaus Pevsner to this estate, I might end up haunted for the rest of my days. Neither man would take kindly to the attempted Tudor style, each house cast in red brick. Some owners have tried their best with the postmodern identity crisis and added boards and stucco to the upper floor, but this makes matters made worse. At least with the exposed red brick, the pretence of age has been abandoned. What fascinates me is just how little relationship these streets bear with earlier parts of the landscape, notably Cwm Farm. It is as if, in making this a patch of Cymru, the estate's original, upwardly mobile inhabitants lost sight of the real South Wales all around them – if they even knew all about it from childhood.

Towards the uppermost part of Coed-y-Cwm is a road-cum-footpath which leads through to Ynysybwl. Tarmac recedes and nature begins to take over. With the estate behind me, I cannot yet see the village, everything is obscured by ferns and hedgerows and the light begins to fade as it does in the moments before a thunderstorm. Occasionally, I glimpse drystone walls in the farmland, those upland boundaries that are common all over Britain. The route I'm on now is an old one, one of those taken by tenant farmers who have lived up here decades, if not centuries, all before the discovery of coal. The tithe map tells me that the land was owned by the Clive family, which explains why it was that the colliery and the village that sprang up around it took on all-too-familiar names from the Windsor-Clive dynasty. Two farms lie either side of me. The first, Pen-y-parc, simply means 'top of the park' – it was once called New Park or Parc Newydd – the other, Gellifendigaid, has a more romantic meaning akin to sacred grove or a glorious copse.

When at last the darkened road breaks out into open country-side, my eyes squint and I am blinded temporarily by the light of the sun. After a few moments of adjustment, they open again to reveal a landscape that I find difficult to describe, in part because I know it so well. It is easy, up here on the hillsides, all too easy, to fall into the trap laid out for us by that notorious charlatan and fabricant of the London Welsh, Richard Llewellyn, a literary success story that I cannot stomach. What he envisaged in his famous novel of 1939 was a paternalistic South Wales, not an American one as I have it, a place unencumbered by the politics of the South Wales Miners' Federation or by immigration. Throughout the novel, England and the English are used as antagonists, or they are referenced by those whose character and behaviour is unsavoury. Men such as Mr Elias, the chapel deacon and greengrocer, who threatens on several occasions to 'have the English law on you'. The worst of the schoolteachers is no differ-ent. 'How green was my valley,' Llewellyn concludes, 'and the valley of them that have gone.'

With a verdant view like this, we might be tempted to nod along with that sort of thing, tempted to agree that this post-industrial landscape is our way back to the lost land of pre-indus-trial Glamorgan, which is something else Llewellyn meant with his appeal to some green untouched ancestry, but there is no going back. Coal has been and gone. It is in the past, but it is still the past - it happened, it is history now, and that is how we understand and how we come to terms with its legacy.

I have a choice, here, at this junction on the mountain, to walk down towards the village, or to continue my ascent and come off a different way. The path before me has been known for generations as the Roman Road. It has never mattered to me whether it is, or is not, in fact, Roman; it just is. With its straight precision, what else could it be but that. The background of the name lies in the doubtful legend (nothing more) about a bloody battle at Glyncoch between legionaries and Silurian natives, all for control of these valleys north of Pontypridd. The Romans prevailed, albeit not without a human cost, and so they built a marching camp on the hillside at Llanwonno overlooking the Rhondda to assert their authority. This was, so the story goes, one of the roads that led there. On the opposite side of the valley there lies a set of earthworks that just might be the remains of an Iron Age hillfort. Britons to the left of me, Romans to the right. Suddenly I feel the need for some magic potion from the druid Getafix.

No kidding: I'm almost three hundred metres up in the air, about as high as it gets in greater Pontypridd. As the Roman Road stretches before me, I stop to admire the view. I know what to expect, of course, but it still takes the breath away: from here, as the river below bends to follow the curve of the mountain, you can observe the entire valley and marvel at its beauty. There's the village and its paralleled terraces, horizontal in Roberttown, vertical in Clivetown. There's the house that I grew up in, the shops I knew as a child, my old primary school, and even the rugby field on which I scored my first - alright, only - try. If I was given the choice to go back to 1989 and to stay by the beach or to move here into the hills, then I am certain now that I would hesitate, for I am a product of both. It has just taken me a while to come around to that fact.

A little further along, I come to another crossroads. I can go right, then along a pathway which leads to Pontycynon Farm Road and Cynon Bridge, and into a different valley. That way lies Abercynon. Carry on and I'll eventually reach Perthcelyn Reservoir, from where I can walk, with ease, into the terraces of Mountain Ash. Or left, then, and down off the mountain at last, and on past Tylar Fedw Farm and Dee Plant and the mine manager's house at Ty'n-y'wern and the main entrance to what was, but is no longer, the Lady Windsor Colliery. This is the way. Above me, a red kite is circling. They are a common sight in this valley. As someone who is not even an amateur ornithologist, it looks rather majestic as it swoops and lifts, but these birds of prey were not well regarded. Shakespeare thought of them as scavengers and so used them in his plays as symbols of greed and cowardice. Perhaps he meant the black kite, though, which makes more sense in a line like 'the city of kites and crows'. That was his description of London in *Coriolanus*.

It is as I ponder this subject that I meet a group of hikers coming up the road, they are clad in synthetic fibres, fleeces and the like, and are armed with walking poles in each hand. Whatever cannot be stored in their rucksacks is attached to the strapping with a shiny carabiner. In typical Bwl fashion they stop me to say:

'Wrong way, Dar!'

I splutter a reply, something about walking over from Coed-y-Cwm, and we all giggle as I catch my breath.

'Won't keep you then.'

They're soon back on the march, two by two. As for me, I'm on a go-slow and so I stop again by the colliery memorial just up the hill from Windsor Place.

It's hard to imagine that this was ever an industrial site but for a hundred years this was home to one of the finest steam coal collieries anywhere in the world. There's quite a lot of film footage of the place: for various reasons, some of them political, film crews, directors, and television stars often came to shoot on location. Documentary maker Humphrey Jennings made his 1945 film *A Diary for Timothy* here. Thirty years later, it was the turn of Cilla Black, who arrived in the spring of 1976 to film a segment for her eponymous Saturday night television show. She was taken underground and on her return to the surface told a waiting reporter that 'it was cold but not as bad as that programme *When The Boat Comes In*. Those scenes down coal mines were awful.' Something tells me that Cilla got celebrity treatment. Surprise, surprise.

3.

I am stood now on the square opposite the Roberttown Hotel. Behind me is the garage or, to give its proper name, the Robert-town Service Station. Established 1970. I remember the old design, with its canopy and petrol pumps, but this square metal and brick edifice has been around for more than a decade and looks set to survive for quite some time yet. This is where the two landed estates once owned by Robert Thompson Crawshay and Robert Windsor-Clive, Earl of Plymouth, met, apparently in harmony. One part of the village was known, briefly, as Roberttown (or Tre-Robart); the other took the name Clivetown.

To force myself not to walk these streets on autopilot, to pay attention to what has changed in the years that I have been away, is no easy task. The chippy is still there as is the Vision-Regeneration Project, which I once served, and Cresci's Café, the local Italian. Founded by John Cresci sometime around 1905, the business has been going for nearly one hundred and twenty years (with a few breaks here and there). Many residents fondly remember its earlier location at No. 9, Robert Street. There have been other alterations on this stretch, too, the bakery has become a kebab house, for instance, and the pet shop has disappeared as has the pizzeria that sprang up for a while, but not so many things have changed as to be disconcerting.

Moving on past the old Spar, run for decades by Leighton and Margaret James, and the former Barclays Bank, which survived until the early 1990s, when the demise of the colliery made a small outpost of financial services like this redundant, but is now a house, I can feel myself slipping into old habits. You need detective skills to spot the other bank that once maintained a presence in Ynysybwl: Lloyds. No. 7, Windsor Place, has been attached to the neighbouring Fu Kwai Chinese takeaway for so long that its existence as a bank is almost completely forgotten. But buildings, like people, retain their scars, however much they fade, they remain, and this one is no different.

Taking refuge on the island by the war memorial, kitted out by the local community council with benches and some attractively planted metal containers, I survey the scene. I am a young boy again, walking down one of the hilly streets to my right towards the telephone box which stood outside the Constitutional Club opposite me. Without a landline at home and long before mobiles became an extension of our arms, this was the only way we could ring the outside world. Mum would drop ten-pence pieces into the slot, dial her parents, or Dad's, then read out the number and wait for a call back. My sister and I would pile into the kiosk and have our minute or two with Granny and Grampa, and then Mum would take up the conversation. As Bob Hoskins kept telling us back then, 'it's good to talk'.

Taking the lower road to my left, back through Windsor Place, I reach Clydach Park, site of Butcher's Pool. It's not a pond, nor is it a full-size swimming pool suitable for all ages, but rather a paddling pool. The ankle wash, according to some of the more sarcastic inhabitants. Built during the late-1960s, early-1970s rush of civic-mindedness, when a dying district council wanted to leave its mark and an energetic replacement wanted to make certain of voters' loyalties, Butcher's Pool has been entertaining villagers since about 1968. It was installed as a replacement for an even smaller paddling pool at the Recreation Ground. These days, with the council no longer able to do so, it's a community-managed facility run by a hard-working cohort of volunteers to whom I pay tribute here. Lottery funding enabled renovation and renewal in the 2010s, and in the summer sunshine of the 2020s – assuming any summer sunshine at all that is – it now beams as bright as ever it has done.

Whenever I'm here, I think it's the mid-1990s, the peak of my own childhood. The sun blazed in the summer, there was talk of heatwaves, and for the six weeks of school holidays, give or take a washout or two, the entire village camped out on the grass. We queued up for our 99s – ice cream with a flake – from the yellow van, whose owner must have paid for a year's worth of holidays from the collected proceeds of our daily, or was it bi-hourly, need for sugar. The young mothers marvelled over men in string vests, noting with a certain glee that they wore fresh ones every day and that it was nice to see muscles now and then, and from the portable, battery-powered cassette-radio glued to the life-guard's deckchair and kept perma-tuned to Red Dragon FM, there rang out the unmistakeable sounds of Pulp's 'Common People', 'Boom, Boom, Boom' by the Outhere Brothers, or Edwyn Collins' omnipresent hit, 'A Girl Like You'. The only competition for its guitar-driven melody was the shrill blast of a whistle, the jingle of the ice-cream van, or the inevitable squeal of a toddler going headfirst over their own left foot.

Exiting the park via the upper gate, I am soon at the junction of Clydach Road and Old Ynysybwl Road. A bus rushes past on its way back into town, so I follow it at a more pedestrian speed. It is soon out of sight, however. To my right, as I traverse Glanffrwd Terrace and then Tai Newydd, is the municipal cemetery, this one is of 1890s vintage. The boundary wall marks the precise limits of a field that can be seen on eighteenth-century estate plans and which the tithe commissioners recorded, perhaps figuratively, as Graig Canol – the middle rock. There's no chapel inside, for unlike many municipal cemeteries of the period, the then Bishop of Llandaff, Richard Lewis, a nationally prominent Freemason, insisted that he would only do the unveiling if the council did not build one. They used the money saved to put up lodgings for the caretaker instead – Ynysybwl's first council house.

I follow Heol-y-Plwyf, the Parish Road, which takes me past the entrance to the cemetery, past Y Waun, Leighton Rees Close – named after the darts champion and Ynysybwl native – and the rugby club. There's another boundary wall, which begins as the rise levels out. This one belongs to the recreation ground, our own gift from the Miners' Welfare Fund of the 1920s and opened in the summer of 1924 as no less than the first fully completed miners' welfare project anywhere in South Wales. It stretches for as far as the eye can see and this, the rugby-cricket field, is just one part of the leisure complex. You need to go inside to view the rest, to grasp properly the progressive vision of miners and teachers and other residents, those who planned this site a century ago as Ynysybwl Recreation Association. And so, that is what I do.

Someone has painted *Croeso i'r Rec* on the right-hand corner of the grandstand. A nice welcome as I walk through the main gates. The Rec was essential to the story I told in my doctoral thesis as well as in my first book, which I had planned to call *Up The Rec!* in its honour, but was told no one would get the reference, so it was called *Fields of Play* instead. I grasped from the history of this place that what made social democracy a living, breathing form of politics in these valleys – one quite removed from the system we have now, whether the politicians base themselves in Cardiff or London – was investment in communities and people. This was quite literally politics from the ground up. Had a different set of plans come to fruition, this would all have been a garden village, but the developers grew frustrated and so the landowners handed the site over to the local miners' federation lodge to do something, if they could.

I take the left-hand path alongside the bowling green, the only part of the ground I have never been in, although I have peeped through the hedged fence. To my right is the grandstand. It's not the original one; that burned down in the 1950s. This is the replacement, opened in 1957. The old tennis courts have had an upgrade from the council and have been turned into a colourful MUGA. It's all empty as I walk through, though. The fields below contain a rugby pitch and a soccer pitch and some forlorn cricket nets, I'm not being rude – they've always looked forlorn in this, their out-of-the-way spot at the far end of the field. In the distance, in the boggy wastes of the Waun, I see the remains of the sunken houses, a misguided attempt (and not the only one) to build on that most unforgiving piece of wetland. I exit through the children's play area and am back on Heol-y-Plwyf.

Before I reach the crossroads, I spot a lane, which I know takes me behind Christ Church and onto Church Street. Names start to come back to me: the Sussats, the Nixons, Sheila and Rob Grant, and a (now lost) Happy Shopper store. I'm hoping to get a three-sixty view of the church, at least from the outside. Built in the mid-1880s, when the colliery spurred a population explosion in this valley and completely reorientated the focal points of human activity, this was originally a chapel of ease for St Gwynno's. It was put up cheaply to a plain design by the Cardiff architect Edwin Montgomery Bruce Vaughan but, I suggest, it is not an unattractive building for a not unattractive place. The last time I ventured inside was for a village fete circa 1992. I came home with a copy of a *Doctor Who* novelisation: *Tom Baker and the Robots of Death*.

In truth, the reason for halting at Christ Church is to enjoy perhaps my favourite view of all. It pays to be here in the autumn, just as the trees and bushes enter their long slumber, because you then are rewarded with the prospect of the entire valley. Below me the busy activity of the square, to my left the covered slag heaps and the colliery site left for nature to make of what it can, and to my right terraces and the hint of a field where men and women once stood together to proclaim ideas and principles of faith. Not religious faith, as it happens, but their newfound and growing belief in a social democratic future. It is in unmarked places like this that one can hear the earliest echoes of Labour Country. I grew up around the corner.

4.

I cannot objectively explore *these* streets. There are too many neighbours, some since moved away or passed on, whose shadows I see as I pass their old front door. Phyllis, Steve, Vicky, and Melanie. Jeanette, David, and Susan. Caroline. Sam and Phil. Sadie. Derek, who lived in the cottage at the top of the hill and who never failed to regale me with stories of his adventures as a batsman for Glamorgan. Penry, the diminutive window cleaner, who pushed his wooden cart and ladder up and down these hills, no matter the weather. Brian Arnold, the county councillor, who would stop me to ask what I thought of this or that. Mary Hier, who knew the answer to every problem or the people who would. Llinos at Pen y Banc, who gave me a tea towel with the landmarks of Pontypridd on it the week I left for Oxford, all so I would remember where I came from, where I belonged.

New folks have come, some of them have gone too, but in the village of my childhood, I am still nine years old, and it is 1995. That was the year Michael Jackson went to number one at Christmas with a song about the damage humans were doing to the natural world, Robson & Jerome ushered in the summer with a double A-side revival of 'Unchained Melody' and 'White Cliffs of Dover', although I insist that we were all listening to Edwyn Collins as I said earlier, and Robbie left Take That. Mum was devastated. So now she preferred Shane from Boyzone and listened to M People instead. She was very young still: twenty-seven that year and, with my sister and I both in school, beginning to find out who she was as a person. When we came to Ynysybwl, Mum was about to turn twenty-one with her entire adult life ahead of her. If she was still alive, she would only be fifty-five, a decade and more from retirement, and some distance from genuine old age.

There were times growing up when her youth came to the fore, like when she accidentally ran over a toad with the lawn-mower and was upset at having claimed the life of a creature that just happened to be in the wrong place. She cradled it in her hand right to the end. There was her enthusiasm for Christmas, which meant trimming the house up with garlands and chains dangling from the ceiling and throwing herself into building up Santa sacks for my sister and me. But there were also times when her epilepsy triggered a fit and I had to react by ringing the ambulance and hoping that she would come around again. She did, of course, but only moments before the knock at the door signalled the arrival of the paramedics and we were whisked away to the hospital under a siren and flashing lights. The nurses fed my sister and I some cheese sandwiches in their staff room and the doctor said that I had been brave dialling 999. I cannot have been much older than six or seven.

The happiest year was when street parties were organised to mark half a century since the end of the Second World War – one last hurrah to the twentieth century and its darkest corridor. You could never get a trestle table on a street these days, there are just too many cars. Besides, to borrow from Bob Dylan, things have changed. But back then, we dressed in our oversized clothes, surrounded ourselves with Union flags, which draped from every conceivable cranny, and kicked off Cool Britannia with a cider lolly, a handful of jammy dodgers, and gallons of own-brand cola and three-stripe Neapolitan ice cream. No wonder we were optimistic, we were on a synthetic sugar rush. Even the sun seemed to want to play, gifting us a heatwave that our parents likened to childhood memories of 1976. I'm not making it up, I checked this really happened. Day after day we basked in sunshine; we packed our sandwiches, bathers, and a towel, and headed off to the Rec or to Butcher's Pool – we had no reason to leave the village.

As for me, I dreamed I was a member of International Rescue, the World Aquanaut Security Patrol, or an officer in Spectrum battling the Mysterons alongside Captain Scarlet. The *Radio Times* put it best. 'Just as *Thunderbirds* and *Stingray* have been introduced to a new, young public by recent BBC Two screenings, so *Captain Scarlet* awaits a fresh audience, as well as thirty-somethings anxious to feast on nostalgia.' It was the same with *Star Trek*, which celebrated its thirtieth anniversary in 1996, and the *Flintstones* which was of a similar vintage. A few hundred years ago, doctors thought nostalgia was an illness, something which affected individuals – and perhaps whole societies – who are uprooted from their places of origin, whose social and cultural lives have atrophied, and who feel frustrated or alienated. Perhaps that's what we were supposed to feel, but I'm not sure it was the case, at least not then, though it is now.

With little money around, our toys came from the Warehouse, a former chapel that sold all sorts of weird plastic, ranging from Christmas decorations and tinsel to the latest in imported, likely counterfeit and therefore toxic, action figures. I had a Lion-O and Panthra, heroes from the *Thundercats* cartoon series, and one or two from *Defenders of the Earth*, as well. Flash Gordon and the Phantom. They're long since lost but my memory of them is fresh. Standing outside what was the Warehouse, I see something that I was not expecting to see, a Ukraine flag flying outside one of the houses on Robert Street. It is a reminder that no matter how far The Bwl, as it is affectionately known, can seem from world events, and often is, those same events resonate here just as much as anywhere else.

I take the incline leading towards Trerobart Primary School and instinctively list my teachers from nursery through to year six. Eirlys Edwards and Yvonne Eveleigh, Jill Price and Kim Jones, Carole Barraclough, Nan Howells and Jayne Coleman, Andrea Hedditch, Mike Allen, Emma Lewis, Steven Johnson, and the headteacher, Enfys Hanks. Primary school has such an effect on us all that we can, even from the distance of decades, recall with absolute precision those who taught us when we were five or six years old. Staring through the gates, which are locked, I can see in my mind's eye those games we played on the yard: British bulldog, touch rugby, rounders, and the occasional kiss chase. I see the face of the only girl who chased me, her name was Charmain, but we always seemed to miss. I can see others from my class: Natalie and Kimberley, James and Kenneth, Mark and Nathan, Lee, Nicky, Gareth, Matthew, the twins Kathleen and Kimberley, four Daniels, David, Jonathan, Lindsey, Nia, and others whose names I have forgotten. I see the space in the yard where the nursery used to be, a temporary building that stood for decades. I see us crossing the road to go to the old canteen on Crawshay Street and imagine the smell of scoops of mashed potato, meat gravy, and ship's biscuits or chocolate cake and pink custard, all served to us on grey-green plastic trays by white-uniformed staff. This was Term 3 Catering at its finest.

I am surprised by the survival of a sign, now painted over in a deep green. It is at least fifty years old; Glamorgan County Council was a dozen years deceased before I was even born. This is what it says:

THIS SITE IS THE PROPERTY OF THE
GLAMORGAN COUNTY COUNCIL
LEGAL ACTION WILL BE TAKEN AGAINST
ANY PERSON COMMITTING ANY ACT
OF TRESPASS OR DAMAGE

T. V. WALTERS
CLERK OF THE COUNTY COUNCIL

Walking along Grove Terrace, I notice the canteen has been demolished too. All that remains are the yellow bricks which once formed the corners of the building, they have been tastefully incorporated into the school's new boundary wall. I cross into Crawshay Street and into an unending battleground. The street sign on No. 60 says Crawshaw and you will often hear it so named, but the three parallel terraces – Robert Street, Thompson Street, and Crawshay Street – were named for an individual (Robert Thompson Crawshay), the last member of that family of ironmasters to live at Cyfarthfa Castle in Merthyr Tydfil. Crawshaw entered the vernacular in the 1940s, where it has stubbornly remained. A parallel world of its own.

At the far end of Crawshay Street, turning left from Grove Terrace, is a small park. There is nothing here to indicate why it exists, nor that it is the oldest public recreation facility in the village, opened before the First World War. The miners fought for this space, too. It tends to get overlooked by the younger upstarts, the Recreation Ground and Clydach Park, but I have a soft spot for what we used to call, logically enough, Green Park. (Aren't all parks green?) With its proximity to the school, teachers would often bring us here for PE, for geography and environmental lessons, and for history. Mr Allen especially favoured the view from the playing field. He would point out where the colliery had been – demolished about five years before – where the railway had been and the importance of the co-operative society and how it all began here. 'This is important, children,' he used to say to us, aware that my age group would serve as a bridge between those generations able to remember these things, though they had begun already to disappear, and those who came after us who would not. This is now my duty as a historian.

5.

On another day, I return to Ynysybwl to explore its northern edge and to walk to Llanwonno. I alight the bus on Rock Terrace. The junction here has long had a bench in the middle of it. Once upon a time, you could sit, assuming you were brave enough to dodge the cars and buses, that is, and pass the day by staring out at the wilderness like a latter-day W. H. Davies. But the owners of the house opposite have put up a fence, their trees have matured, and now all you get out of sitting on the bench is a puzzled look from passing drivers. Rock Terrace, like so much of this village, is a steep incline with houses either side. Some belong to the Buarth-y-Capel estate, you can spot those by their uniformity of design; the others are one-offs put up whenever someone was feeling flush. Rock Terrace proper, built in about 1890, is a genuine valleys terrace situated a short distance up the hill. The original residents, traceable on the 1891 census returns, were coal miners and their families. When they moved in, and for decades afterwards, there was nothing but empty fields opposite.

It would have been a view familiar to John Wesley, the Methodist preacher, the terrace aside. I have downloaded a copy of his diary to my phone. Wesley made this journey by horse on 6 April 1749. He was on his way from Cardiff to Aberdare via Llantrisant but stopped off at 'a hard-named place on the top of a mountain'.

It is generally thought he meant Llanwonno, but it could have been any of the hills overlooking Ynysybwl, even this one. There were certainly enough 'honest, simple people' around, folk already caught up in the spirit of nonconformity, who came to listen to his sermon. They 'recompensed us for our labour in climbing up to them,' Wesley later wrote. There was no chapel here in those days, so dissenters met in various of the farmhouses dotted around the place. Methodists at Rhyd-y-Gwreiddyn and Pwll Helyg, Presbyterians at Mynachdy, the General Baptists at Gelliwrgan, and the Particular Baptists at the Old Ynysybwl Inn. We can date most of these congregations to around 1810 or so. The Particular Baptists, following the teaching of Jean Calvin, believed that Christ had died to atone only for the sins of an elect group of people. If you were in, you were in, but if you were not, you were not, and, well, good luck to you. My Scottish ancestors took a similar view as members of the Free Kirk.

The Methodists were the first of those nonconformist sects to grow large enough to invest in a chapel building of their own: Capel Fanheulog, which opened in 1786. It's still there on Rock Terrace, although it has been residential property since worshippers moved out to the neighbouring Capel Bethel in 1876. That second chapel closed exactly a century later in 1976 and is now a private residence. Details about the eighteenth-century chapel are alas scarce. By all accounts the interior was austere. Even in the 1850s, there were just ten seats, sitting being the exclusive privilege of the leading families of the congregation. Everyone else had to stand. Glanffrwd, who attended the chapel as a boy but later became an Anglican vicar at St Asaph Cathedral, wrote of hearing 'voices in song and praise hundreds of times between the walls of the old Fanheulog'.

He is something of a local celebrity, Glanffrwd that is. His real name was William Thomas, and he was born in Old Ynysybwl in 1843. As it happens, he was an ancestor of Alun Richards.

Glanffrwd's fame rests on a volume of poetry, some articles of an antiquarian nature, and a history-cum-travel book he wrote towards the end of his life called *Hanes Plwyf Llanwonno*. In it he takes the reader back to a time before industrialisation began to alter the parish (which in those days extended into the Rhondda and down to Pontypridd). It is not that he was an anti-modernist, so much that he was keen to preserve the culture and society of upland Glamorgan in the mid-nineteenth century, before it was too late. I feel an affinity for him because we share a landscape and we have grown up on the cusp of change: industry in his case and post-industry in mine.

Just down the hill from the chapel is the lane which leads in and out of Buarth-y-Capel Farm. To me, this is just like any other pre-industrial farmstead, so I ignore the lane in favour of the road leading into the housing estate, which is just a little bit further on, but I thought I had better tell you that it's there just in case you visit. When locals talk about Buarth-y-Capel – listen carefully and you'll note they say 'Beth Kapull' – it is likely they mean the housing estate. It was unveiled in its original form in February 1948 as a development of just five streets. These were called The Hendre, Heol Bethel, The Avenue, The Crescent, and The Close. There were around one hundred and thirty houses, that is, prefabricated aluminium bungalows each with their own small plot of land, and all to meet the demands of a post-war housing shortage.

In the 1960s, the prefabs gave way to permanent housing stock and inevitable compromises were made at the planning office. Some private outdoor space was sacrificed to allow for an increase in motorcars and to squeeze in a few more houses. At around this time, too, another housing estate was built, this one by the National Coal Board at the lower end of the village. Dan-y-Cribyn, as it is now known, was all part of the offer made to miners from the Durham coalfield to move south and start over in Ynysybwl. When they first arrived, their new 'house' proved to be no more than a static caravan, as the television journalist, Vincent Kane, discovered when he visited on assignment for the BBC's *Wales Today* programme in 1963.

I wander along to look at the former Glanffrwd Infants School, now Ty Coch Special School. This pleasant, red-brick edifice replaced its namesake on Heol-y-Mynach. This place is a single-storey design with a feature made of the chimney, all surrounded by green open space. Luxurious, especially in an age of playing field sell-offs. My primary school best friend, Stephen, went here because his mum, Enid, who came from the northeast of England, was the deputy headteacher. Her boss was the marvellously named Mrs Valentine. Stephen and I met on the annual exchange visit for Year 2, which was designed to smooth the transition for Glanffrwd pupils as they moved into the junior department at Trerobart. We would be in the same class for the rest of primary school and were almost inseparable.

On my way out of the estate, I think of the people I have known who have lived here over the years. Most have moved on, some have sadly passed away, only a few remain in residence. The Billingtons: Margaret and Bruce. The Gregories: Elin and Josh. The Colliers: Hannah, Mal, and Gill. The Williams-Joneses: Andrew and Christopher. I have forgotten which houses were theirs, but that doesn't matter. Instead, I chuckle to myself recalling that Bruce would introduce himself to us as Bruce Billington the Third.

6.

By good fortune, a white minibus passes as I reach Glanffrwd Terrace. I wave and the driver toots the horn to say hello. Then it stops. The window winds down and my name is called. An arm reaches out of the passenger window and beckons me over.

'Hop in, Dar.'

'Okay.'

I get into the back section of the bus, push the door shut, and sit down.

'Well now,' says a familiar voice. 'That's a stroke of luck.'

I've been borrowed by Jill and Wynford, retired schoolteachers, one primary, the other secondary, who have turned their career inside the classroom into one very much outside and in all weathers. They are the leading lights of the outdoor pursuits centre at Daerwynno. I've been volunteered, happily, to house-sit while the day's activities carry on at the site and in the surrounding forestry, joining in as needed.

Daerwynno Outdoor Activity Centre, with its instantly recognisable metal window shutters and solar panels, is a survivor. Set in the heart of the Llanwonno Forest, the nineteenth-century building out of which the centre operates is all that remains of a once-thriving hilltop farm. The rest, including the seventeenth-century farmhouse, was demolished after the Second World War as superfluous to the needs of its then owner, the Forestry Commission. The staff and volunteers at Daerwynno have delivered outdoor education to community groups, schools, and passers-by for more than twenty-five years and I am very proud to have played my own part in its story, first as a junior member and as an intermittent volunteer ever since.

As kids we were inspired to pick up essential skills like erecting a tent, how to pitch it properly on the ground to avoid a headache in the morning, how to check for stones that would dig into your back, how to fry an egg on a camping stove, how to rely on others to navigate a trail in the forest armed only with a map and compass, and how to cope if anything went wrong. The best gatherings were the summer camps held over the long weekend at the end of August. I get caught up in happy memories as we drive down the hill and then through the main gate.

The day's activities are soon in full swing. There's pond dipping under the watchful eye of the centre's third musketeer, Mary. She was a primary school teacher, too. A dragonfly hovers above the water for a moment, almost a moment too long as a net swoops down. Off goes the insect, liberty intact, as the net plops into the water abandoned in a youthful sulk. Someone else shouts for attention:

'Miss, miss.'

They've captured a four-spot ladybird and are busy showing it off to anyone and everyone. In the distance I can see Hannah and Richard, the next generation, one a teacher, the other an ex-Royal Marine turned paramedic, and the wiry, bearded Cyril, who is busy fixing something as he so often is. Colleen and Kevin are on their way. There are gaps in the roster from the old days, and friends scattered far and wide, but I sense their presence all the same.

I make my way into the house, where I spot Jill adding wood to the Aga and checking on the water boiling atop the stove, Cyril has got things going already. When the centre opened in 1997, there was no electricity. After dark, it was candle power or torches, an eerie magic. But green innovations in recent years, including solar panels on the roof and a miniature wind turbine, have brought the lightbulb and, I notice, a fridge. What luxury we now know. Electricity is a concession to modernity, to be sure, but it is also an essential tool for education: school groups can be shown the direct relationship between their energy use and the need for a sustainable supply. I pour myself a cup of coffee and sit on one of the dark green benches, which are a cross between those of the House of Commons and those which would once have graced a workmen's club.

'I'm glad I saw you,' I say. 'I was on my way up here as it happens.'

'What brings you to us,' says Jill.

As I dunk a biscuit, I tell her about this book, and she moves off towards the shelf to the right of the Aga.

'This will keep you busy.'

She hands me a photograph album before heading outside to lead one of the team-building challenges. I flick through the pages of the volume. They chart the history of the centre: there are photographs of me here aged fifteen or sixteen climbing the gable end of the house, kayaking down on the reservoir, learning the ABCs of first aid, there's even one of my going-away party, thrown at the Brynffynnon just before I left for Oxford in 2004.

Being outdoors, in this woodland idyll, was how I began to come to terms with losing Mum. Everything that had made sense in my life up to that point no longer did. What remained unaltered were memories of childhood escapes to Llanwonno to stand in falling snow or to eat a picnic of paste sandwiches in the sunshine or a bag of crisps as we watch fireworks from the car park of the pub on a sharp November evening. When I'm up here in the forest, even now, I sometimes hear Mum's voice. After so long it is feint, as though the volume is stuck on its lowest setting. But I am grateful that it has not been switched off entirely.

During a break I ask Jill and Wynford if they know anything about the various phases of the house since it was taken over by the Forestry Commission in the 1930s - for a while they ran it as a tenanted farm. I have some notes of my own, which I line up with what I'm told. There was an outdoor pursuits place here in the 1970s, then an Explore Glamorgan visitor centre in the early 1980s. After that, various attempts were made at outdoor pursuits until, at last, Daerwynno took off in the 1990s. Explore Glamorgan was a curious venture. It attracted flies - I mean planners - who came down from Birmingham and suggested a large development of log cabins run on a timeshare basis. That was in December 1983, a few months later the miners' strike broke out and the planners and their cabins were never seen or heard from again.

7.

Just to the west of the outdoor centre, on the mountain road leading down into Blaenllechau and Ferndale in the Rhondda Fach, is a view utterly unique to this part of Glamorgan. On a clear day, you can look north to the Brecon Beacons, south to the Bristol Channel, and west to the pilgrim's Penrhys. Below, terraces string out along the hillside. Most are in parallel but occasionally an adventurous builder has made a dash for it and constructed a street at a forty-five-degree angle to the neighbouring one. At the end of the 1960s, Gwyn Thomas filmed a good part in a documentary for the BBC's *One Pair of Eyes* series on this spot. His pieces to camera bookend the programme. I can see him in my mind's eye.

'My growing-up place,' he says, his face in profile to the camera. 'Monstrous and beautiful.'

Apart from the scars to the landscape, those thinly disguised tips which altered the natural roll of the hills, for instance, you would never know, now, that the Rhondda, the Cynon, and the Taff together fuelled the world with their steam coal. As Gwyn would put it, the cover up is all part of a great joke.

'We hear the laughter all right,' he says in voiceover at the end of the documentary. 'But we are never quite sure about where it's coming from.'

After his death in 1981, Gwyn's ashes were scattered in a grove near Daerwynno and so the laughter from the dark might yet be his. There's another set of ashes in the soil up here. They belong to the actor Stanley Baker. In the summer of 1976, with Harry Secombe, the football referee Clive Thomas, Lady Baker, and others, all in attendance, Baker's remains were laid to rest overlooking his own growing-up place. There is a wind blowing and the greying clouds seem mournful, much more so than they were at Daerwynno, so I linger awhile and think of the journey made by those two men, the actor and the writer, and about the journey from this place and back again at the end.

8.

Onwards we go to St Gwynno's Church. This forms part of what Gwyn Thomas called his earth's warm centre. He had a point. If you were to press me on the subject, I would say the same thing. This is one of my favourite places in the world and has been ever since I first discovered it at three or four years old.

If it began picking to snow in the village – Ynysybwl, that is – as autumn turned to winter, there would be a collective rush into cars so that we, the villagers, could be here on the mountaintop in the twilight as the flakes began to settle on the ground. If someone was given a small telescope as a present, they would be driven here to test it out on the blanket of stars that fill the night sky, that give true darkness its hue. Every so often, rally cars could be seen here, and in the village, particularly during the late 1990s when the RAC Rally and its successor, the Rally of Great Britain, used the forest as a special stage in the annual championship. There was a thrill to be had celebrity spotting favourite drivers like Colin McRae and his brother Alister, the Finn Tommi Mäkinen, or the Welshman Gwyndaf Evans. But the forest is silent now. No rally cars have been through here since 2001 and they are unlikely to be back.

Beneath my feet, deep underground, are the miles of complex tunnels and what remains of the coal seams that once criss-crossed between the Rhondda and Cynon valleys. Dug out over generations, these tunnels were held up by sturdy pit props made first from the trees that covered the uplands of Glamorgan and then from imported Scandinavian pine. The families who lived up here were deliberately oblivious to that industrial transformation, insofar as they could be. They farmed the land, kept flocks of sheep or cattle herds, and raced horses for fun. If they needed to go into town, into Pontypridd or Mountain Ash or Ferndale, they travelled by horse and trap, moving in and out of modernity as they went up and down the hills. You can still be oblivious to the rest of the world up here: mobile phones work only in certain spots and you can forget about accessing the internet with any speed. Downloads take hours to complete. At night it gets so dark that you can see stars such as city dwellers will never know and gets so quiet you can hear your own heartbeat and the call of an owl. Pipistrelle bats duck and dive in the gloaming.

This old church, one of two buildings which stand opposite on a T-junction – the other is the Brynffynnon Hotel – is largely a figment of the late-Victorian imagination. Before a series of costly refurbishments, which were embarked upon in 1893, completed in 1894, and paid for by Olive Talbot of Margan, St Gwynno's looked more like a Viking longhouse, a barn, or perhaps a modern- day community centre. A low profile kept in the heat in the long winter months when temperatures up here frequently fall below zero and snow and ice together turn the hills into a beautiful but precarious wonderland. The belfry and western porch, which give the church its modern profile, were added by the architect George Eley Halliday, a Londoner who made a life for himself in Cardiff, as well as a successful business. He was keen to reinvent this otherwise isolated parish church using the then popular Gothic style.

Inside, I am presented with a scene of austere stonework, a far cry from the loud orange of St Catherine's. It reminds me of a trendy city wine or coffee bar, the sort that makes a feature of its exposed bricks and a virtue of uncomfortable retro seating. The stained glass in the windows is all Victorian, of course, paid for by the well-to-do, anti-modern and big-c Conservative parishioners who lived and worked the nearby farms: the Llewellyn family of Daerwynno Farm among them.

Stiff wooden pews completed the puritan's idea of the medieval world, a Protestant rendering of the old Catholic spirit. Societies tend to cast earlier centuries in black and white, so that the present may believe in progress, in the technicoloured exclusivity of our modernity. But the past was always brighter and louder than that, so I look again at the fabric of this place to be sure. In the southern part of the building, there are relics of the earlier, medieval structure and of those ancient ideas about faith and Christianity. These ancient carvings amount to no more than a few centimetres of worked stone, easily missed by the casual unknowing eye, but there they are. This is art that is more than a thousand years old. I got shown them first as a teenager at the end of a wedding ceremony. I'd played violin in a small band - flute and guitar to accompany - and as we were packing up, a voice in the crowd said, you must come and see these. And so, I did.

9.

After a cuppa and some biscuits, or some blackcurrant squash for the juniors, we set off from the Daerwynno house in groups and make our way down to the former Clydach Reservoir, making use of our map-reading skills and a compass. We eventually reach one of the forest's calmest spots. Water ripples with a light breeze and the occasional dog walker passes with a woof and a hullo. You can walk around the perimeter quite easily, and so get a close look at the release mechanisms that add water into a channel running down towards Ynysybwl, or cast an eye over the conning tower dominating the scenery. The warning signs - danger, danger (but no high voltage) - point to a favourite activity of teenagers: jumping off the top. There are none today, the water is far too cold.

Our next destination-challenge is to find our way to the Pistyll Goleu waterfall. In the early days, before the centre had its climbing wall, we would abseil down the rockface in the summer, or come and look at the ice formations in the winter. It is not on the scale of Niagara or the Victoria Falls, to be sure, but this miniature chute, formed by the drop of one mountain stream into another, suits us just fine. After heavy rainfall, or in the winter when it freezes, this is one of the great wonders of St Gwynno's sylvan grove. The myriad routes that dart in and out of the trees can make a romantic flaneur of even the most agoraphobic of us. After waterfalls, reservoirs, and the great Norwegian firs and pines which make up the working woods of this place, I half expect to run into a hobbit or an elf as I make my way through with my group. No such luck. Back at the house, we're preparing for our departure. We're all tired, so there's not much chatter, a quiet moment that gives me the chance to look out the window.

This stretch of road between the turn off to Llanwonno and the point at which we arrive in Ynysybwl is called Pleasant View, an understatement if you ask me. The houses are obnoxiously large, of course. They are bourgeois in the truest sense of the word. Don't let anyone convince you everyone who lives in the valleys is dirt poor and surviving hand to mouth. Far from it. At least one of these mansions has the sort of manicured grass you get from a sit-on lawnmower. Laid out on auctioned-off parcels of land, the houses are a reminder that even when South Wales was not doing so well, economically, someone living here was and is doing just fine.

Any innate jealousy on my part is soon shaken when I catch sight of the coal tips a few metres further along the road. King coal may be dead and buried but like Ozymandias his empire can still be looked upon. As a very young child, travelling along this road in a tiny, royal-blue Ford Fiesta, Dad driving and Mum in charge of the cassette tapes, I marvelled at the sudden appearance of these little black hills. I wondered what they were, since there were none in Weston, but never got to the chance to ask.

Instead, as I got older, I sought out the answer for myself. I had heard talk of coal; some of the people in the village still burned the stuff for fuel and a delivery lorry appeared every few weeks dropping off sacks filled with a substance no one thought of as gold anymore. I realise as an adult how old-fashioned this was, a relic not of the 1990s but of decades long since passed, but as a child it was the way. That's the thing about coal in the valleys, it is all around us, even today when the pits are gone. Most of the time the industrial waste is hidden away, covered in a kind of experimental moss imported from the continent, but never so completely hidden as to be unknowable. There is no mistaking the artifice of a rubbish dump for a natural tump that has always been there. As I inspect the tip, I notice that there is a little of that Common Market moss poking out of the extremities; a lack of successful growth, though, so it suggests the crossing of a moulting pet and its owner who suffers from alopecia. I'd have asked for my money back.

10.

It is not long before we arrive at the edge of Ynysybwl itself. This area, defined by Mynachdy Farm, Cyncoed Housing Estate, and the main thoroughfare, Heol-y-Mynach (which has never been known by its English translation, Monk's Road), is deliberately undramatic. I lean forward and ask to be let out. More research for the book, I say, when Jill asks am I sure.

At the bus terminus-cum-turning-circle, the 106 pulls off heading towards Pontypridd. It is empty for now. I follow in its wake, down the short but steep incline that takes me past the site of Ynysybwl British School, which opened in 1868 with funding from the British and Foreign School Society. It was better known to locals as Glanffrwd Infants School, which was its name for much of the last century. The buildings were knocked down some years ago, however, declared surplus to requirements after a modern facility was built at Buarth-y-Capel in the 1980s. There are two substantial redbrick houses on the plot instead. Something stirs in my memory, a note of regret from one of the older residents of the village I knew as a boy: about how the original school had been paid for by the people. So, I wander back to the bus stop and sit on the bench, the cold metal gives me a start but soon warms up. On my phone I type in a combination of terms linking Ynysybwl and the charity in whose name Glanffrwd was originally built. I find what I am looking for and, sure enough, the old man's memory was right.

> *Ynysybwl.* This is an agricultural district, a short distance from Ponty-pridd. There has been a school of some kind here for many years, but it is anything but suitable to the wants of the neighbourhood. Seeing this, a gentleman farmer in the place resolved to attempt to form a good British school. ... The people were most enthusiastic. Some of the poorest in the locality contribute[d] their half-crowns towards the building fund.

That was the view of David Williams, the British and Foreign Schools Society's local agent, as published in the Society's annual report for 1866. The older school he mentioned had its roots in the circulating schools founded by cleric Griffith Jones in the early eighteenth century. It also means that, in the not-too-distant future, Ynysybwl can celebrate an impressive three hundred years of continuous provision for the education of its residents.

While I am in the vicinity of Mynachdy, I set myself the challenge of following in the footsteps of those pedagogical pioneers, the ones who established themselves somewhere in this part of Ynysybwl and began teaching local people how to read the bible. The oldest clues, dating to the 1730s and 1740s, are cryptic. *Welsh Piety*, the regular accounts published by Griffith Jones about his circulating schools, describes the location as being either Ynys y Bool in Llanwynno or near Ynys y Pool in Llanwynno. I take the first one to mean the Old Ynysybwl Inn, rather than a location called Ynysybwl, so I am in the right area. The other key piece of information from these early reports is the number of pupils: forty-nine in 1738–9, forty-two in 1741–2. Pont-y-ty-Pridd had just forty pupils at that time.

Only in the records from the 1750s do we get more (apparently) concrete clues of a location. This time they point towards a barn at Mynachdy Farm. I am none the wiser, however, because the full extent of the land belonging to the farm was much larger in the eighteenth century than it is today. Fields lying behind the Old Ynysybwl Inn and alongside the Nant Clydach were all included, so every clue might well point to the same building. A building that has long since disappeared. Most of the speculative enquiry has focused on a structure near the main house at Mynachdy Farm. It has attracted the attention of archaeologists several times, in fact. What they found when they came to visit was certainly old but there was nothing certain about its connections with education. And so, we may never know the truth.

I schlep up the hill towards the farm anyway, since nothing ventured, nothing gained. The road, known officially as Mynachdy Road but colloquially as Corpse Road, apparently because this was the route taken by funeral processions up to St Gwynno's, is quite narrow. It is a country lane, after all, albeit one that leads past some rather beautiful old houses.

There are hikers coming down off the hills and we stop for a chat. 'Hiya Daryl, haven't seen you for a while,' they say.

'Where are you to these days?'

'Only town.'

'Ponty is it? Different world that is mun. You don't fancy moving back to the Bwl?'

'Maybe.'

After enquiries about family and work and all that, we separate, and I carry on. Before me is a substantial metal gate, which screams keep out but doesn't say it aloud – there is no sign. The farmer is progressive and civic-minded, not at all like the cartoon Elmer Fudds of yester-year. You know the sort, those who carry their shotguns and sing 'shoot the wabbit' in Wagnerian style. The gate is a necessity of security rather than a harbinger of doom.

Fortunately, the road arcs to the left and so I could carry on if I wanted to. But I'll save that for another time. I head back down the hill to the main road. This time I want to look more carefully at the terraced houses. Only half remain. One of them was the village shop, in existence since the late nineteenth century. It was eventually to be known as the Ffrwd Stores and in the 1930s became a branch of the Ynysybwl Co-operative Society. Expansion in the middle years of the Depression? Well, the YCS had four branches in its natal village by then, plus a new headquarters in Pontypridd, and so completely dominated the shopping experience of all who lived in the village. There is no physical trace of the 'Kwop' in Old Ynysybwl anymore, though, just human memories which are themselves fast fading. Soon all that will be left are the ghosts seen by historians like me.

I round the corner and come to a grove. To my left lies Mill Road, to my right the route towards Buarth-y-Capel. But I have a different idea of what to do next. I cross over and head into the greenery past some signs telling me tipping no longer allowed and no tipping. This is a footpath. No, let me rephrase that. This is what remains of an old colliery tramway, and it leads to the remnants of the Mynachdy Colliery. Sadly, there is no longer very much. Decades of decay, natural recovery, and the battering of Storm Dennis, have destroyed almost everything, but it was not all that long ago that one could see the powder stores and the gated-off and padlocked colliery entrance.

Following the path, which is rather more hazardous and squelchy than I had expected, I listen to the rumble of the Nant Ffrwd beside me and spot some snagged sheep's fleece billowing in the wind but otherwise stuck on the wire fencing above. I walk slowly, following an Edwardian map as best I can. The experience is surreal: to be walking to a colliery site hidden by woodland. At the same time, it is one of the privileges of knowing the area as well as I do. What a shame it would be to drive past and pay it no heed. Admittedly, you would need to know that there was a mine here at all, and even with a bird's eye view, you would have to be taught how to spot the subtle changes in the landscape. The place where the trees do not grow quite as tall, where the under-growth is stained black, where industry has left its indelible mark, and that sort of thing. But such a skill is easily taught and easily learned. I survey the damage done by Neptune, full of regret for what was lost.

Doubling back, I rejoin the main road and this time follow the line of the tramway with my eye. I imagine colliery horses pulling coal drams across and onwards towards the junction with the railway or pulling empty ones back to the pit. It is a track, now, leading on towards Llechwen Farm and people seldom go that way at all. There is no reason for me to do so. Better instead to take Mill Road and to head to the pub.

II.

Wandering along Mill Road, I delight in its quaint character. This was the first place that was not a museum I ever saw a waterwheel.

Using the fast flow of Nant Ffrwd, the wheel once powered the grinding stones of a corn mill and survived long after the millers had moved out. It was something to look for on a trip from the new village to the old, for it was as if you had somehow passed into history and could now glimpse this valley as it might have been had coal never been found.

I'm not so romantic as to believe that the valleys would have been better off without the mines, without the associated processes of industrialisation, immigration, and social and cultural change. Quite the opposite, in fact. I embrace modernity, just as our ancestors did, no matter where they came from. Despite ongoing debates among historians about the standard of living during the early years of industrialisation – and on balance things were, albeit temporarily, worse in the factories and iron-works than they were in the countryside of the 1820s and 1830s – by the time industry arrived in Ynysybwl in the 1880s, there was no doubt that families were better off with a breadwinner working underground or on the railways than they had ever been out in the fields.

And yet for women, this transition had a different character. The novelist Jack Jones writes affectingly about this aspect of the past in his best novel, *Black Parade*. Published in 1935 and set in late-nineteenth-century Merthyr Tydfil, the story draws on the life of Jones's parents, who had themselves progressed from the rural to the urban. The protagonist, Saran Morgan, is a mother and a homemaker but never a domestic servant or a housewife, she is one who encapsulates the once-powerful idea of the Welsh Mam, the family matriarch. Towards the end of the story, after watching a parade of soldiers marching off to war, Saran is asked by a friend whether she would like to go for a walk. To enjoy some leisure time. But her home is foremost in her mind, as a place to live and as a world of labour, and so she says no. The men are off to war, and she is off to fight with a mangle:

'With all the washing as I've been leaving and leaving wanting to be done?'

When we first moved to the village as a family, we had no washing machine at home. My parents had to save up for one – there was no spare to be had from among our relations – as there had been excess furniture – and so for several years we made use of the laundrette on Robert Street. It's gone now, the front has been re-rendered for use as a domestic property, but in such a way as you can tell that it was once a shop. Remarkably, it survived the 1990s and the 2000s, the name above the front door, which read *laundrette*, went on fading year after year. As did its number: 50. The interior was little different from the more famous domain of Dot Cotton on *EastEnders*, with stacks of washers and driers and plastic baskets on a shelf above. I remember being fascinated by the coin slots on the machines and wanting to be the one to put the money in – there was a necessary combination of ten-, twenty-, and fifty-pence pieces, as with the public telephone box. I was less enthusiastic about carrying the basket or the bags of clean clothes home again or hanging things on the line to dry.

This was the thing about valley life in those days, it was communal, at least in certain ways, and so felt connected to the past. The total privatisation of domestic labour had not happened, especially for those who were young or had the lowest incomes. That was yet to come.

12.

The thing that comes to mind now that I'm at the Old Ynysybwl Inn is just what Ynysybwl means in English. I looked this up when I was working on my doctorate and discovered several translations, all of them problematic. The issues begin with *ynys*.

In Welsh it is a noun commonly translated as island. Hence Ynys y Bari or Barry Island. The dictionary gives other meanings as well: a meadow alongside a river, a rising piece of ground-cum-dry patch set in marshland. The middle *y* is easy enough because it is definitively 'the'. Which leaves *bwl*, or should it have a circumflex and so be written as *bŵl*? Both are continental in origin. The first derives from the papal bull, a document sent out from the Vatican to issue orders to the clergy; the second comes from the French word *boulle*, and so suggests a ball of some kind — it was originally written in Welsh as *bool*.

But what if *bwl* is a mutated form of *pwl*? Well, that changes things. Has it lost an 'l' at some point and so should be pooled as *pwll*. That is what the tithe map suggests, when it gives the pub name as *Ynis y Bwll*. An older map, made by George Yates in 1799, insists on *Ynis y Bwl*, however: one 'l' and no circumflex. One meaning of *pwl* (the single 'l' version) is a fit or bout of illness, another is a steep drag, a pull if you will, there's one of those nearby. As for *pŵl* with the interloping circumflex, I think the dictionary is trying to tell me something: 'blunt, obtuse, without edge or point.'

The best that can be made of this lexical jumble is a translation I have borrowed from the will of Thomas Moses, a former owner of what is now the Old Ynysybwl Inn, who died in 1798. He gives us 'Bowling Greens'. This was not bowling in the sense of immaculately kept lawns and old people clad in white. Oh no. This was handball: the fast-paced folk game once played against the left-hand gable of the Old Ynysybwl Inn. The most useful account comes from the antiquarian and local mythmaker, Glanffrwd. In his history of the parish, first published in the pages of the newspaper *Tarian y Gweithiwr* in the 1880s, he tells of fierce matches taking place here, of talented local players like Daniel Thomas and Iantws the Mill, and of inter-parochial showdowns between noble natives and rougher upstarts from the Rhondda or Aberdare.

Fast forward to the 1990s, when I was growing up, handball had been replaced by Trerobart's annual duck race. A legion of numbered, yellow plastic ducks bobbed along the Nant Clydach towards their moment of glory and the award of a box of chocolates or a small cash prize to the winning family. The evening's highlight was the race, of course, but there was a carnival atmosphere, too, with raffle prizes, tombola stands, and parents desperate not to let on to the teachers just how much they'd drink if they could. Teachers were in a similar position. I can still smell the boiled, slightly metallic hotdog sausages and fried onions, cooked on one of those two-ring hotplates that came from the school staff room. Ketchup for me, no onions; and you?

In the middle of it all there was us, the kids, running around exploring, all while avoiding falling into the river or covering the seat of our trousers in mud. We're allowed into the pub but only as far as the toilets.

'You've got to wear them again tomorrow,' I hear a parent cry, amid a communal look of disapproval. One of the Year 3s is tumbling down a footpath at the same time. I feel Mum's gaze as if to say, don't you dare, you'll fall. We both know you will.

I don't suppose there is a duck race here anymore. Just like those handball matches chronicled by Glanffrwd, it is gone. But it is worthy of history. And so, speak memory.

13.

As I stand in this empty car park outside a pub at the bottom of a hill, I am reminded once more of Laurie Lee. There's a passage in one of his memoirs where he looks back on his life from the vantage of old age. When he left his valley as a teenager in the early 1930s, he set out believing that everywhere else in the world was the same, and so what difference did it make where he went.

What he wanted was to be free, and in Slad he was not. But on his return in the 1960s, after living in London and, for a time, in Spain, where he was caught up in the Civil War, he understood that nowhere else was ever quite the same as his growing-up place, that the village in the valley of his childhood was where he should be and where, if truth be told, he had always been in spirit. Dennis Potter felt this way about the Forest of Dean.

I leave Old Ynysybwl and make my way back to the square to catch the bus into town. On this final leg of my journey, I ponder what I have learned about the past, the present, and my own future. I began uncertain of where I fit in. I do not yet know if I shall remain here, and settle at last, or if I shall make another attempt to flee, to step into the unknown and start over once more. It is not too late, I tell myself. Perhaps I was right after all, that something better does lie elsewhere, outside of the valleys, outside of Wales. I know that I am not Welsh. That I am something else instead, yet unnamed. But I shall never know anywhere as well as I know Pontypridd. I shall never have an instinct for somewhere as I have for Ynysybwl. I shall never forget that my schooldays were spent in Cilfynydd on the site of a once-deadly coal mine. When all is said and done, this is where my parents came to rest and where my sister has too. My roots on earth are these.

Alighting at the bus station, I walk to the Old Bridge. I take one step after another, not the two or three as usual, climbing little by little until I reach the top. Then I turn to face the river, which flows serenely beneath my feet. A queue of traffic is lined up beside the library, stopped at a red light. Temporarily in charge, a group of pedestrians makes its way across the road, with shopping trolleys tugged along behind them. Up here I reflect that writers need somewhere to call their own, somewhere their spirit of creation is at its strongest, that there is something special about the place in which a writer grows up, and that this is where they belong.

'A writer, then,' I hear someone say. 'Is that what you made of yourself?'

I am alone on the bridge. The voice must be a figment of my imagination. A trick of the mind. Yes, I am a writer, I reply. Because after all that has happened - and all that may yet happen, or, in its own way, has not - it seemed the natural thing to do.

THE END

AMERICAN AIRWAYS

join the jet-set...

in PONTYPRIDD

PARTHIAN

WALES: ENGLAND'S COLONY?

Martin Johnes

From the very beginnings of Wales, its people have defined themselves against their large neighbour. This book tells the fascinating story of an uneasy and unequal relationship between two nations living side-by-side.

PB / £8.99
978-1-912681-41-9

RHYS DAVIES: A WRITER'S LIFE

Meic Stephens

Rhys Davies (1901-78) was among the most dedicated, prolific and accomplished of Welsh prose writers. This is his first full biography.

'This is a delightful book, which is itself a social history in its own right, and funny.'
– The Spectator

PB / £11.99
978-1-912109-96-8

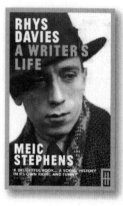

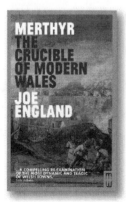

MERTHYR, THE CRUCIBLE OF MODERN WALES

Joe England

Merthyr Tydfil was the town where the future of a country was forged: a thriving, struggling surge of people, industry, democracy and ideas. This book assesses an epic history of Merthyr from 1760 to 1912 through the focus of a fresh and thoroughly convincing perspective.

PB / £18.99
978-1-913640-05-7

TO HEAR THE SKYLARK'S SONG

Huw Lewis

To Hear the Skylark's Song is a memoir about how Aberfan survived and eventually thrived after the terrible disaster of the 21st of October 1966.

'A thoughtful and passionate memoir, moving and respectful.'
– Tessa Hadley

PB / £8.99
978-1-912109-72-2

ROCKING THE BOAT

Angela V. John

This insightful and revealing collection of essays focuses on seven Welsh women who, in a range of imaginative ways, resisted the status quo in Wales, England and beyond during the nineteenth and twentieth centuries.

PB / £11.99
978-1-912681-44-0

TURNING THE TIDE

Angela V. John

This rich biography tells the remarkable tale of Margaret Haig Thomas (1883-1958) who became the second Viscountess Rhondda. She was a Welsh suffragette, held important posts during the First World War and survived the sinking of the *Lusitania*.

PB / £17.99
978-1-909844-72-8

BRENDA CHAMBERLAIN, ARTIST & WRITER

Jill Piercy

The first full-length biography of Brenda Chamberlain chronicles the life of an artist and writer whose work was strongly affected by the places she lived, most famously Bardsey Island and the Greek island of Hydra.

PB / £11.99
978-1-912681-06-8

PARTHIAN

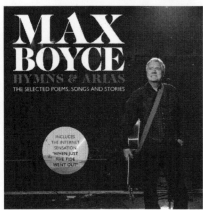

www.parthianbooks.com